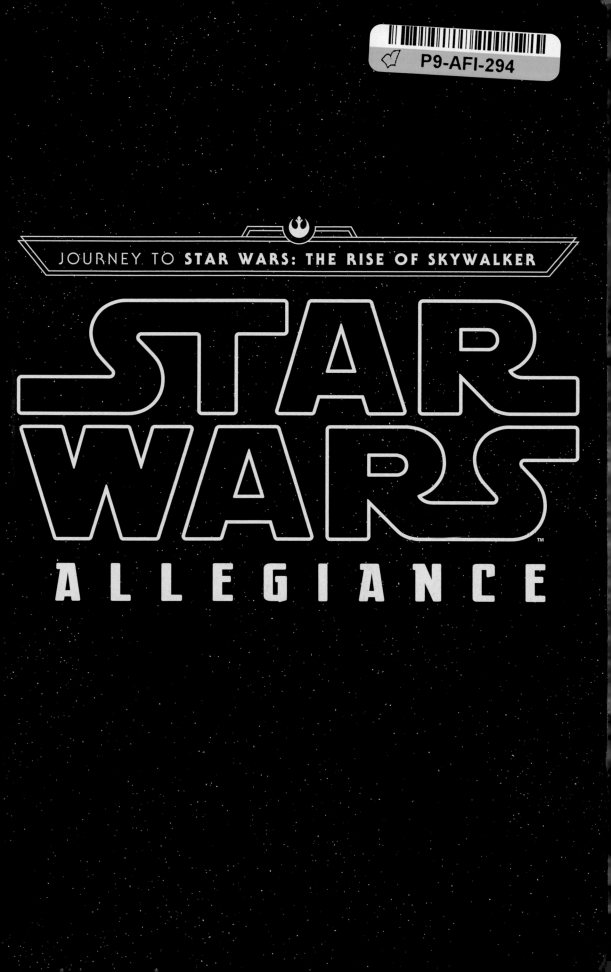

JOURNEY TO **STAR WARS: THE RISE OF SKYWALKER**

STAR WARS

ALLEGIANCE

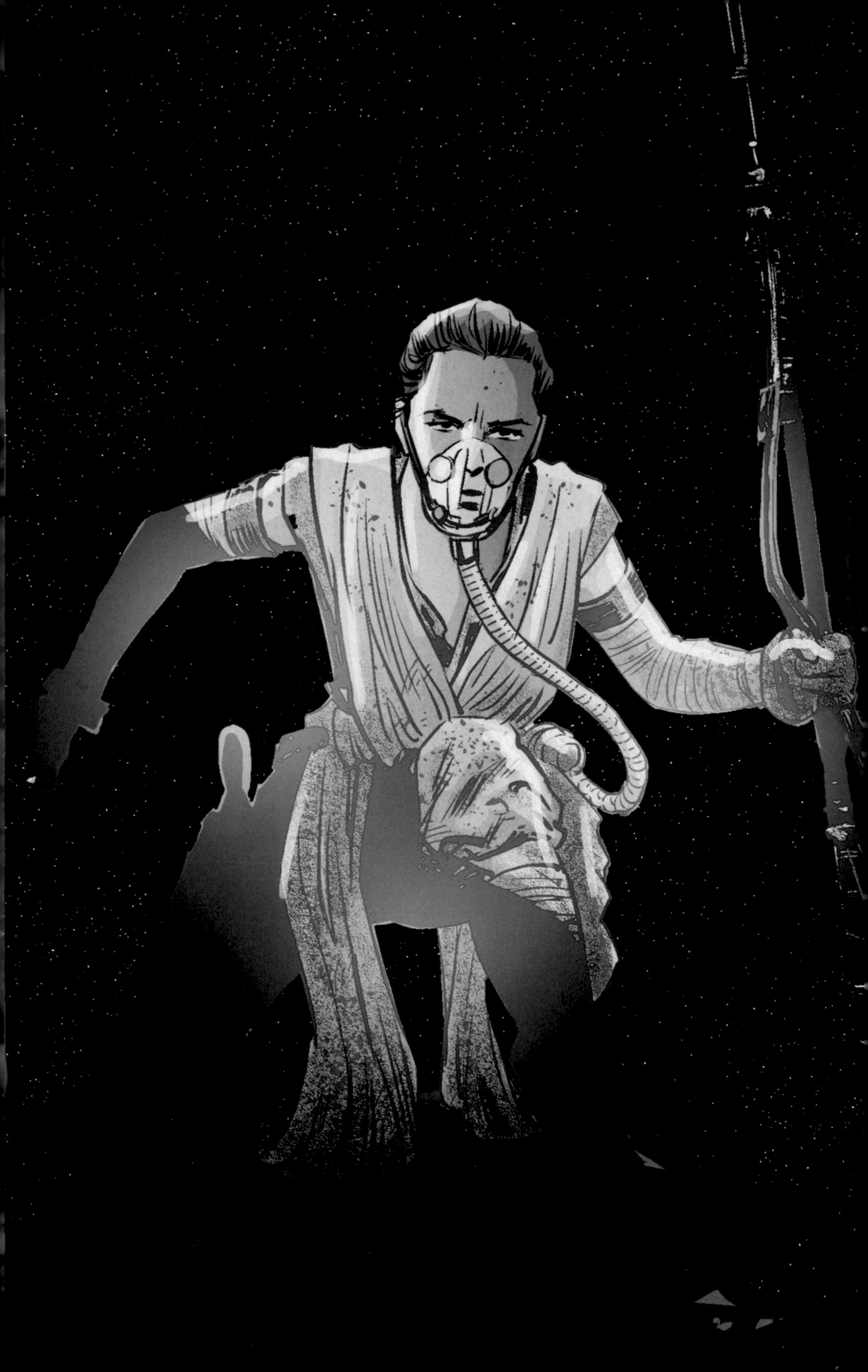

JOURNEY TO **STAR WARS: THE RISE OF SKYWALKER**

STAR WARS™

ALLEGIANCE

Writer	ETHAN SACKS
Artist	LUKE ROSS
Color Artist	LEE LOUGHRIDGE
Letterer	VC's CLAYTON COWLES
Cover Art	MARCO CHECCHETTO
Assistant Editor	TOM GRONEMAN
Editor	MARK PANICCIA
Editor in Chief	C.B. CEBULSKI
Chief Creative Officer	JOE QUESADA
President	DAN BUCKLEY

For Lucasfilm:

Assistant Editor	BEATRICE KILAT
Senior Editor	ROBERT SIMPSON
Creative Director	MICHAEL SIGLAIN
Lucasfilm Story Group	PABLO HIDALGO, MATT MARTIN & EMILY SHKOUKANI
Lucasfilm Art Department	PHIL SZOSTAK

Collection Editor	JENNIFER GRÜNWALD
Assistant Editor	CAITLIN O'CONNELL
Associate Managing Editor	KATERI WOODY
Editor, Special Projects	MARK D. BEAZLEY
VP Production & Special Projects	JEFF YOUNGQUIST
SVP Print, Sales & Marketing	DAVID GABRIEL
Director, Licensed Publishing	SVEN LARSEN
Book Designer	ADAM DEL RE

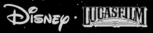

JOURNEY TO STAR WARS: THE RISE OF SKYWALKER — ALLEGIANCE. Contains material originally published in magazine form as JOURNEY TO STAR WARS: THE RISE OF SKYWALKER — ALLEGIANCE #1-4. First printing 2019. ISBN 978-1-302-91924-5. Published by MARVEL WORLDWIDE, INC., a subsidiary of MARVEL ENTERTAINMENT, LLC. OFFICE OF PUBLICATION: 135 West 50th Street, New York, NY 10020. STAR WARS and related text and illustrations are trademarks and/or copyrights, in the United States and other countries, of Lucasfilm Ltd. and/or its affiliates. © & TM Lucasfilm Ltd. No similarity between any of the names, characters, persons, and/or institutions in this magazine with those of any living or dead person or institution is intended, and any such similarity which may exist is purely coincidental. Marvel and its logos are TM Marvel Characters, Inc. **Printed in Canada.** DAN BUCKLEY, President, Marvel Entertainment; JOHN NEE, Publisher; JOE QUESADA, Chief Creative Officer; TOM BREVOORT, SVP of Publishing; DAVID BOGART, Associate Publisher & SVP of Talent Affairs; DAVID GABRIEL, SVP of Sales & Marketing, Publishing; JEFF YOUNGQUIST, VP of Production & Special Projects; DAN CARR, Executive Director of Publishing Technology; ALEX MORALES, Director of Publishing Operations; DAN EDINGTON, Managing Editor; SUSAN CRESPI, Production Manager; STAN LEE, Chairman Emeritus. For information regarding advertising in Marvel Comics or on Marvel.com, please contact Vit DeBellis, Custom Solutions & Integrated Advertising Manager, at vdebellis@marvel.com. For Marvel subscription inquiries, please call 888-511-5480. **Manufactured between 9/13/2019 and 10/15/2019 by SOLISCO PRINTERS, SCOTT, QC, CANADA.**

10 9 8 7 6 5 4 3 2 1

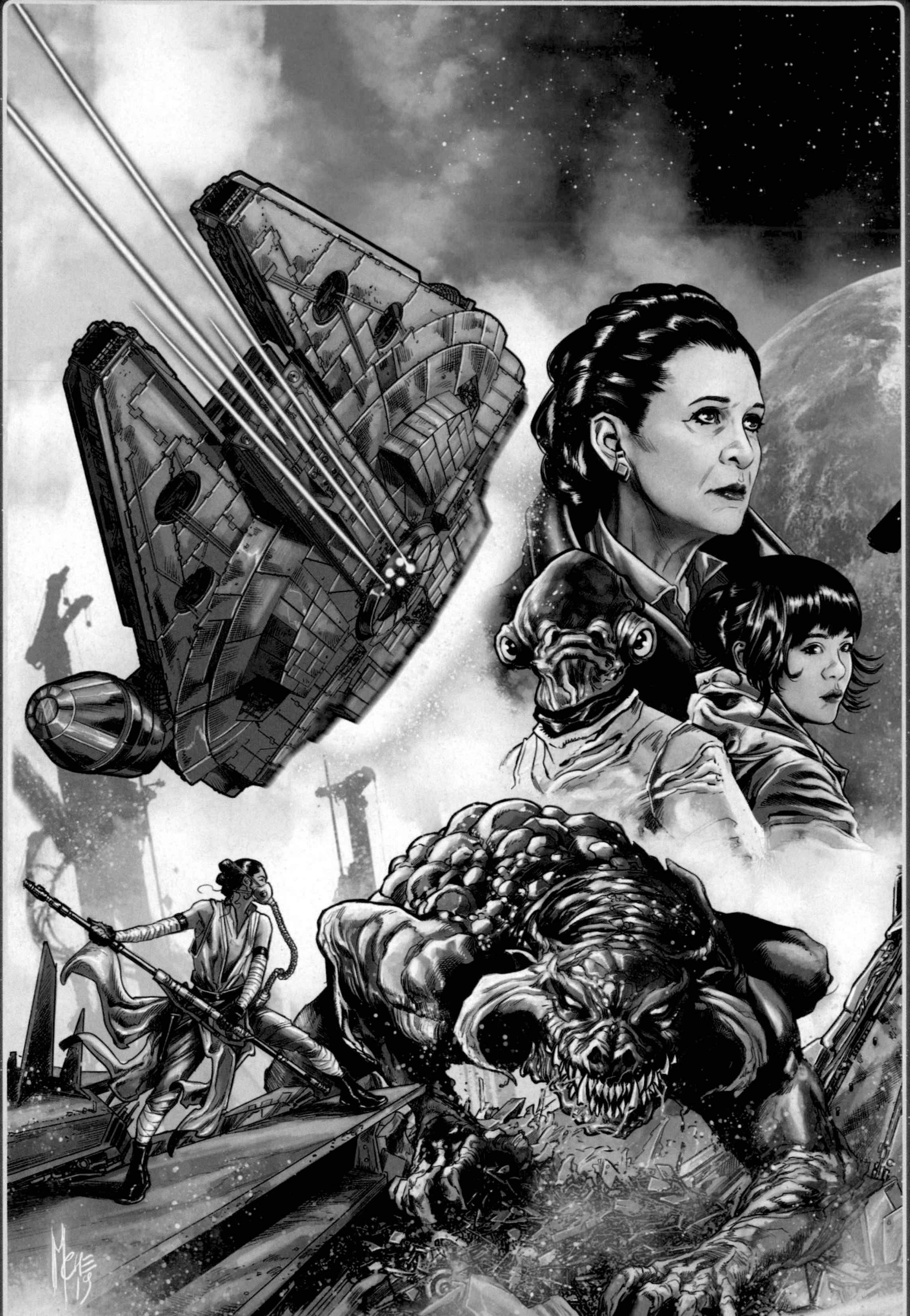

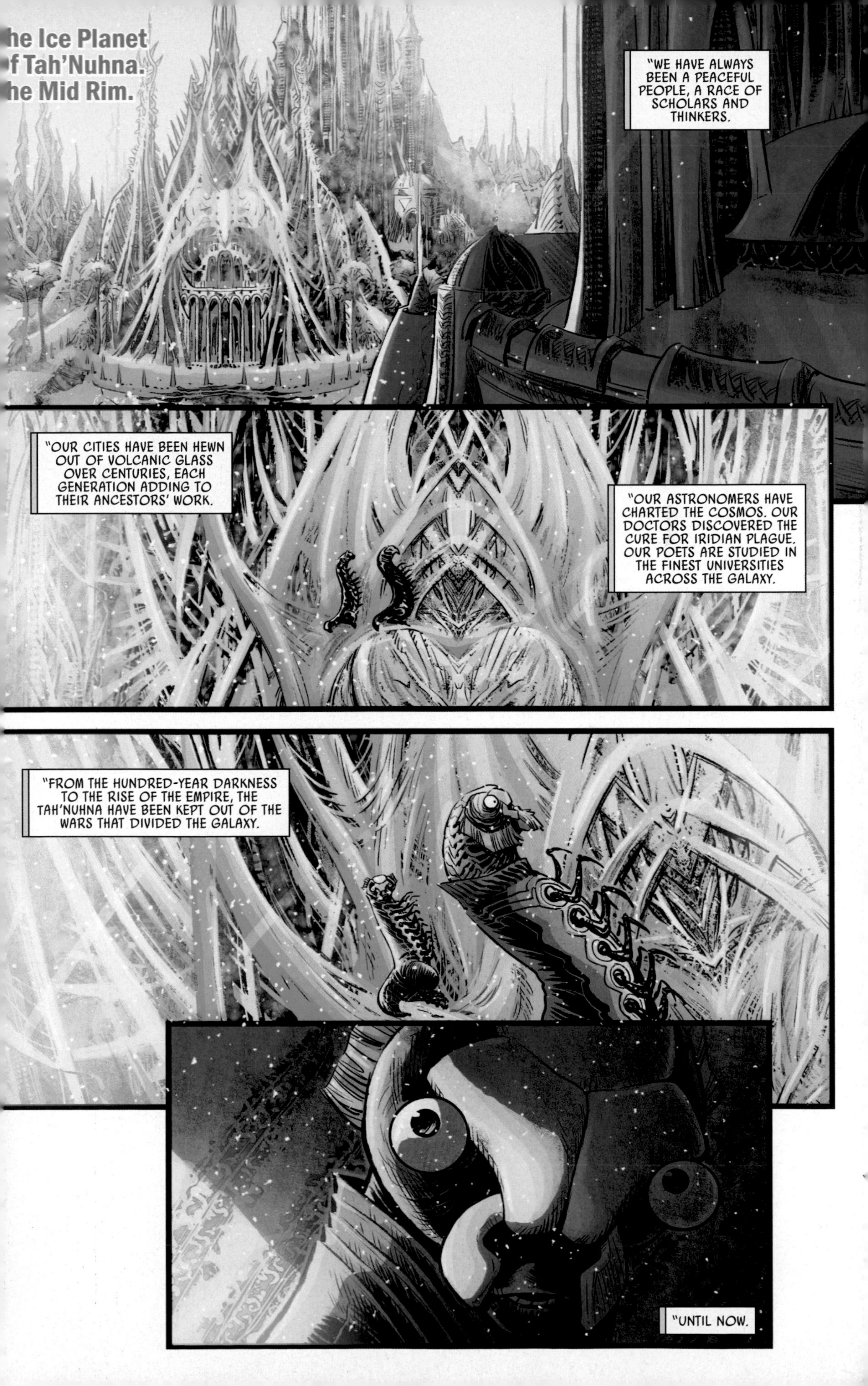

he Ice Planet
f Tah'Nuhna.
he Mid Rim.
"WE HAVE ALWAYS BEEN A PEACEFUL PEOPLE, A RACE OF SCHOLARS AND THINKERS.
"OUR CITIES HAVE BEEN HEWN OUT OF VOLCANIC GLASS OVER CENTURIES, EACH GENERATION ADDING TO THEIR ANCESTORS' WORK.
"OUR ASTRONOMERS HAVE CHARTED THE COSMOS. OUR DOCTORS DISCOVERED THE CURE FOR IRIDIAN PLAGUE. OUR POETS ARE STUDIED IN THE FINEST UNIVERSITIES ACROSS THE GALAXY.
"FROM THE HUNDRED-YEAR DARKNESS TO THE RISE OF THE EMPIRE, THE TAH'NUHNA HAVE BEEN KEPT OUT OF THE WARS THAT DIVIDED THE GALAXY.
"UNTIL NOW.

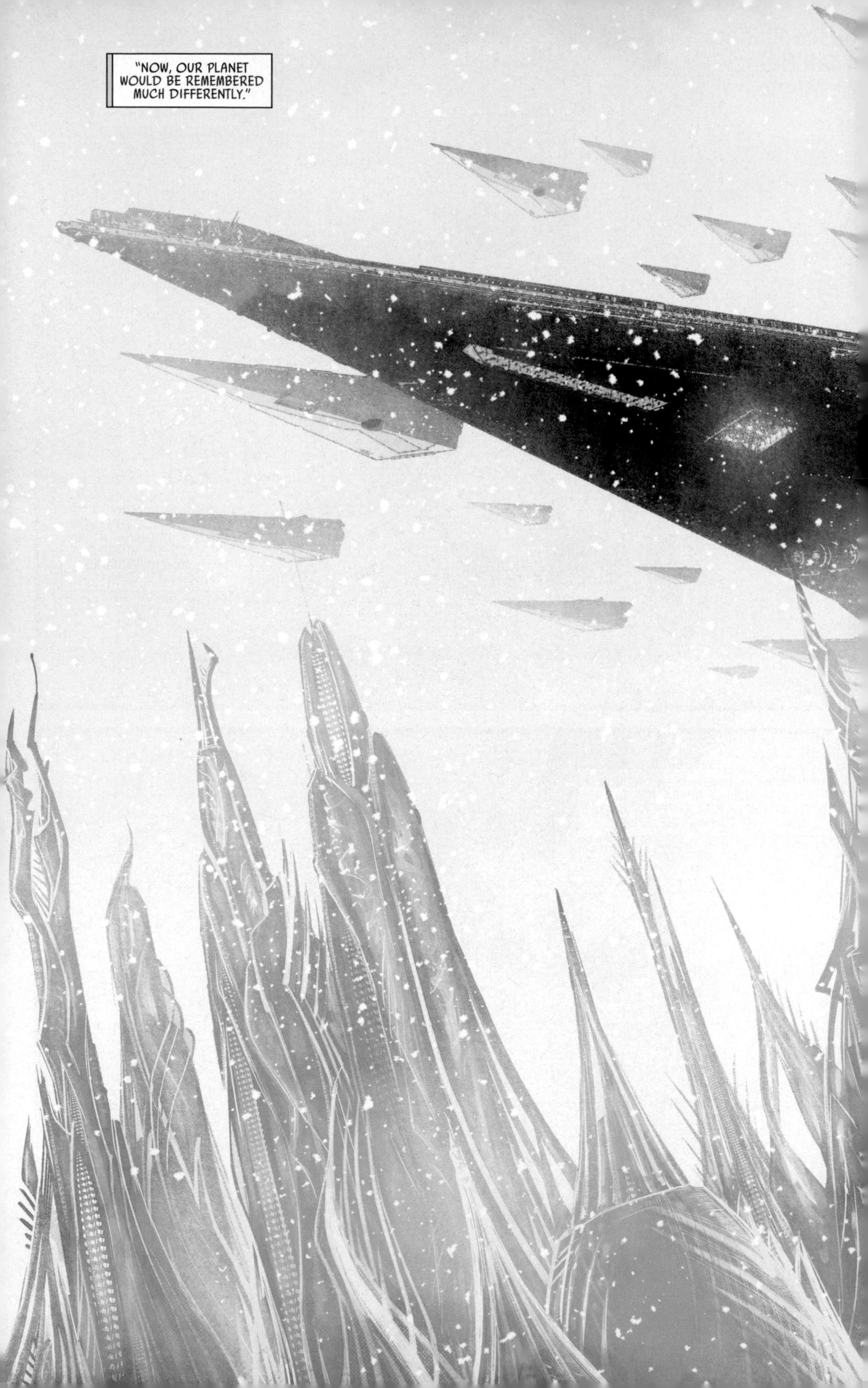
"NOW, OUR PLANET WOULD BE REMEMBERED MUCH DIFFERENTLY."

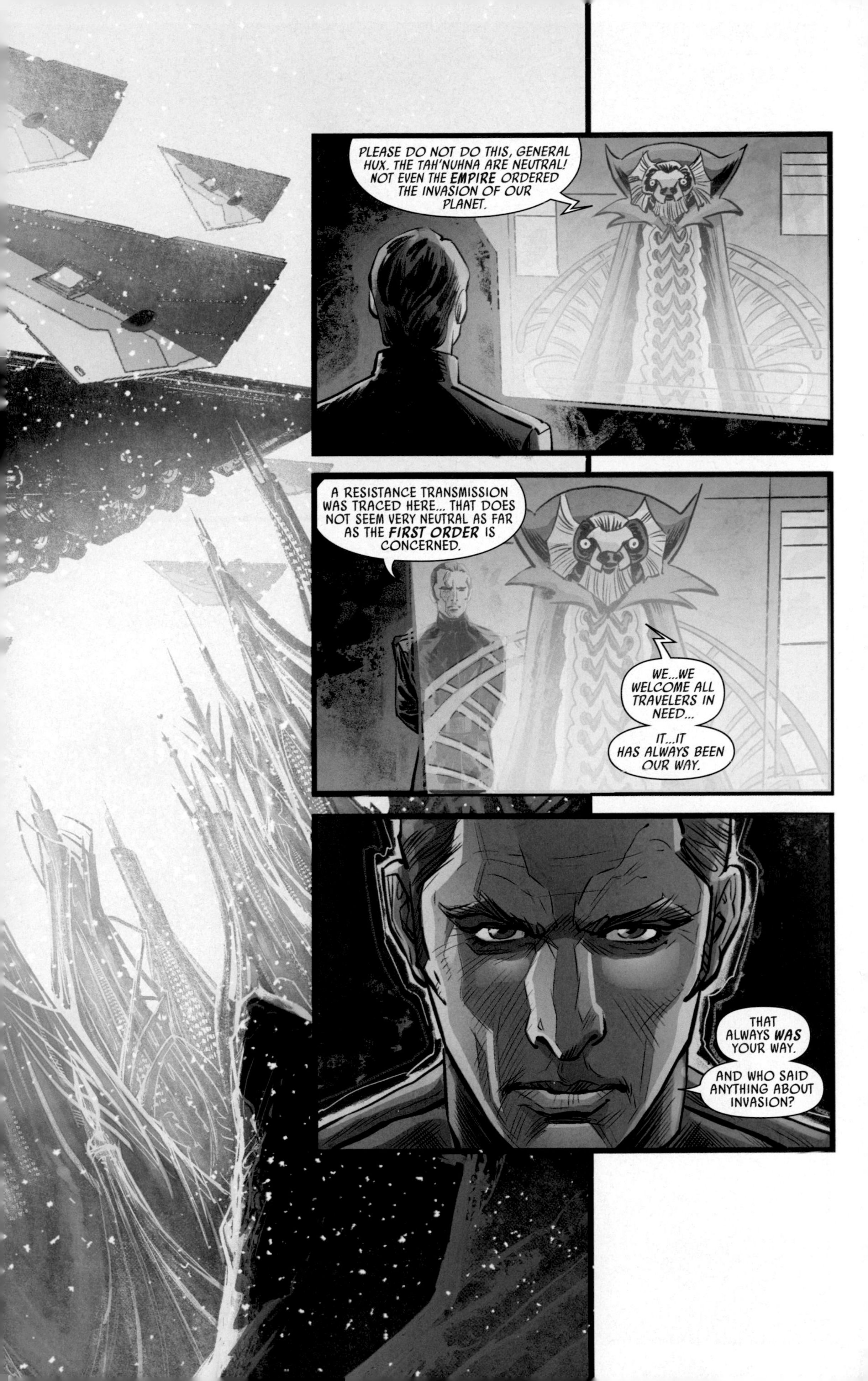
PLEASE DO NOT DO THIS, GENERAL HUX. THE TAH'NUHNA ARE NEUTRAL! NOT EVEN THE EMPIRE ORDERED THE INVASION OF OUR PLANET.
A RESISTANCE TRANSMISSION WAS TRACED HERE... THAT DOES NOT SEEM VERY NEUTRAL AS FAR AS THE FIRST ORDER IS CONCERNED.
WE...WE WELCOME ALL TRAVELERS IN NEED...
IT...IT HAS ALWAYS BEEN OUR WAY.
THAT ALWAYS WAS YOUR WAY.
AND WHO SAID ANYTHING ABOUT INVASION?

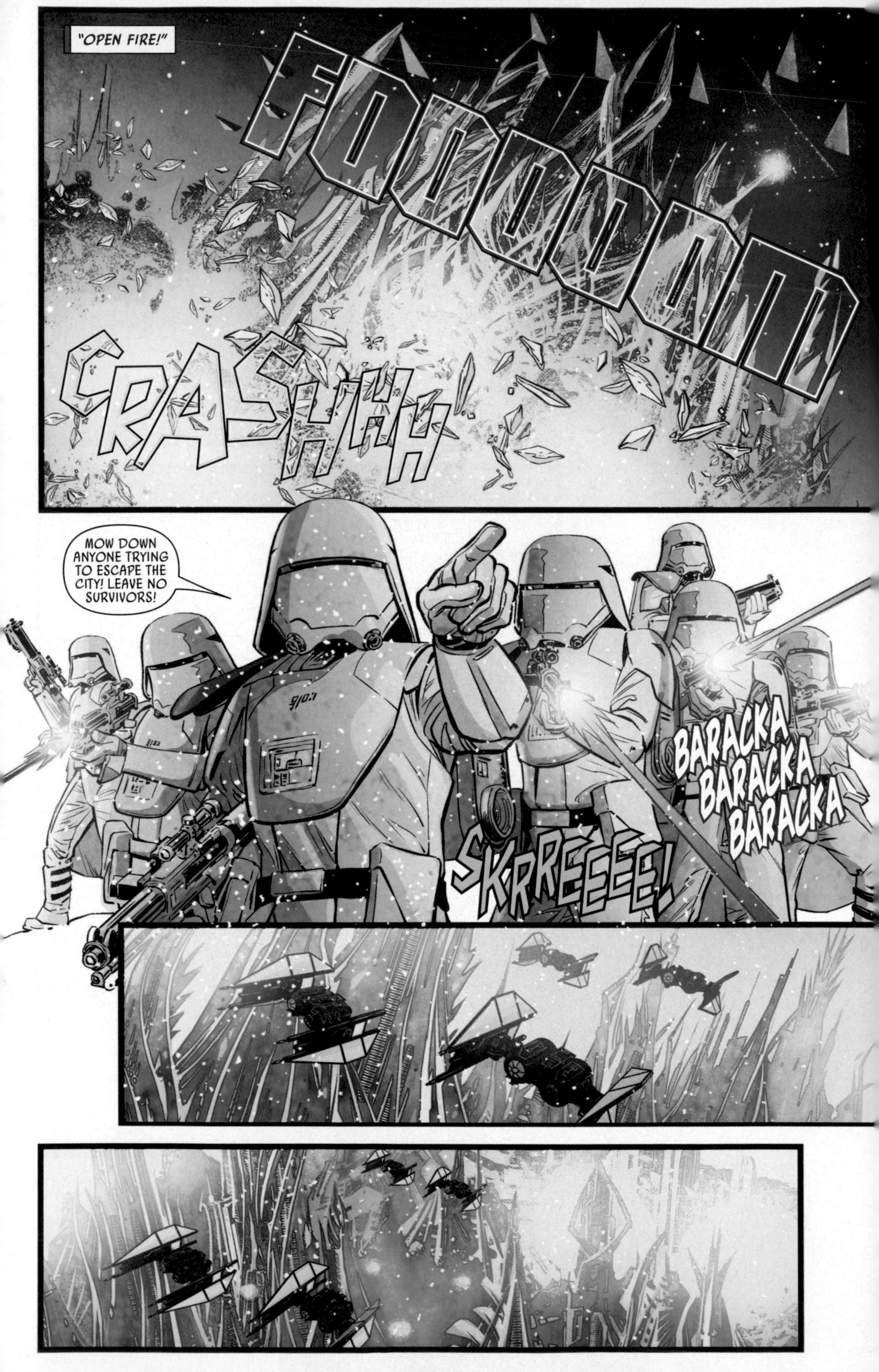
"OPEN FIRE!"
FOOOOOOM
CRASHHH
MOW DOWN ANYONE TRYING TO ESCAPE THE CITY! LEAVE NO SURVIVORS!
SKREEEEE!
BARACKA BARACKA BARACKA

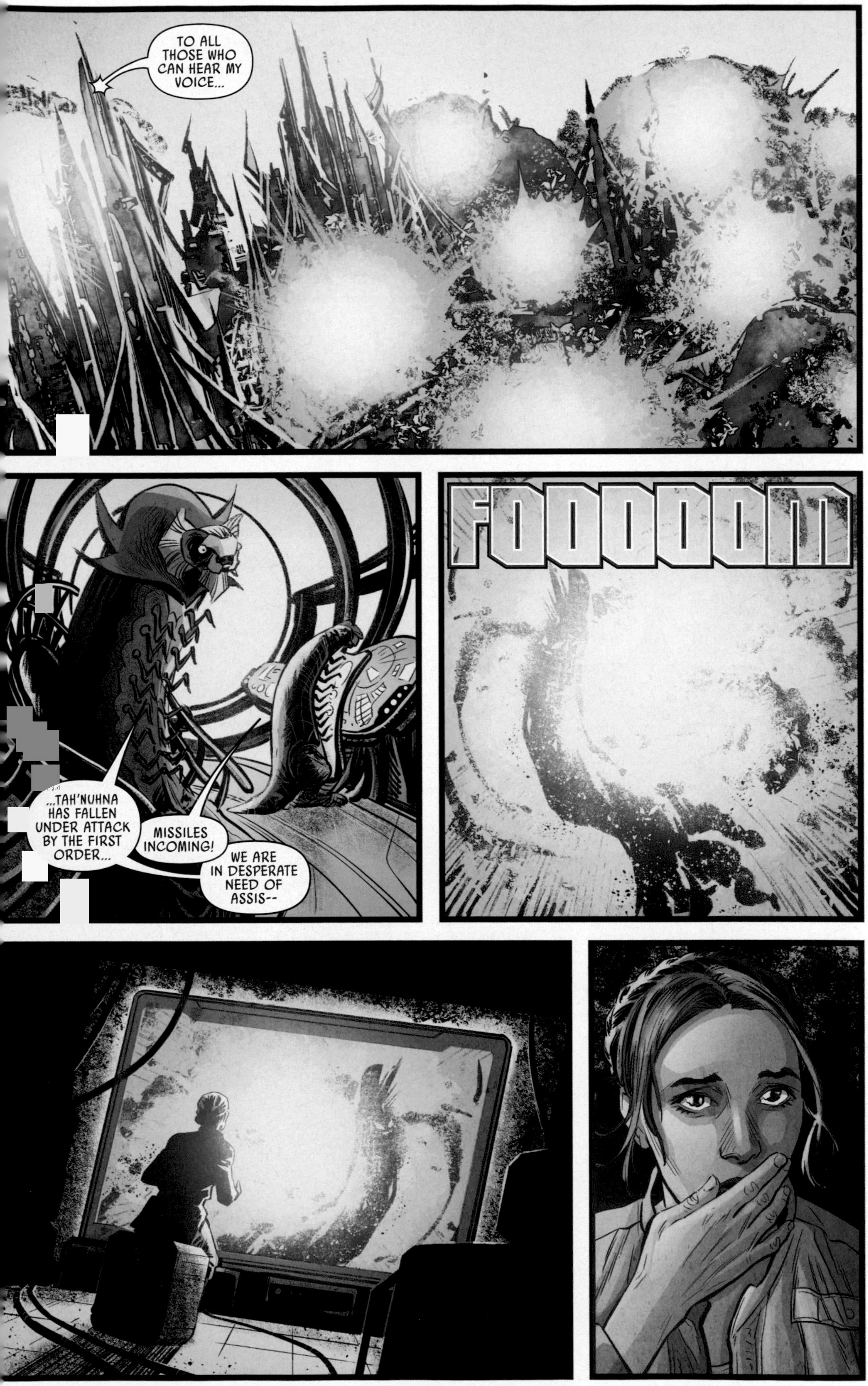
TO ALL THOSE WHO CAN HEAR MY VOICE...
...TAH'NUHNA HAS FALLEN UNDER ATTACK BY THE FIRST ORDER...
MISSILES INCOMING!
WE ARE IN DESPERATE NEED OF ASSIS--
FOOOOOM

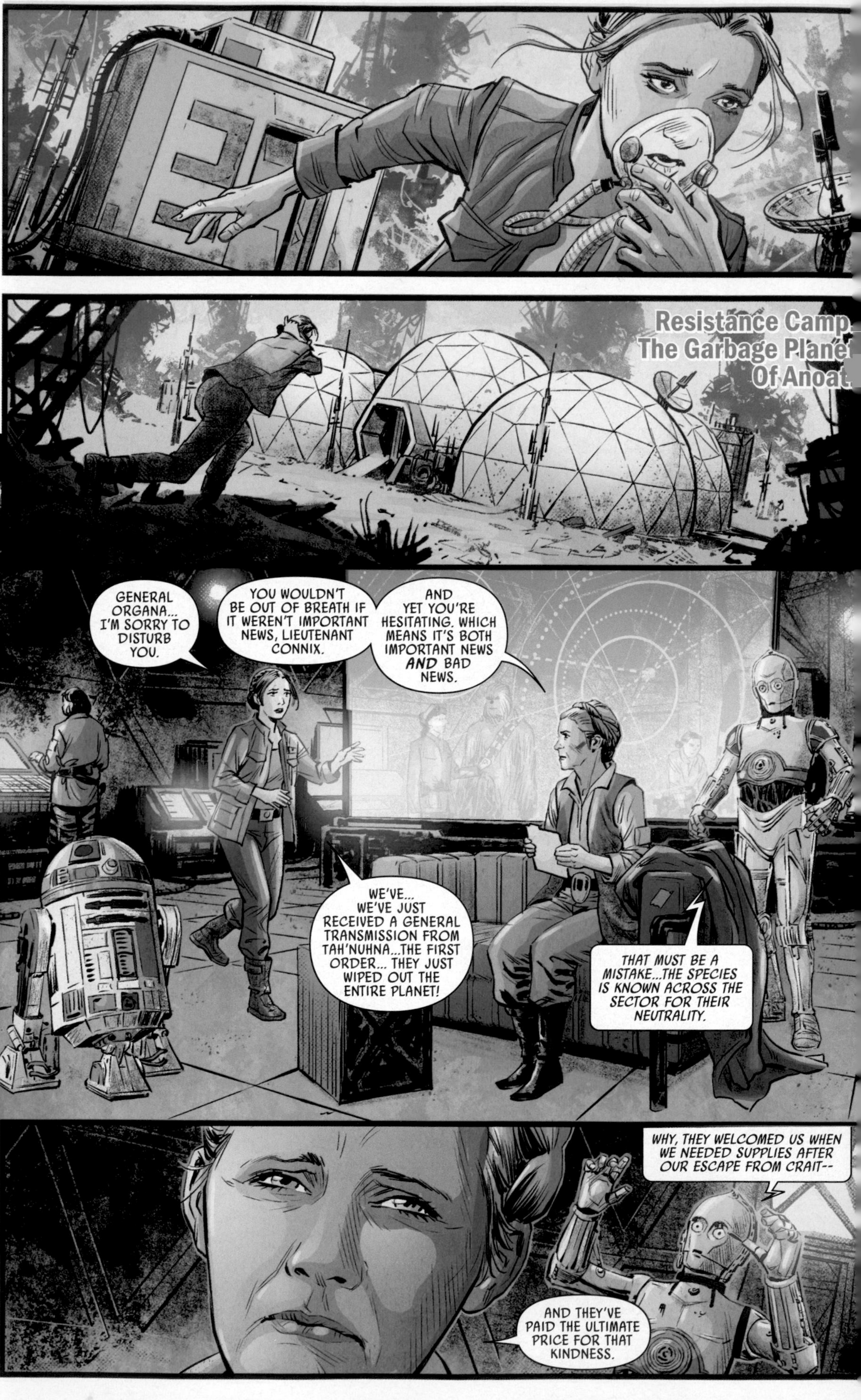
Resistance Camp. The Garbage Planet Of Anoat.
GENERAL ORGANA... I'M SORRY TO DISTURB YOU.
YOU WOULDN'T BE OUT OF BREATH IF IT WEREN'T IMPORTANT NEWS, LIEUTENANT CONNIX.
AND YET YOU'RE HESITATING. WHICH MEANS IT'S BOTH IMPORTANT NEWS AND BAD NEWS.
WE'VE... WE'VE JUST RECEIVED A GENERAL TRANSMISSION FROM TAH'NUHNA...THE FIRST ORDER... THEY JUST WIPED OUT THE ENTIRE PLANET!
THAT MUST BE A MISTAKE...THE SPECIES IS KNOWN ACROSS THE SECTOR FOR THEIR NEUTRALITY.
WHY, THEY WELCOMED US WHEN WE NEEDED SUPPLIES AFTER OUR ESCAPE FROM CRAIT--
AND THEY'VE PAID THE ULTIMATE PRICE FOR THAT KINDNESS.

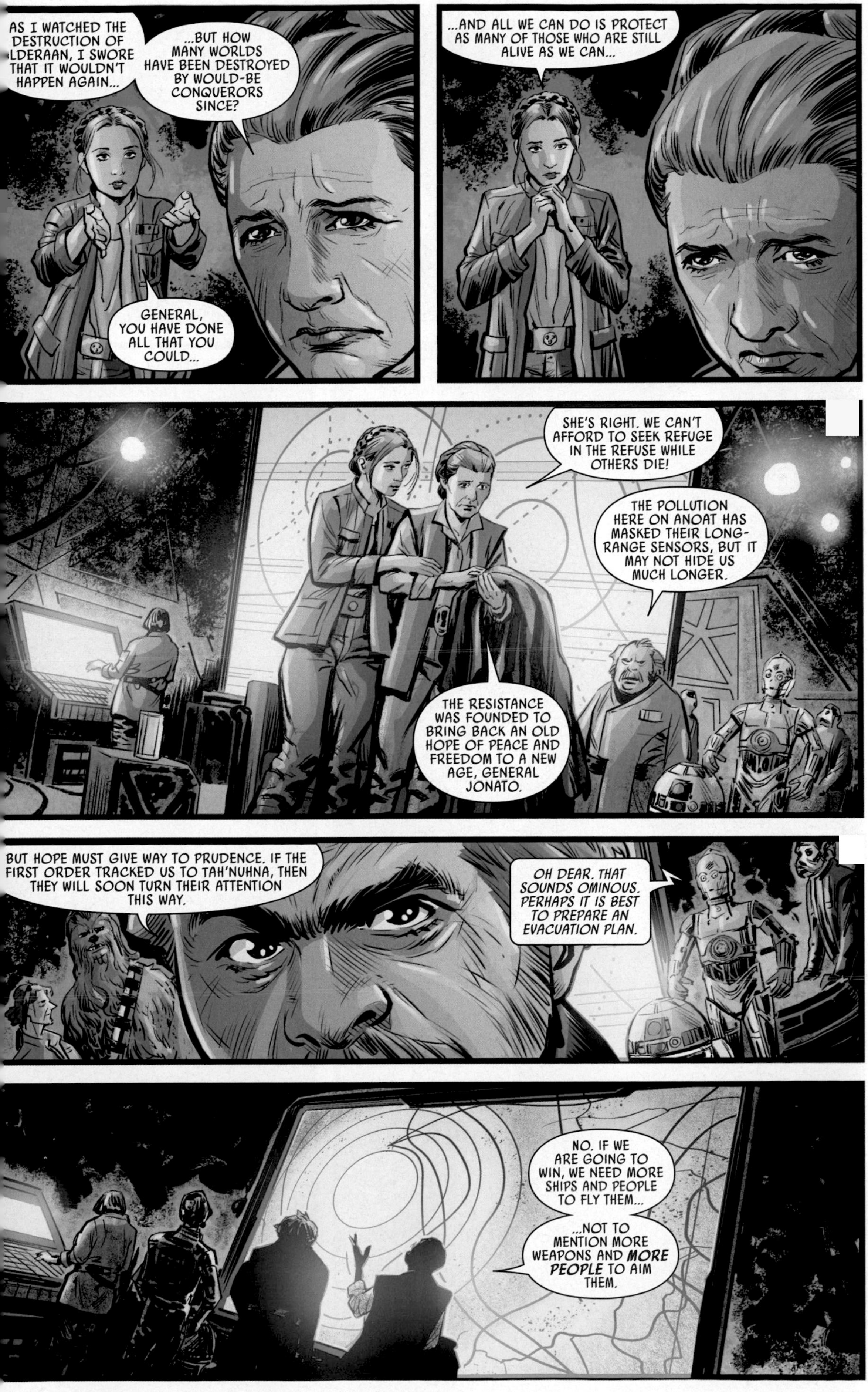

AS I WATCHED THE DESTRUCTION OF LDERAAN, I SWORE THAT IT WOULDN'T HAPPEN AGAIN...
...BUT HOW MANY WORLDS HAVE BEEN DESTROYED BY WOULD-BE CONQUERORS SINCE?
GENERAL, YOU HAVE DONE ALL THAT YOU COULD...
...AND ALL WE CAN DO IS PROTECT AS MANY OF THOSE WHO ARE STILL ALIVE AS WE CAN...
THE RESISTANCE WAS FOUNDED TO BRING BACK AN OLD HOPE OF PEACE AND FREEDOM TO A NEW AGE, GENERAL JONATO.
SHE'S RIGHT. WE CAN'T AFFORD TO SEEK REFUGE IN THE REFUSE WHILE OTHERS DIE!
THE POLLUTION HERE ON ANOAT HAS MASKED THEIR LONG-RANGE SENSORS, BUT IT MAY NOT HIDE US MUCH LONGER.
BUT HOPE MUST GIVE WAY TO PRUDENCE. IF THE FIRST ORDER TRACKED US TO TAH'NUHNA, THEN THEY WILL SOON TURN THEIR ATTENTION THIS WAY.
OH DEAR. THAT SOUNDS OMINOUS. PERHAPS IT IS BEST TO PREPARE AN EVACUATION PLAN.
NO. IF WE ARE GOING TO WIN, WE NEED MORE SHIPS AND PEOPLE TO FLY THEM...
...NOT TO MENTION MORE WEAPONS AND MORE PEOPLE TO AIM THEM.

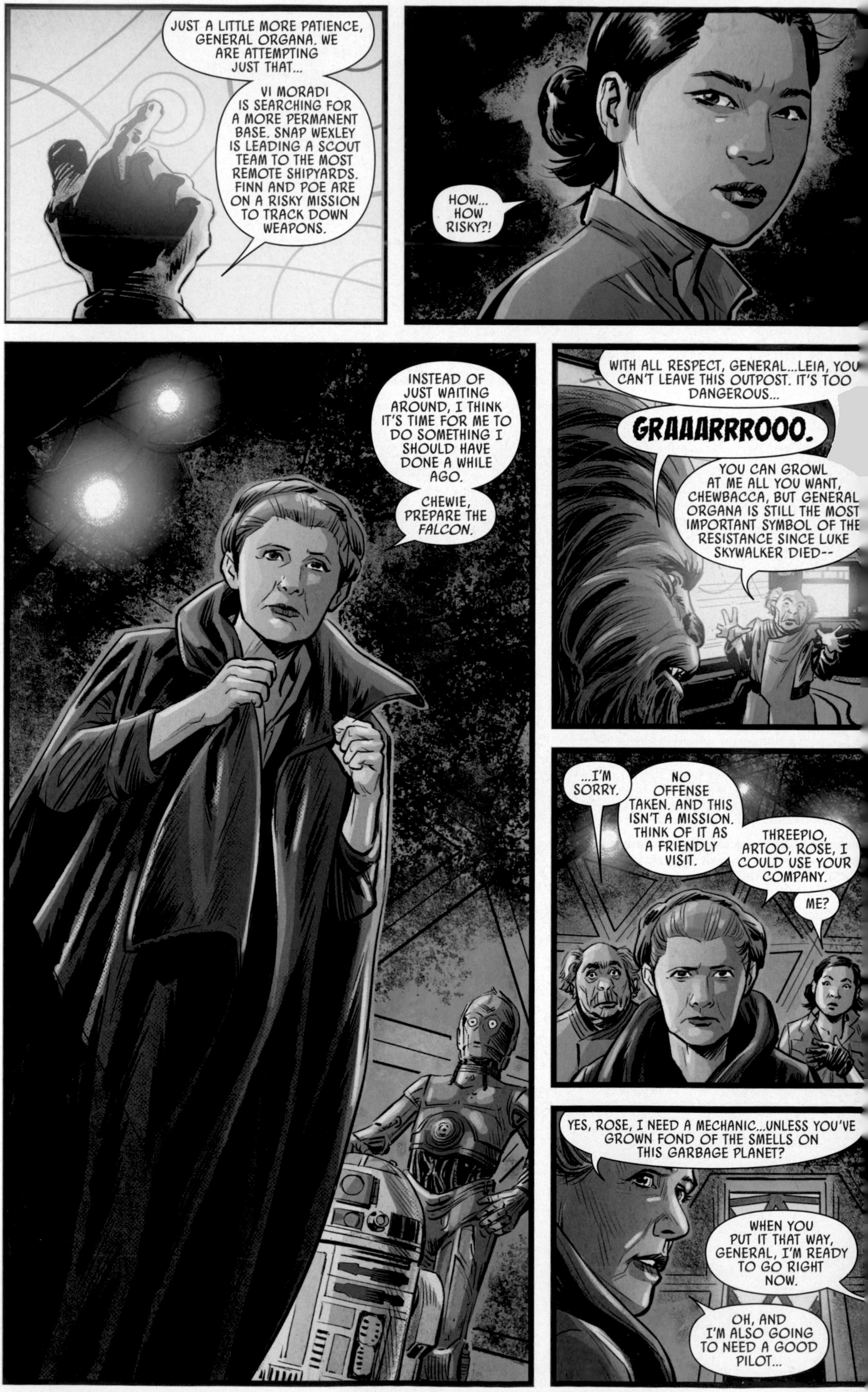
JUST A LITTLE MORE PATIENCE, GENERAL ORGANA. WE ARE ATTEMPTING JUST THAT...
VI MORADI IS SEARCHING FOR A MORE PERMANENT BASE. SNAP WEXLEY IS LEADING A SCOUT TEAM TO THE MOST REMOTE SHIPYARDS. FINN AND POE ARE ON A RISKY MISSION TO TRACK DOWN WEAPONS.
HOW... HOW RISKY?!
INSTEAD OF JUST WAITING AROUND, I THINK IT'S TIME FOR ME TO DO SOMETHING I SHOULD HAVE DONE A WHILE AGO.
CHEWIE, PREPARE THE *FALCON*.
WITH ALL RESPECT, GENERAL...LEIA, YOU CAN'T LEAVE THIS OUTPOST. IT'S TOO DANGEROUS...
GRAAARRROOO.
YOU CAN GROWL AT ME ALL YOU WANT, CHEWBACCA, BUT GENERAL ORGANA IS STILL THE MOST IMPORTANT SYMBOL OF THE RESISTANCE SINCE LUKE SKYWALKER DIED--
...I'M SORRY.
NO OFFENSE TAKEN. AND THIS ISN'T A MISSION. THINK OF IT AS A FRIENDLY VISIT.
THREEPIO, ARTOO, ROSE, I COULD USE YOUR COMPANY.
ME?
YES, ROSE, I NEED A MECHANIC...UNLESS YOU'VE GROWN FOND OF THE SMELLS ON THIS GARBAGE PLANET?
WHEN YOU PUT IT THAT WAY, GENERAL, I'M READY TO GO RIGHT NOW.
OH, AND I'M ALSO GOING TO NEED A GOOD PILOT...

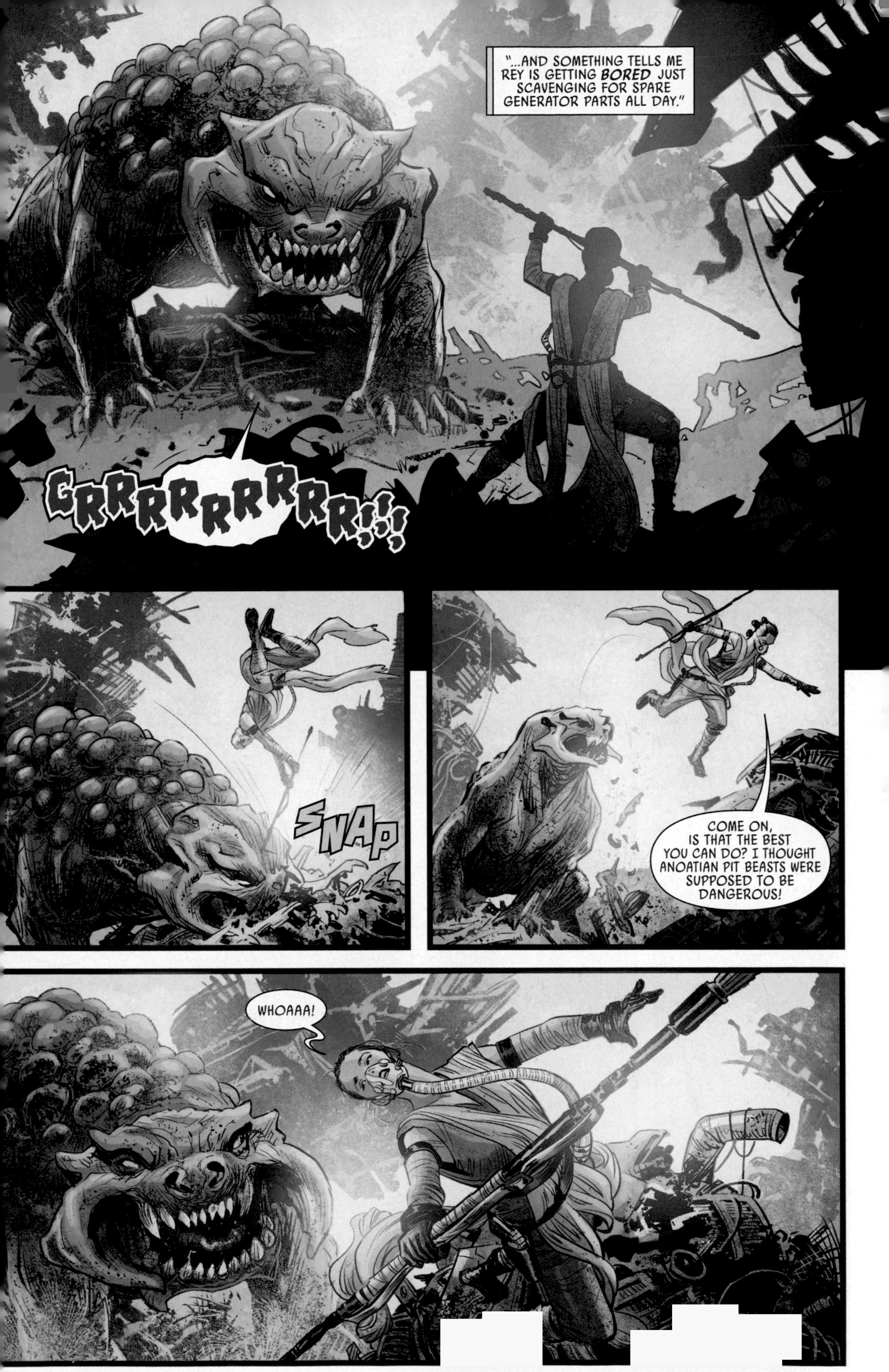
"...AND SOMETHING TELLS ME REY IS GETTING BORED JUST SCAVENGING FOR SPARE GENERATOR PARTS ALL DAY."
GRRRRRRRRRR!!!
SNAP
COME ON, IS THAT THE BEST YOU CAN DO? I THOUGHT ANOATIAN PIT BEASTS WERE SUPPOSED TO BE DANGEROUS!
WHOAAA!

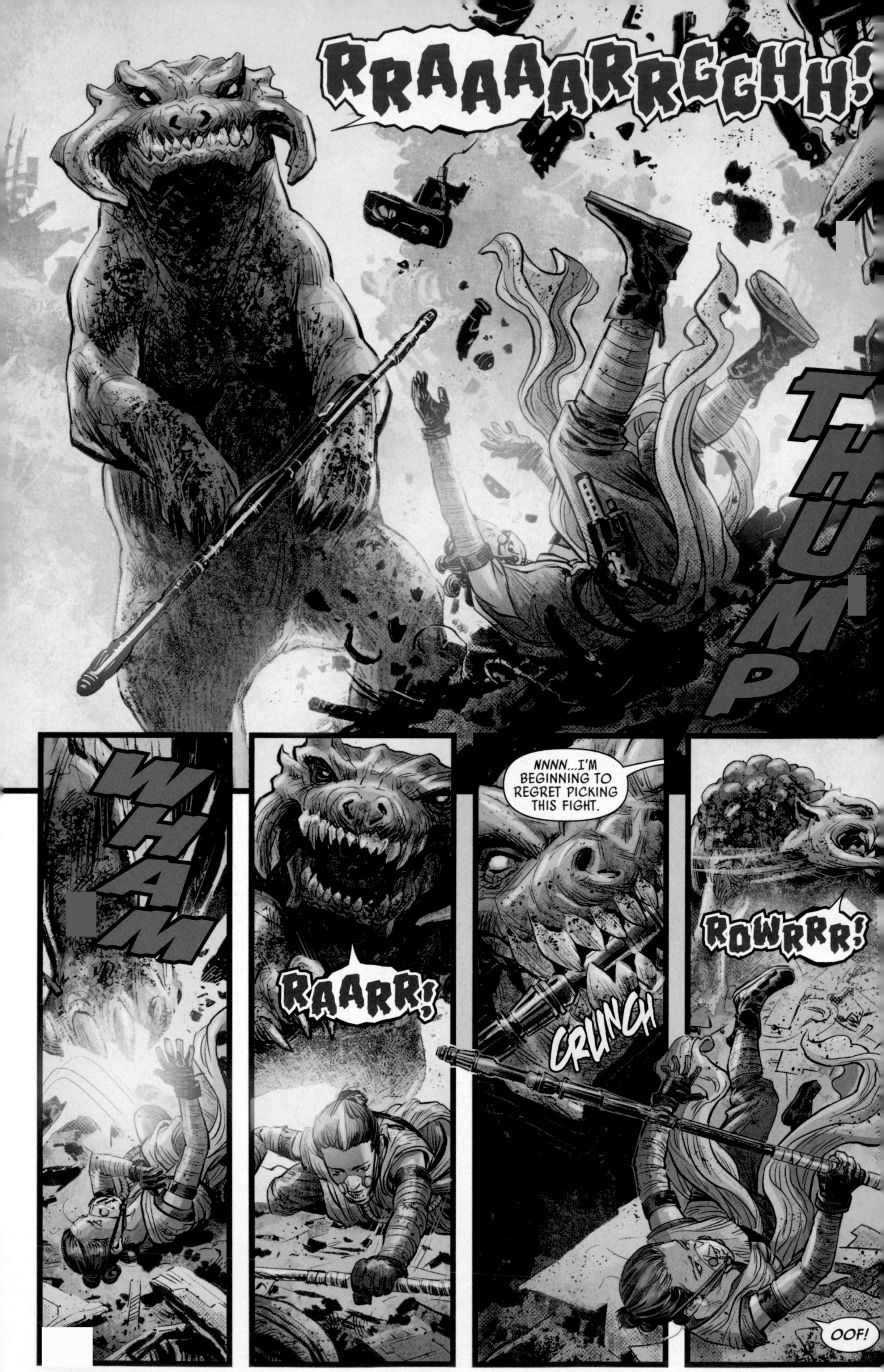
RRAAAAARRRGGHH!
THUMP
WHAM
RAARR!
NNNN...I'M BEGINNING TO REGRET PICKING THIS FIGHT.
CRUNCH
ROWRRR!
OOF!

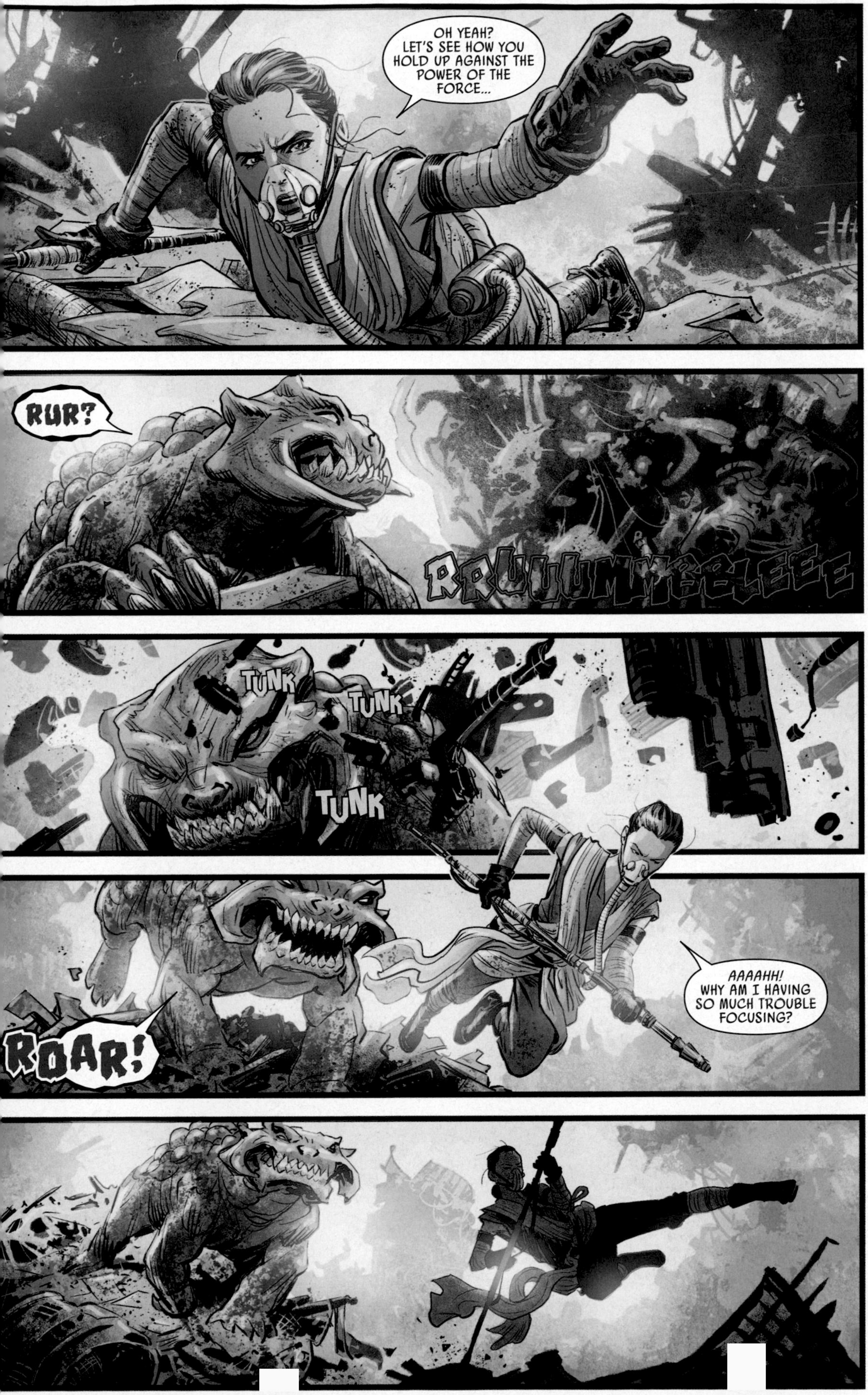

OH YEAH? LET'S SEE HOW YOU HOLD UP AGAINST THE POWER OF THE FORCE...
RUR?
RRUUUMMBBLEEE
TUNK
TUNK
TUNK
ROAR!
AAAAHH! WHY AM I HAVING SO MUCH TROUBLE FOCUSING?

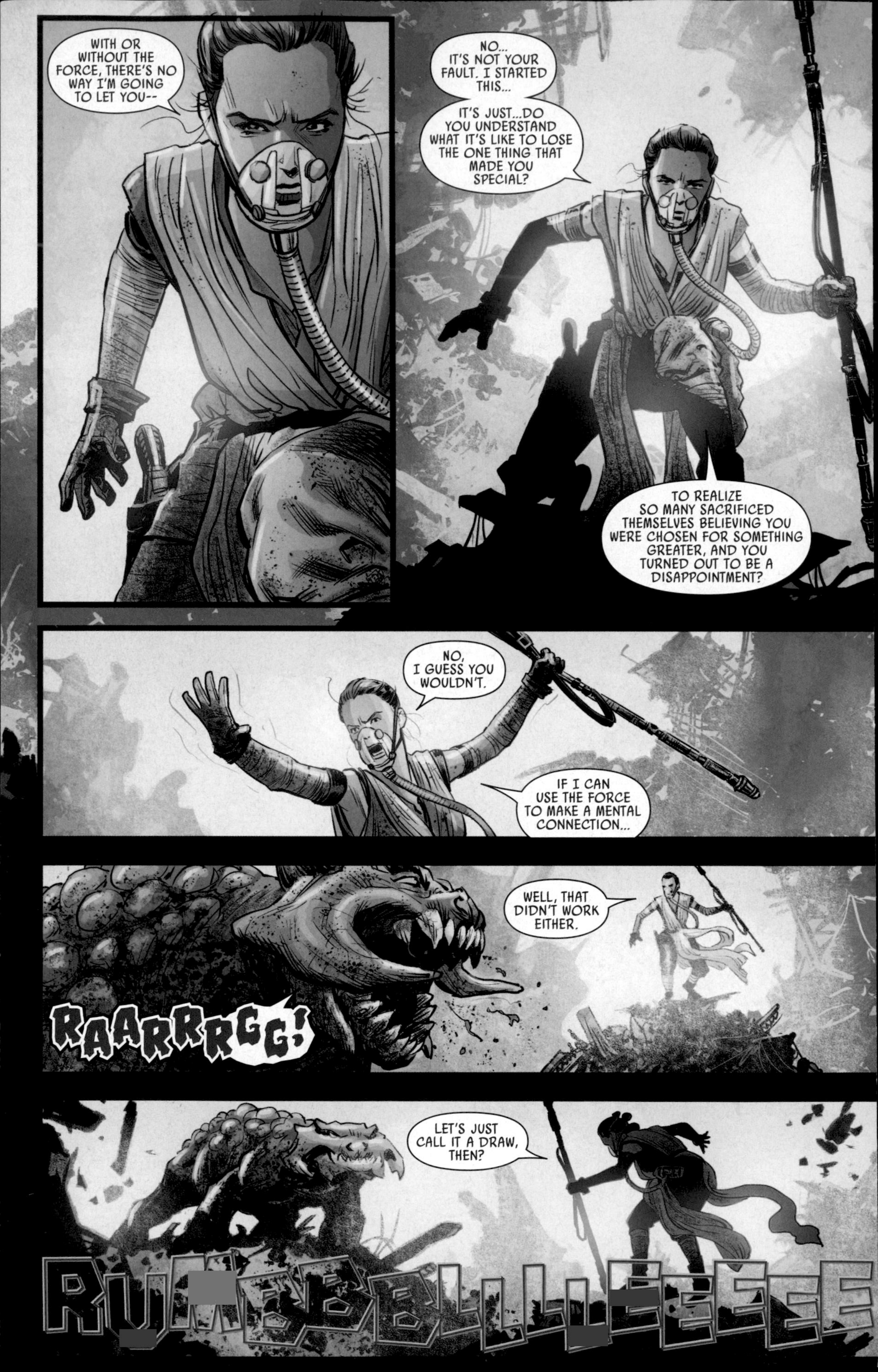

WITH OR WITHOUT THE FORCE, THERE'S NO WAY I'M GOING TO LET YOU--
NO... IT'S NOT YOUR FAULT. I STARTED THIS...
IT'S JUST...DO YOU UNDERSTAND WHAT IT'S LIKE TO LOSE THE ONE THING THAT MADE YOU SPECIAL?
TO REALIZE SO MANY SACRIFICED THEMSELVES BELIEVING YOU WERE CHOSEN FOR SOMETHING GREATER, AND YOU TURNED OUT TO BE A DISAPPOINTMENT?
NO, I GUESS YOU WOULDN'T.
IF I CAN USE THE FORCE TO MAKE A MENTAL CONNECTION...
WELL, THAT DIDN'T WORK EITHER.
RAARRRGG!
LET'S JUST CALL IT A DRAW, THEN?

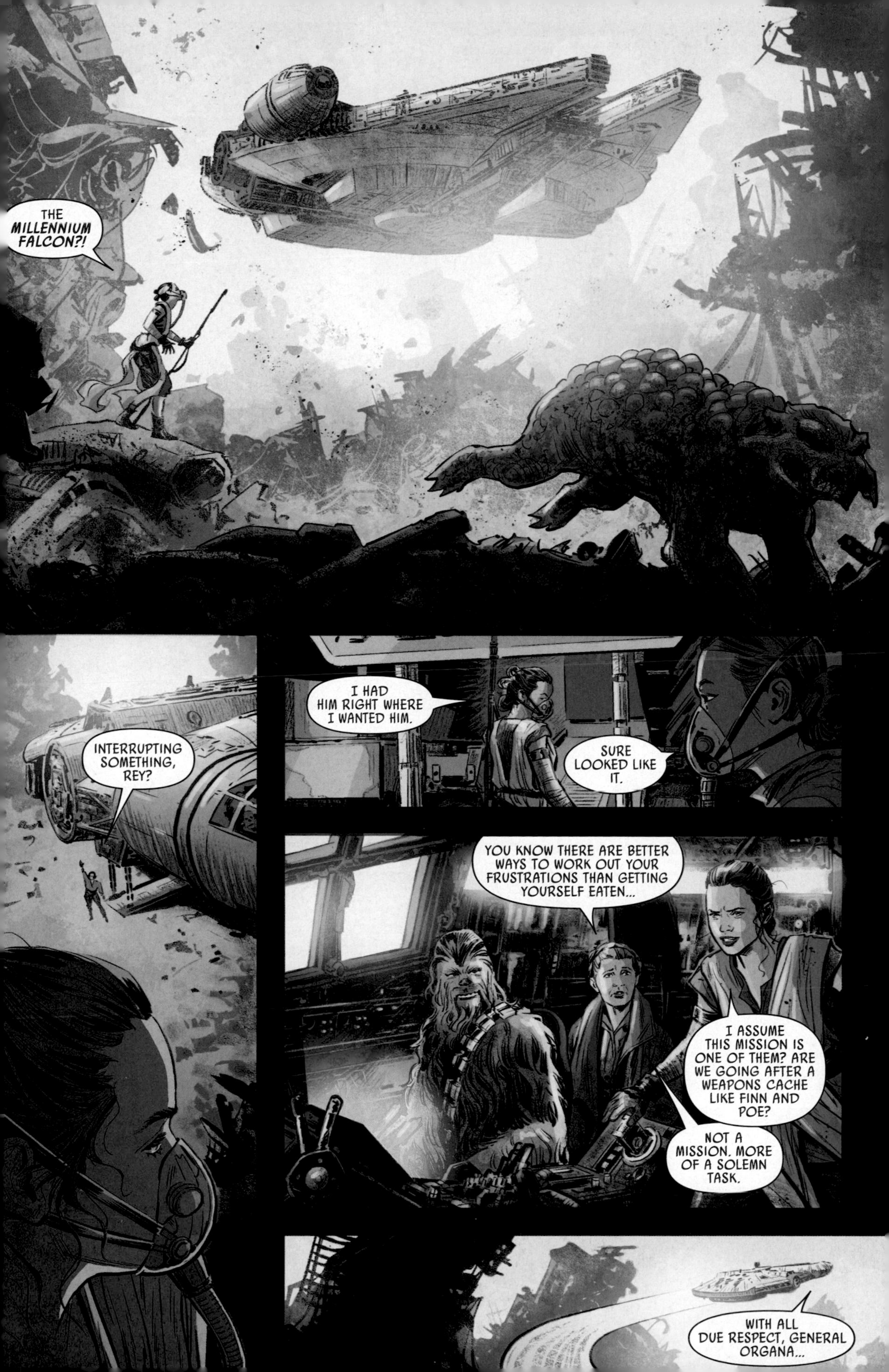
THE *MILLENNIUM FALCON?!*
INTERRUPTING SOMETHING, REY?
I HAD HIM RIGHT WHERE I WANTED HIM.
SURE LOOKED LIKE IT.
YOU KNOW THERE ARE BETTER WAYS TO WORK OUT YOUR FRUSTRATIONS THAN GETTING YOURSELF EATEN...
I ASSUME THIS MISSION IS ONE OF THEM? ARE WE GOING AFTER A WEAPONS CACHE LIKE FINN AND POE?
NOT A MISSION. MORE OF A SOLEMN TASK.
WITH ALL DUE RESPECT, GENERAL ORGANA...

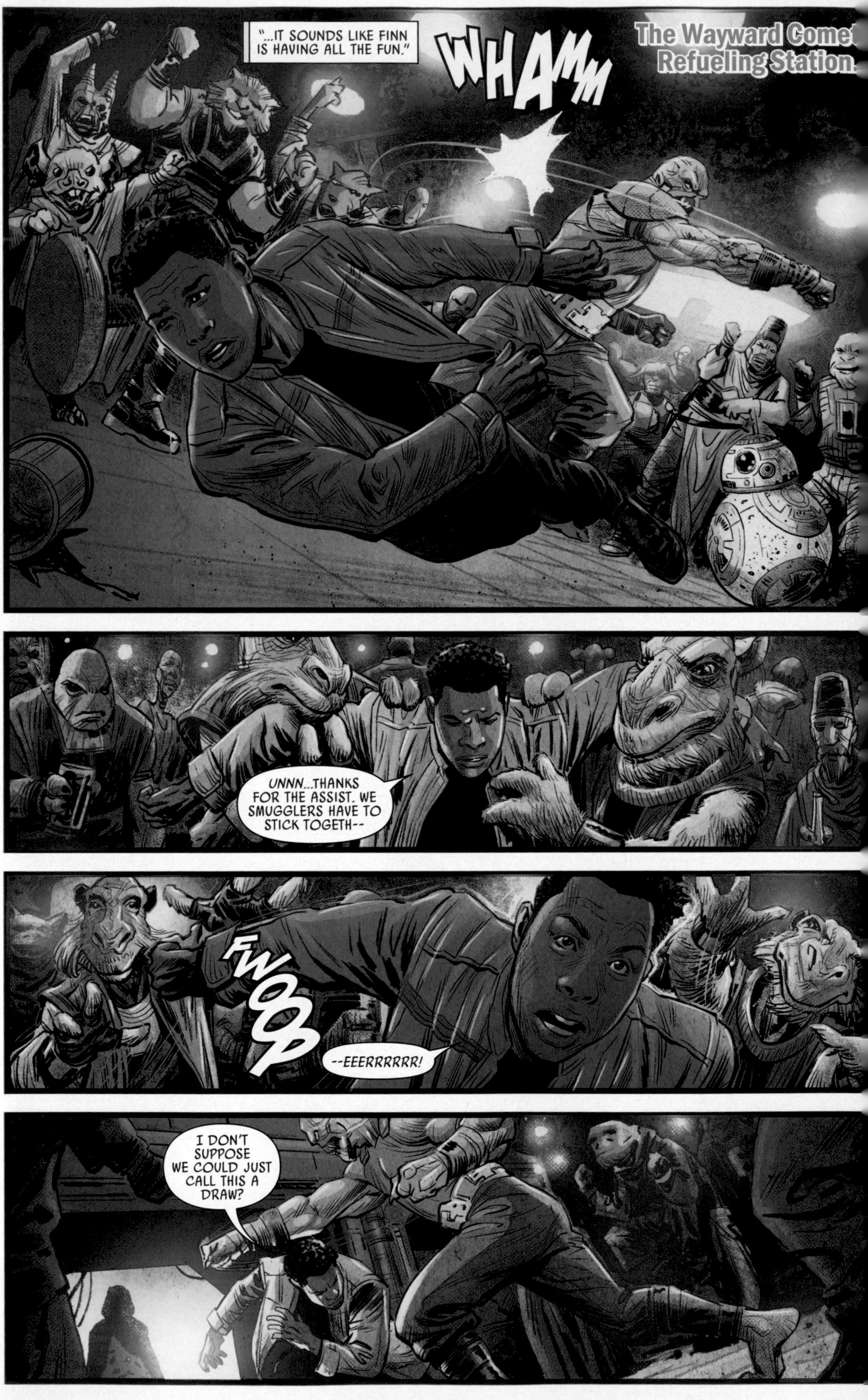
"...IT SOUNDS LIKE FINN IS HAVING ALL THE FUN."
WHAMMM
The Wayward Comet Refueling Station.
UNNN...THANKS FOR THE ASSIST. WE SMUGGLERS HAVE TO STICK TOGETH--
FWOOP
--EEERRRRRR!
I DON'T SUPPOSE WE COULD JUST CALL THIS A DRAW?

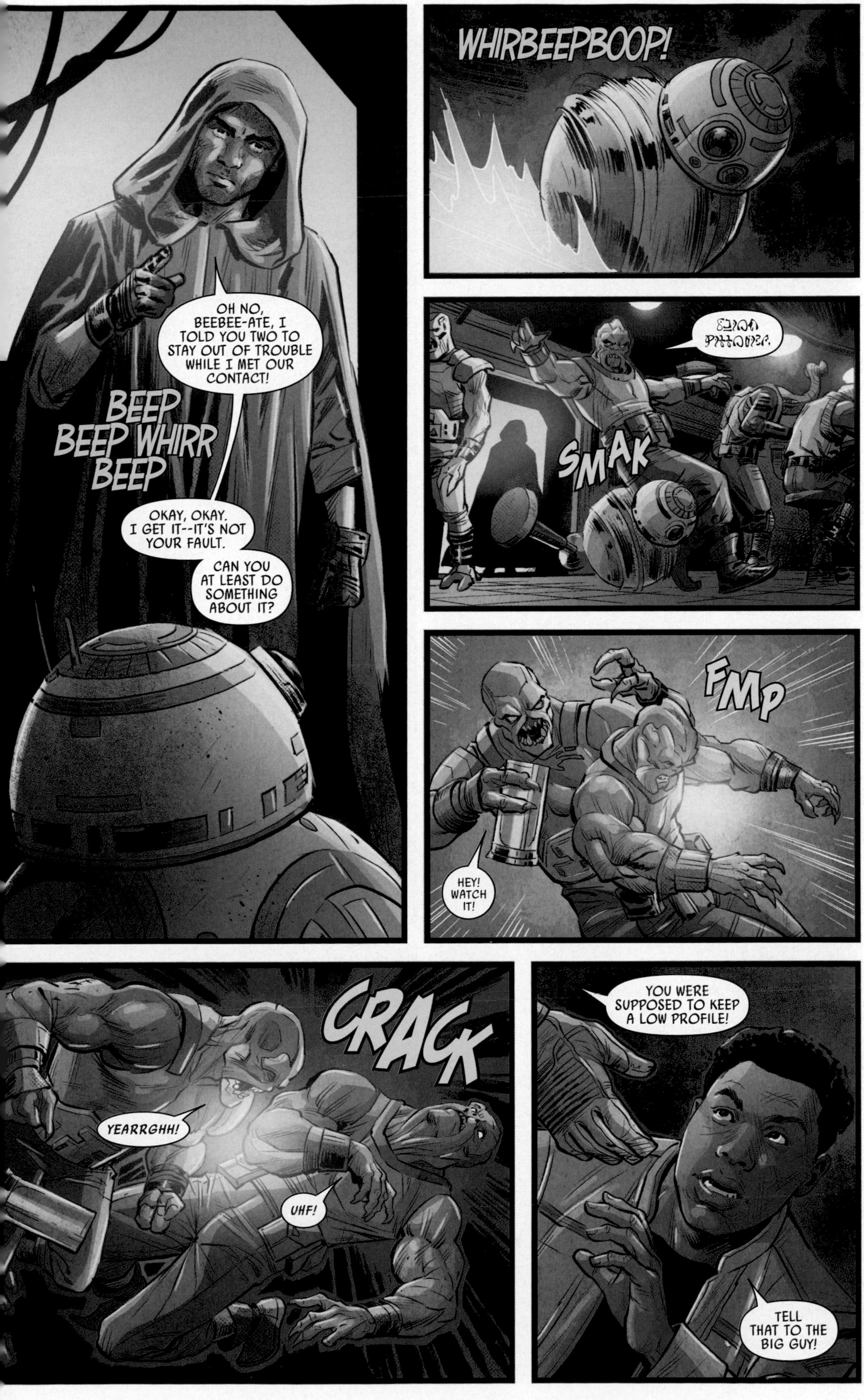

OH NO, BEEBEE-ATE, I TOLD YOU TWO TO STAY OUT OF TROUBLE WHILE I MET OUR CONTACT!
BEEP BEEP WHIRR BEEP
OKAY, OKAY. I GET IT--IT'S NOT YOUR FAULT.
CAN YOU AT LEAST DO SOMETHING ABOUT IT?
WHIRBEEPBOOP!
SMAK
FMP
HEY! WATCH IT!
CRACK
YEARRGHH!
UHF!
YOU WERE SUPPOSED TO KEEP A LOW PROFILE!
TELL THAT TO THE BIG GUY!

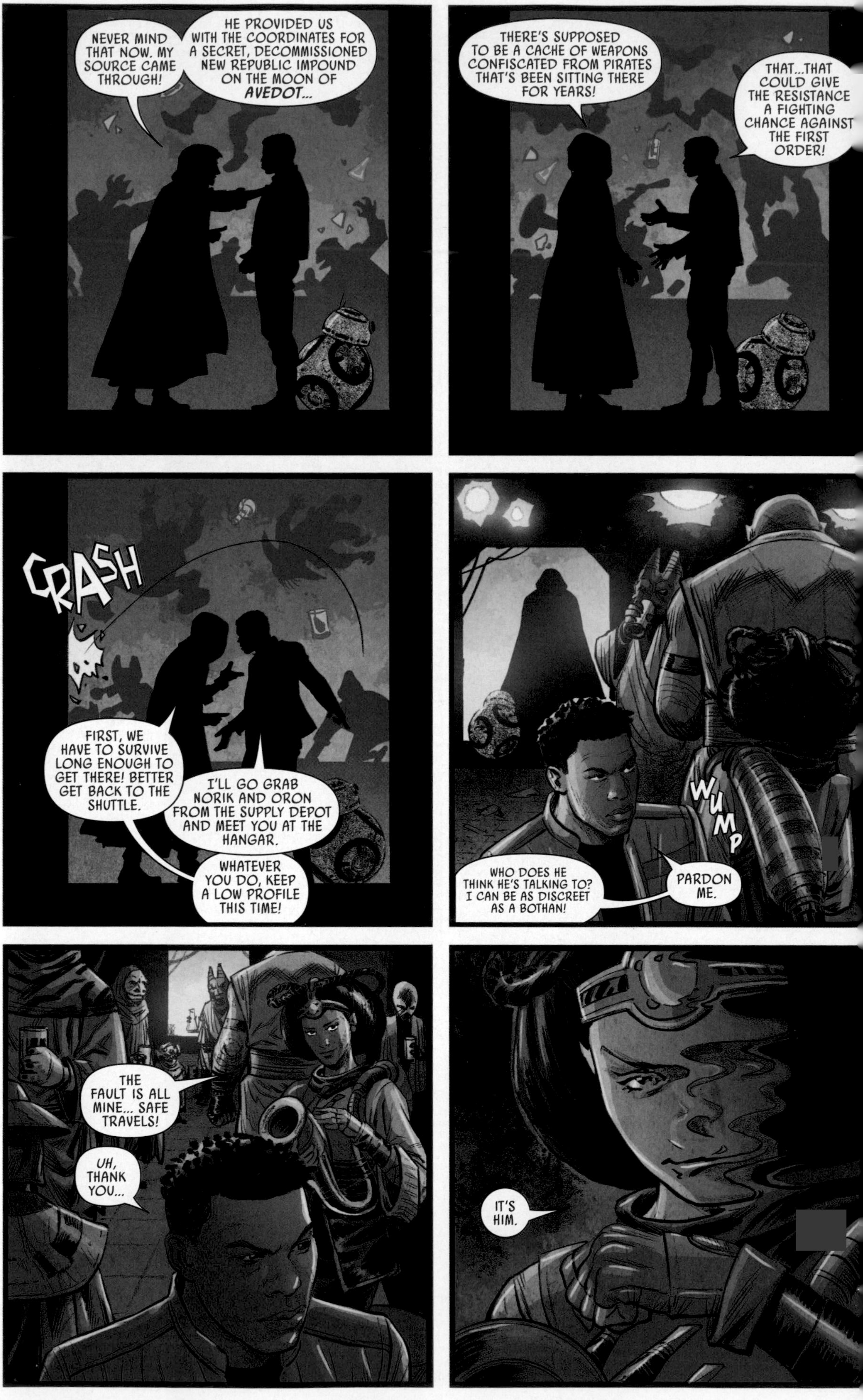
NEVER MIND THAT NOW. MY SOURCE CAME THROUGH!
HE PROVIDED US WITH THE COORDINATES FOR A SECRET, DECOMMISSIONED NEW REPUBLIC IMPOUND ON THE MOON OF AVEDOT...
THERE'S SUPPOSED TO BE A CACHE OF WEAPONS CONFISCATED FROM PIRATES THAT'S BEEN SITTING THERE FOR YEARS!
THAT...THAT COULD GIVE THE RESISTANCE A FIGHTING CHANCE AGAINST THE FIRST ORDER!
CRASH
FIRST, WE HAVE TO SURVIVE LONG ENOUGH TO GET THERE! BETTER GET BACK TO THE SHUTTLE.
I'LL GO GRAB NORIK AND ORON FROM THE SUPPLY DEPOT AND MEET YOU AT THE HANGAR.
WHATEVER YOU DO, KEEP A LOW PROFILE THIS TIME!
WUMP
PARDON ME.
WHO DOES HE THINK HE'S TALKING TO? I CAN BE AS DISCREET AS A BOTHAN!
THE FAULT IS ALL MINE... SAFE TRAVELS!
UH, THANK YOU...
IT'S HIM.

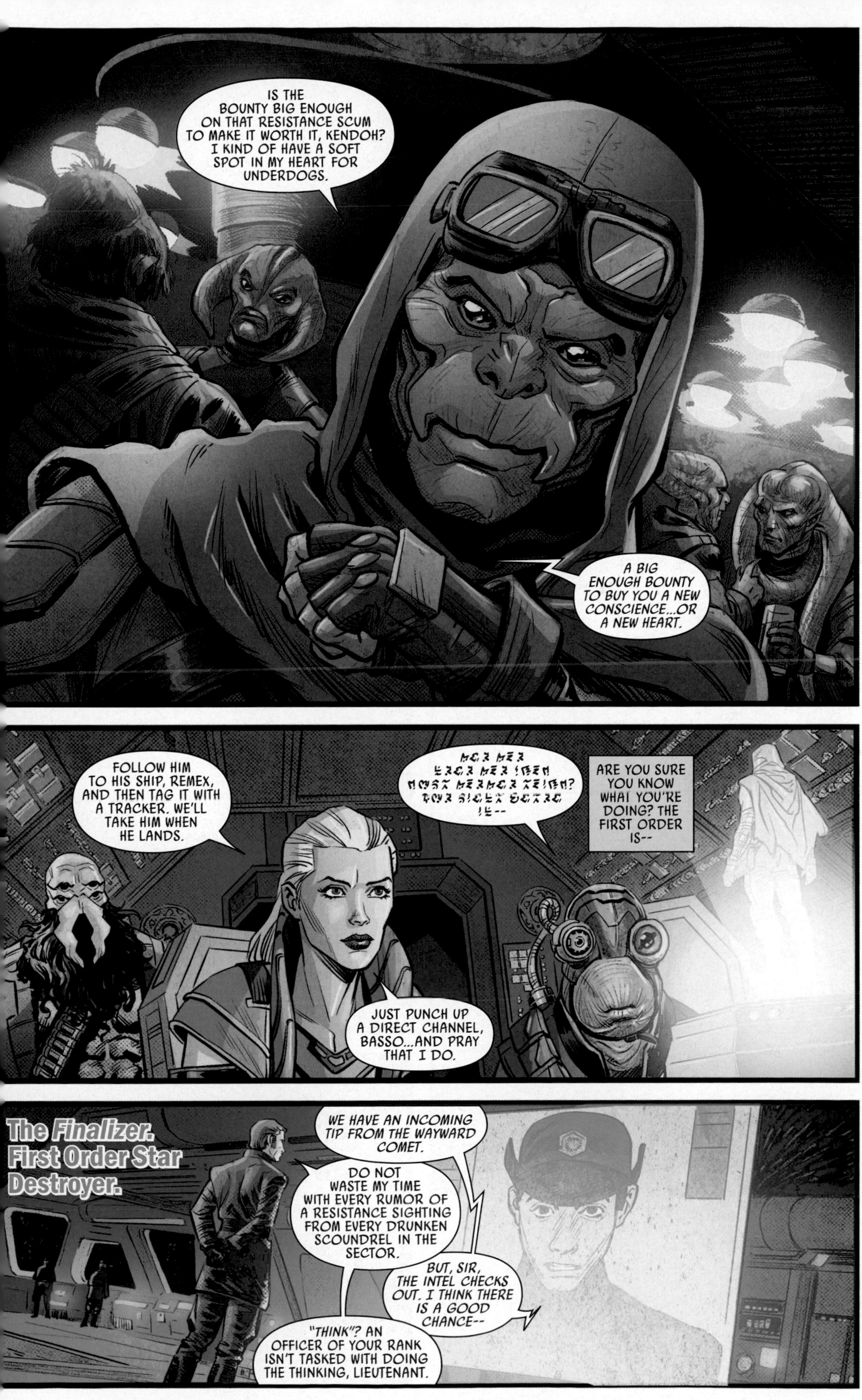
IS THE BOUNTY BIG ENOUGH ON THAT RESISTANCE SCUM TO MAKE IT WORTH IT, KENDOH? I KIND OF HAVE A SOFT SPOT IN MY HEART FOR UNDERDOGS.
A BIG ENOUGH BOUNTY TO BUY YOU A NEW CONSCIENCE...OR A NEW HEART.
FOLLOW HIM TO HIS SHIP, REMEX, AND THEN TAG IT WITH A TRACKER. WE'LL TAKE HIM WHEN HE LANDS.
ARE YOU SURE YOU KNOW WHAT YOU'RE DOING? THE FIRST ORDER IS--
JUST PUNCH UP A DIRECT CHANNEL, BASSO...AND PRAY THAT I DO.
The *Finalizer.* First Order Star Destroyer.
WE HAVE AN INCOMING TIP FROM THE WAYWARD COMET.
DO NOT WASTE MY TIME WITH EVERY RUMOR OF A RESISTANCE SIGHTING FROM EVERY DRUNKEN SCOUNDREL IN THE SECTOR.
BUT, SIR, THE INTEL CHECKS OUT. I THINK THERE IS A GOOD CHANCE--
"THINK"? AN OFFICER OF YOUR RANK ISN'T TASKED WITH DOING THE THINKING, LIEUTENANT.

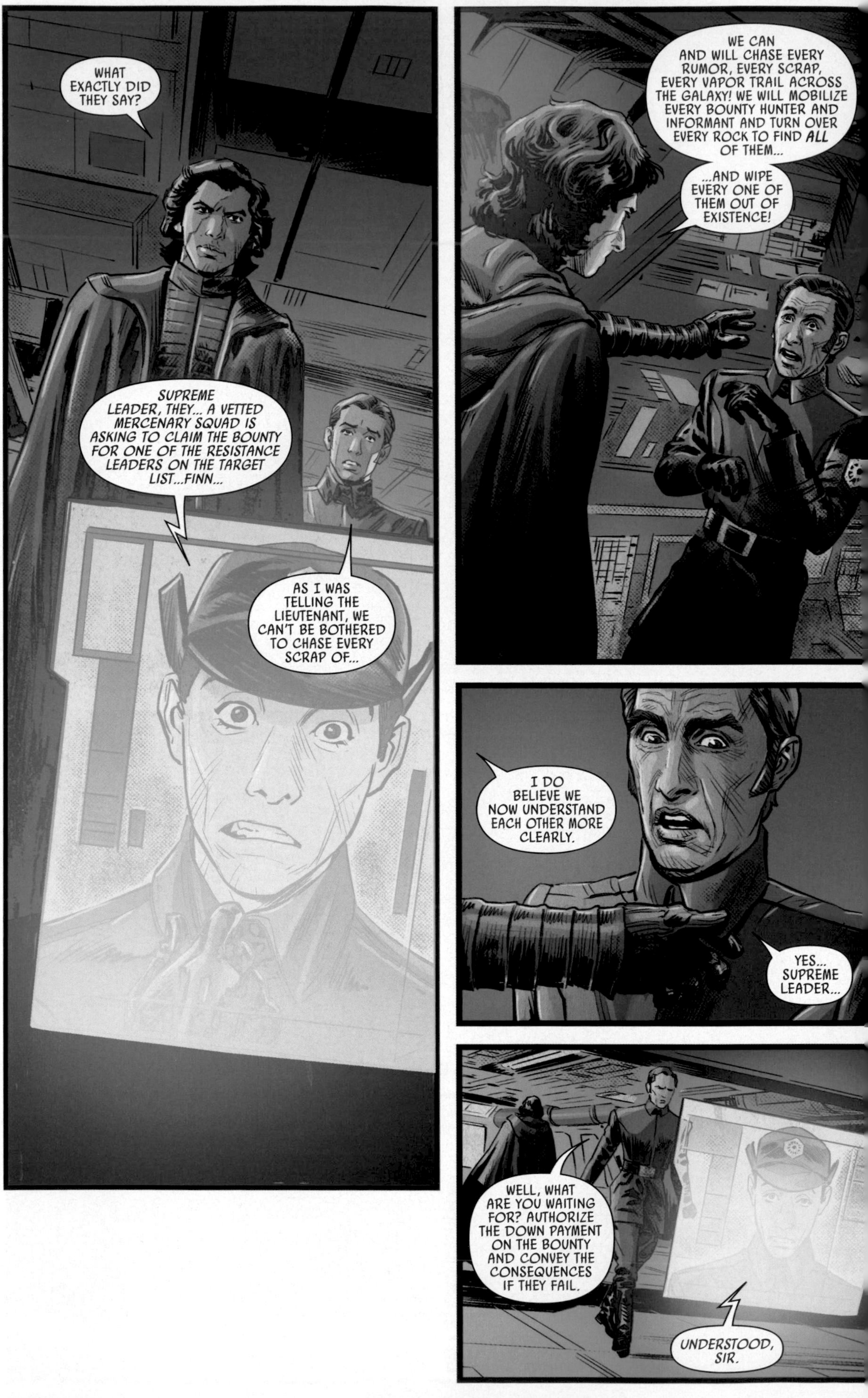
WHAT EXACTLY DID THEY SAY?
SUPREME LEADER, THEY... A VETTED MERCENARY SQUAD IS ASKING TO CLAIM THE BOUNTY FOR ONE OF THE RESISTANCE LEADERS ON THE TARGET LIST...FINN...
AS I WAS TELLING THE LIEUTENANT, WE CAN'T BE BOTHERED TO CHASE EVERY SCRAP OF...
WE CAN AND WILL CHASE EVERY RUMOR, EVERY SCRAP, EVERY VAPOR TRAIL ACROSS THE GALAXY! WE WILL MOBILIZE EVERY BOUNTY HUNTER AND INFORMANT AND TURN OVER EVERY ROCK TO FIND ALL OF THEM...
...AND WIPE EVERY ONE OF THEM OUT OF EXISTENCE!
I DO BELIEVE WE NOW UNDERSTAND EACH OTHER MORE CLEARLY.
YES... SUPREME LEADER...
WELL, WHAT ARE YOU WAITING FOR? AUTHORIZE THE DOWN PAYMENT ON THE BOUNTY AND CONVEY THE CONSEQUENCES IF THEY FAIL.
UNDERSTOOD, SIR.

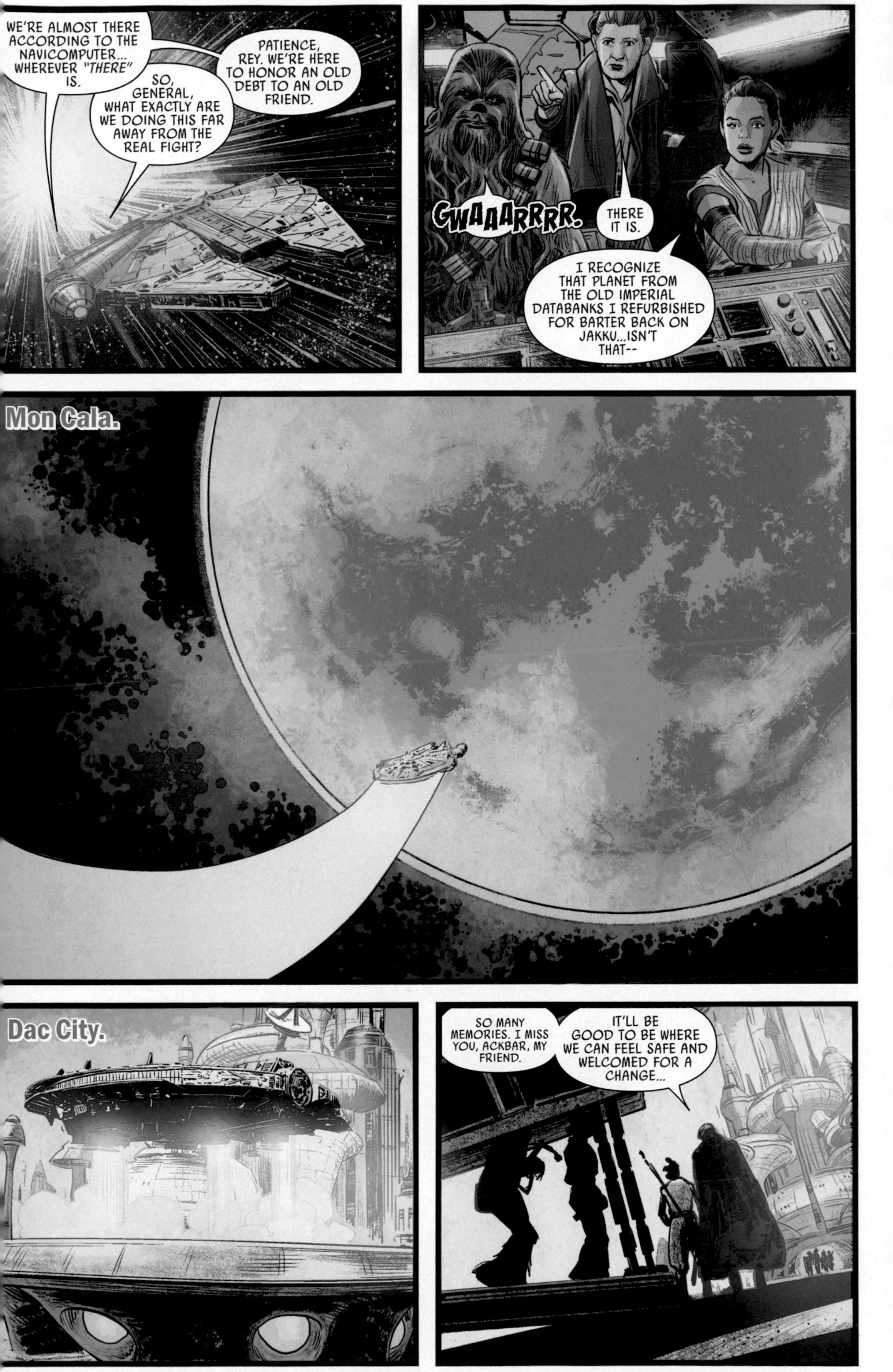
WE'RE ALMOST THERE ACCORDING TO THE NAVICOMPUTER... WHEREVER "THERE" IS.
SO, GENERAL, WHAT EXACTLY ARE WE DOING THIS FAR AWAY FROM THE REAL FIGHT?
PATIENCE, REY. WE'RE HERE TO HONOR AN OLD DEBT TO AN OLD FRIEND.
GWAAARRRR.
THERE IT IS.
I RECOGNIZE THAT PLANET FROM THE OLD IMPERIAL DATABANKS I REFURBISHED FOR BARTER BACK ON JAKKU...ISN'T THAT--
Mon Cala.
Dac City.
SO MANY MEMORIES. I MISS YOU, ACKBAR, MY FRIEND.
IT'LL BE GOOD TO BE WHERE WE CAN FEEL SAFE AND WELCOMED FOR A CHANGE...

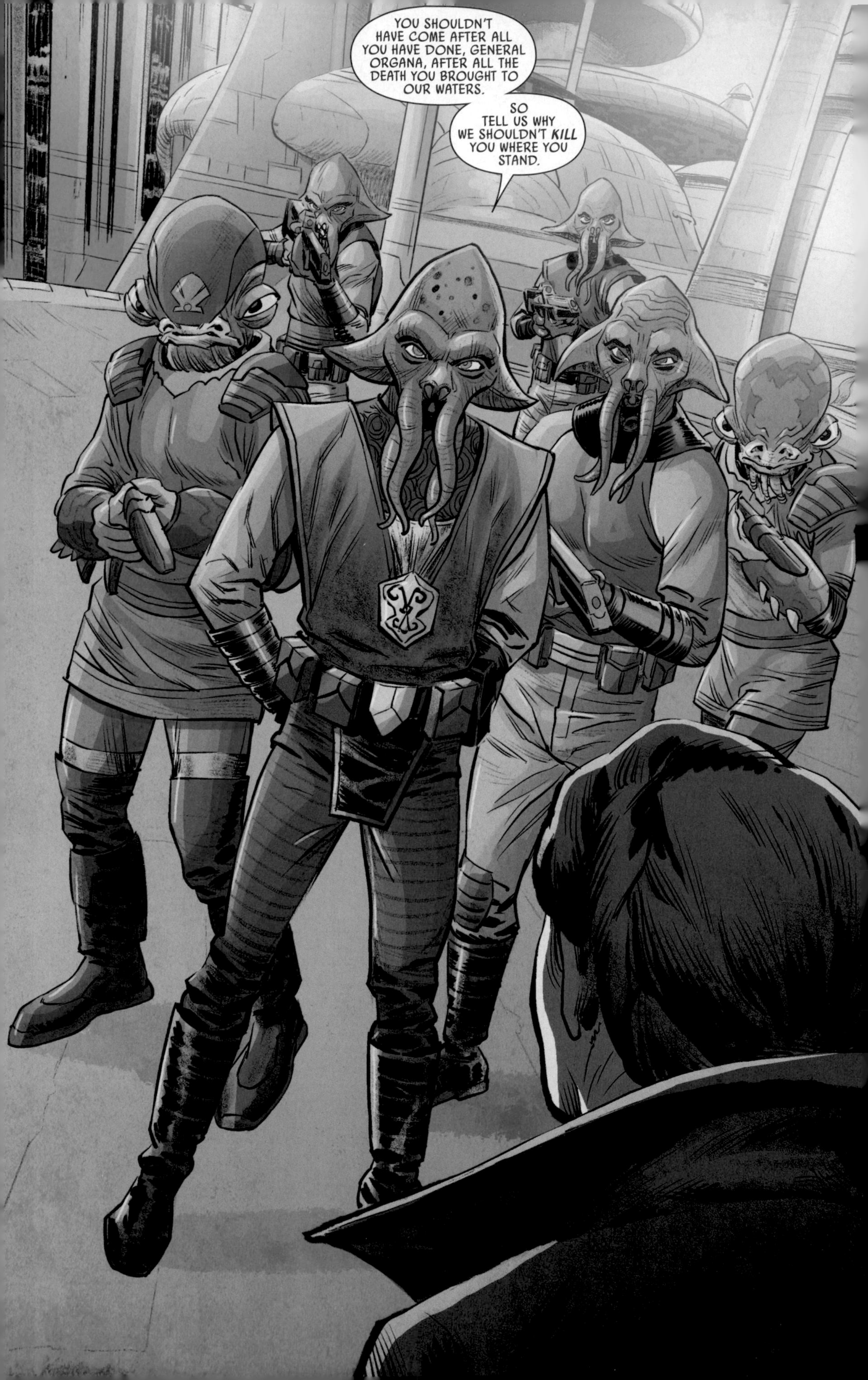
YOU SHOULDN'T HAVE COME AFTER ALL YOU HAVE DONE, GENERAL ORGANA, AFTER ALL THE DEATH YOU BROUGHT TO OUR WATERS.
SO TELL US WHY WE SHOULDN'T KILL YOU WHERE YOU STAND.

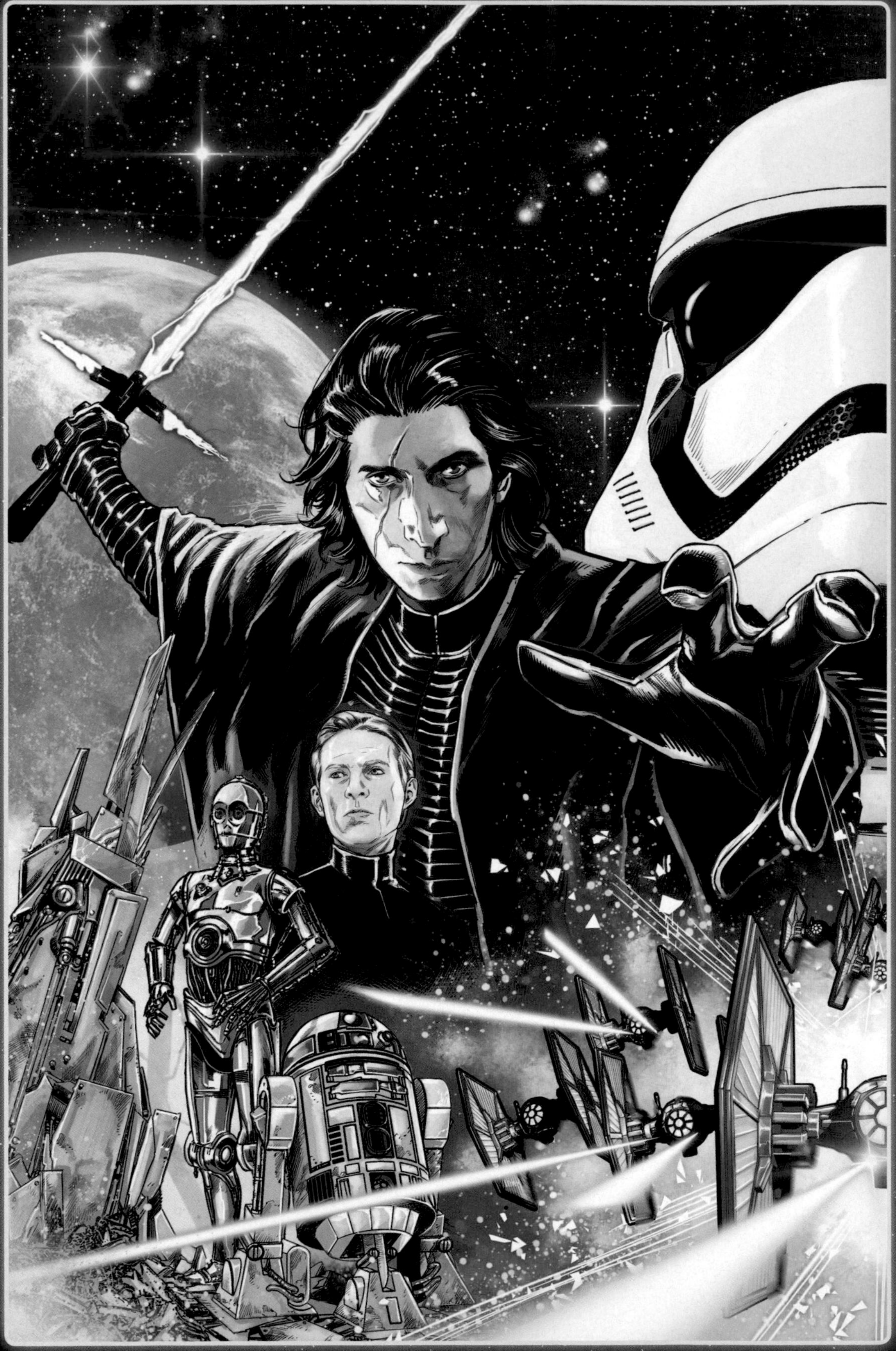

2

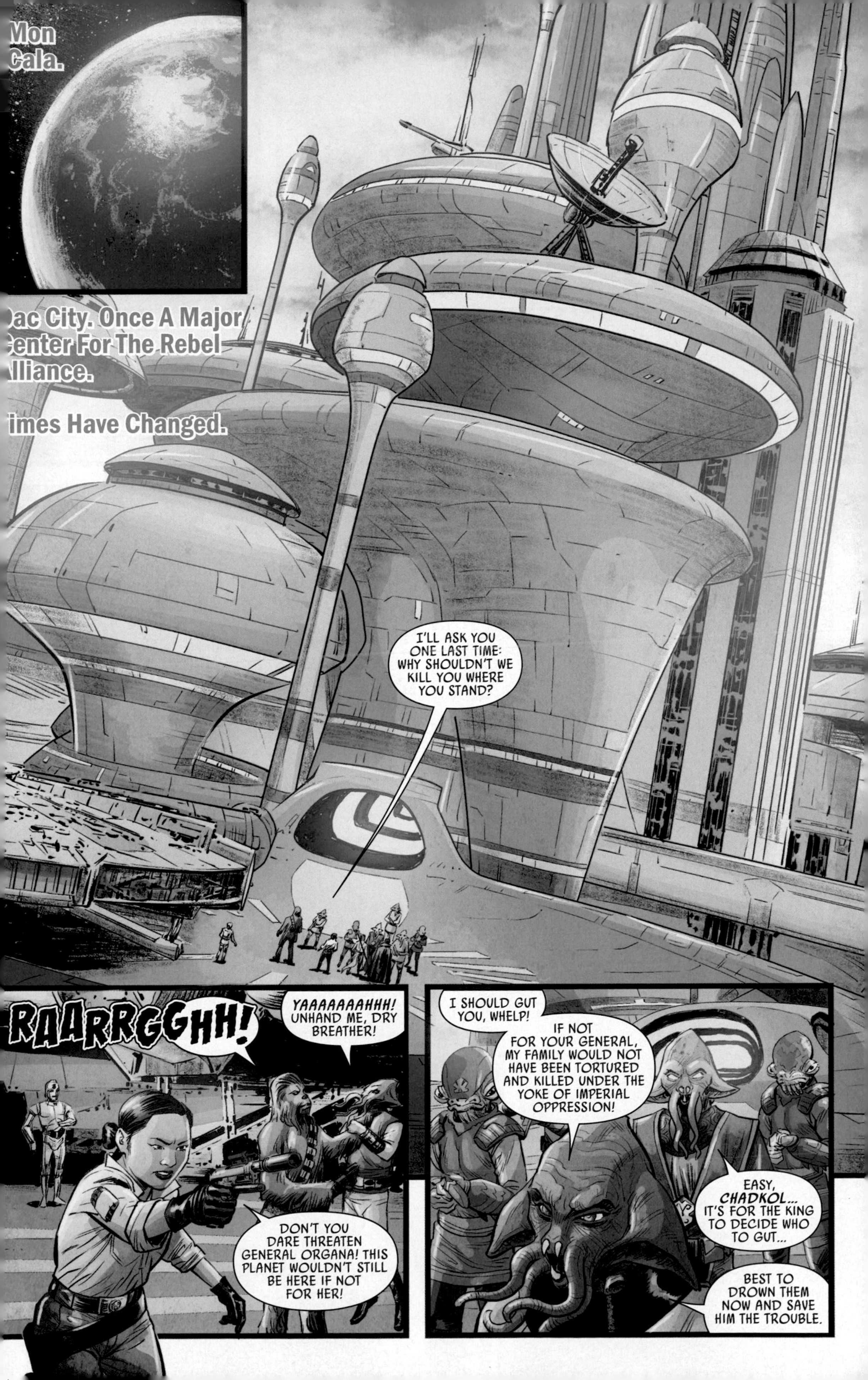
Mon Cala.
Dac City. Once A Major Center For The Rebel Alliance.
Times Have Changed.
I'LL ASK YOU ONE LAST TIME: WHY SHOULDN'T WE KILL YOU WHERE YOU STAND?
RAARRGGHH!
YAAAAAAAHHH! UNHAND ME, DRY BREATHER!
DON'T YOU DARE THREATEN GENERAL ORGANA! THIS PLANET WOULDN'T STILL BE HERE IF NOT FOR HER!
I SHOULD GUT YOU, WHELP!
IF NOT FOR YOUR GENERAL, MY FAMILY WOULD NOT HAVE BEEN TORTURED AND KILLED UNDER THE YOKE OF IMPERIAL OPPRESSION!
EASY, CHADKOL... IT'S FOR THE KING TO DECIDE WHO TO GUT...
BEST TO DROWN THEM NOW AND SAVE HIM THE TROUBLE.

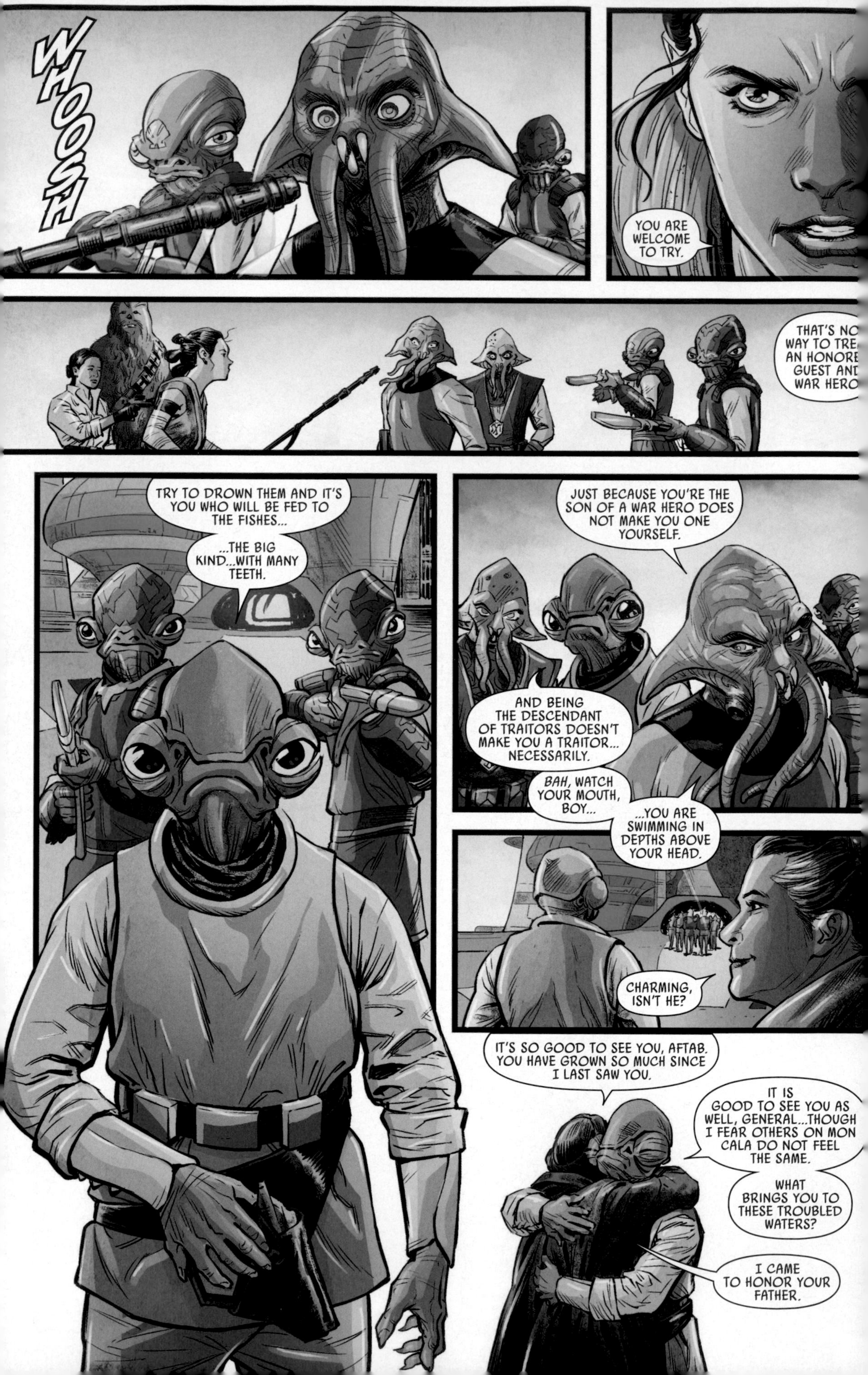
WHOOSH
YOU ARE WELCOME TO TRY.
THAT'S NO WAY TO TRE... AN HONORE... GUEST AND WAR HERO
TRY TO DROWN THEM AND IT'S YOU WHO WILL BE FED TO THE FISHES...
...THE BIG KIND...WITH MANY TEETH.
JUST BECAUSE YOU'RE THE SON OF A WAR HERO DOES NOT MAKE YOU ONE YOURSELF.
AND BEING THE DESCENDANT OF TRAITORS DOESN'T MAKE YOU A TRAITOR... NECESSARILY.
BAH, WATCH YOUR MOUTH, BOY...
...YOU ARE SWIMMING IN DEPTHS ABOVE YOUR HEAD.
CHARMING, ISN'T HE?
IT'S SO GOOD TO SEE YOU, AFTAB. YOU HAVE GROWN SO MUCH SINCE I LAST SAW YOU.
IT IS GOOD TO SEE YOU AS WELL, GENERAL...THOUGH I FEAR OTHERS ON MON CALA DO NOT FEEL THE SAME.
WHAT BRINGS YOU TO THESE TROUBLED WATERS?
I CAME TO HONOR YOUR FATHER.

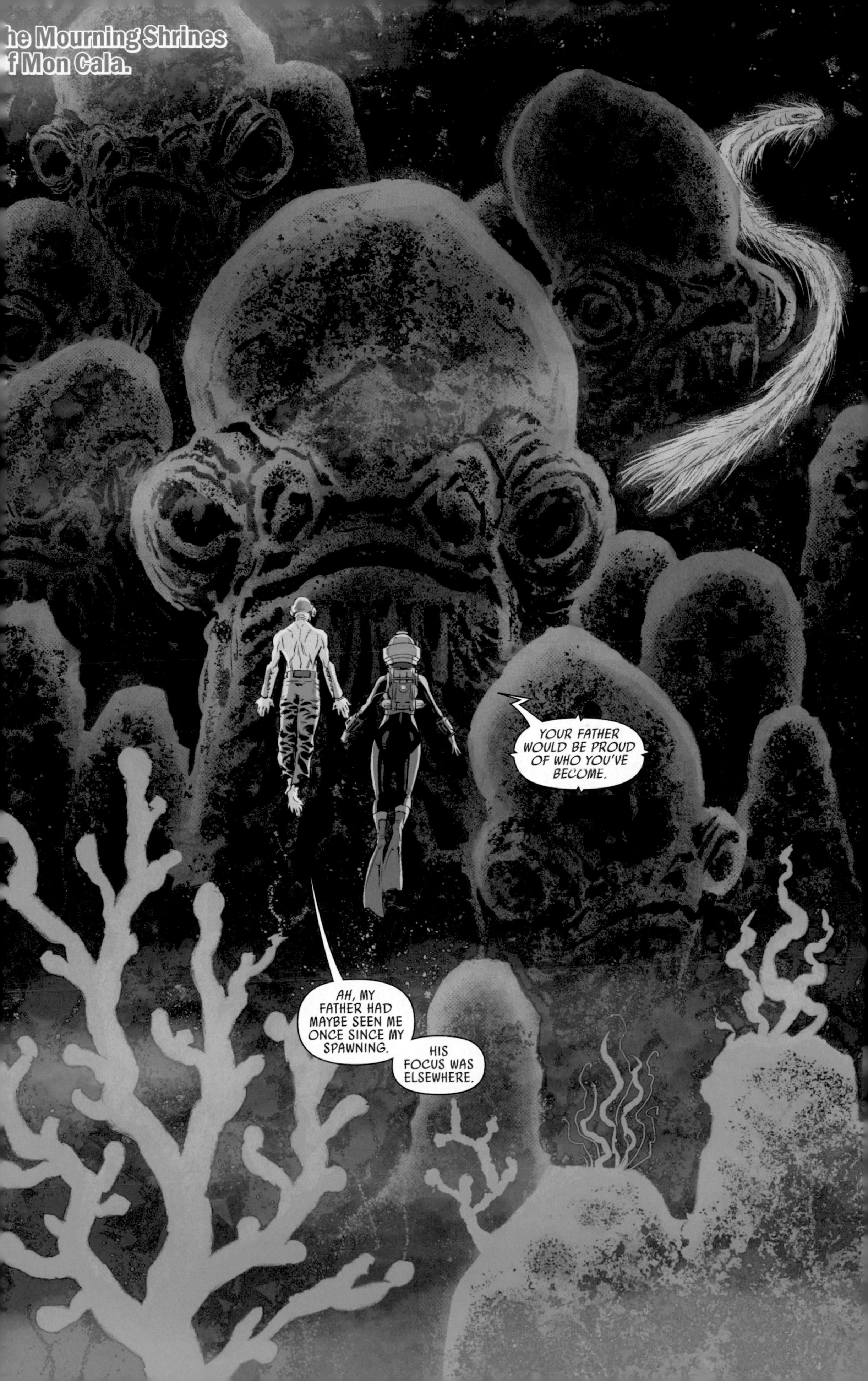
he Mourning Shrines
f Mon Cala.
YOUR FATHER WOULD BE PROUD OF WHO YOU'VE BECOME.
AH, MY FATHER HAD MAYBE SEEN ME ONCE SINCE MY SPAWNING.
HIS FOCUS WAS ELSEWHERE.

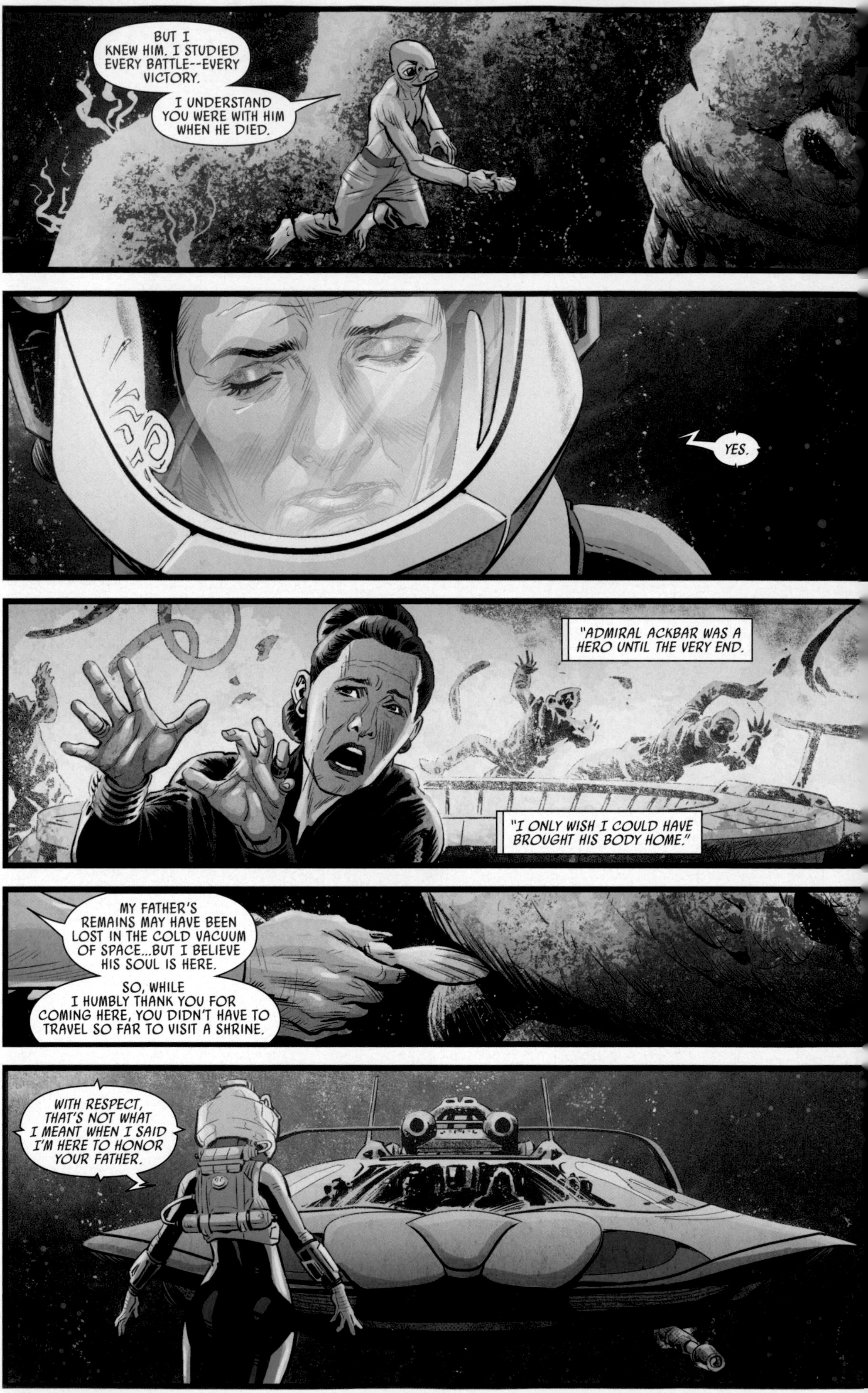
BUT I KNEW HIM. I STUDIED EVERY BATTLE--EVERY VICTORY.
I UNDERSTAND YOU WERE WITH HIM WHEN HE DIED.
YES.
"ADMIRAL ACKBAR WAS A HERO UNTIL THE VERY END.
"I ONLY WISH I COULD HAVE BROUGHT HIS BODY HOME."
MY FATHER'S REMAINS MAY HAVE BEEN LOST IN THE COLD VACUUM OF SPACE...BUT I BELIEVE HIS SOUL IS HERE.
SO, WHILE I HUMBLY THANK YOU FOR COMING HERE, YOU DIDN'T HAVE TO TRAVEL SO FAR TO VISIT A SHRINE.
WITH RESPECT, THAT'S NOT WHAT I MEANT WHEN I SAID I'M HERE TO HONOR YOUR FATHER.

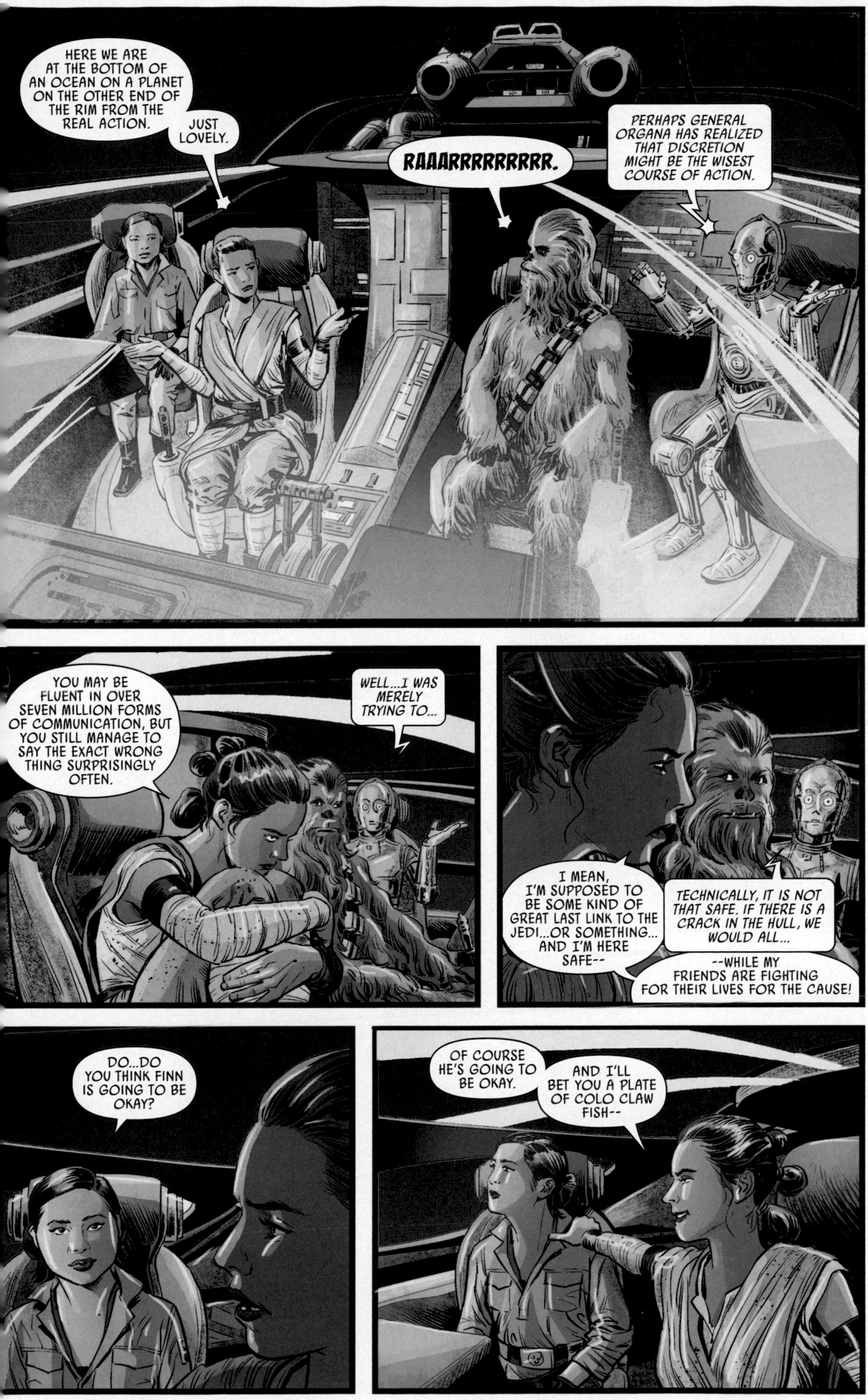
HERE WE ARE AT THE BOTTOM OF AN OCEAN ON A PLANET ON THE OTHER END OF THE RIM FROM THE REAL ACTION.
JUST LOVELY.
RAAARRRRRRRRR.
PERHAPS GENERAL ORGANA HAS REALIZED THAT DISCRETION MIGHT BE THE WISEST COURSE OF ACTION.
YOU MAY BE FLUENT IN OVER SEVEN MILLION FORMS OF COMMUNICATION, BUT YOU STILL MANAGE TO SAY THE EXACT WRONG THING SURPRISINGLY OFTEN.
WELL...I WAS MERELY TRYING TO...
I MEAN, I'M SUPPOSED TO BE SOME KIND OF GREAT LAST LINK TO THE JEDI...OR SOMETHING... AND I'M HERE SAFE--
TECHNICALLY, IT IS NOT THAT SAFE. IF THERE IS A CRACK IN THE HULL, WE WOULD ALL...
--WHILE MY FRIENDS ARE FIGHTING FOR THEIR LIVES FOR THE CAUSE!
DO...DO YOU THINK FINN IS GOING TO BE OKAY?
OF COURSE HE'S GOING TO BE OKAY.
AND I'LL BET YOU A PLATE OF COLO CLAW FISH--

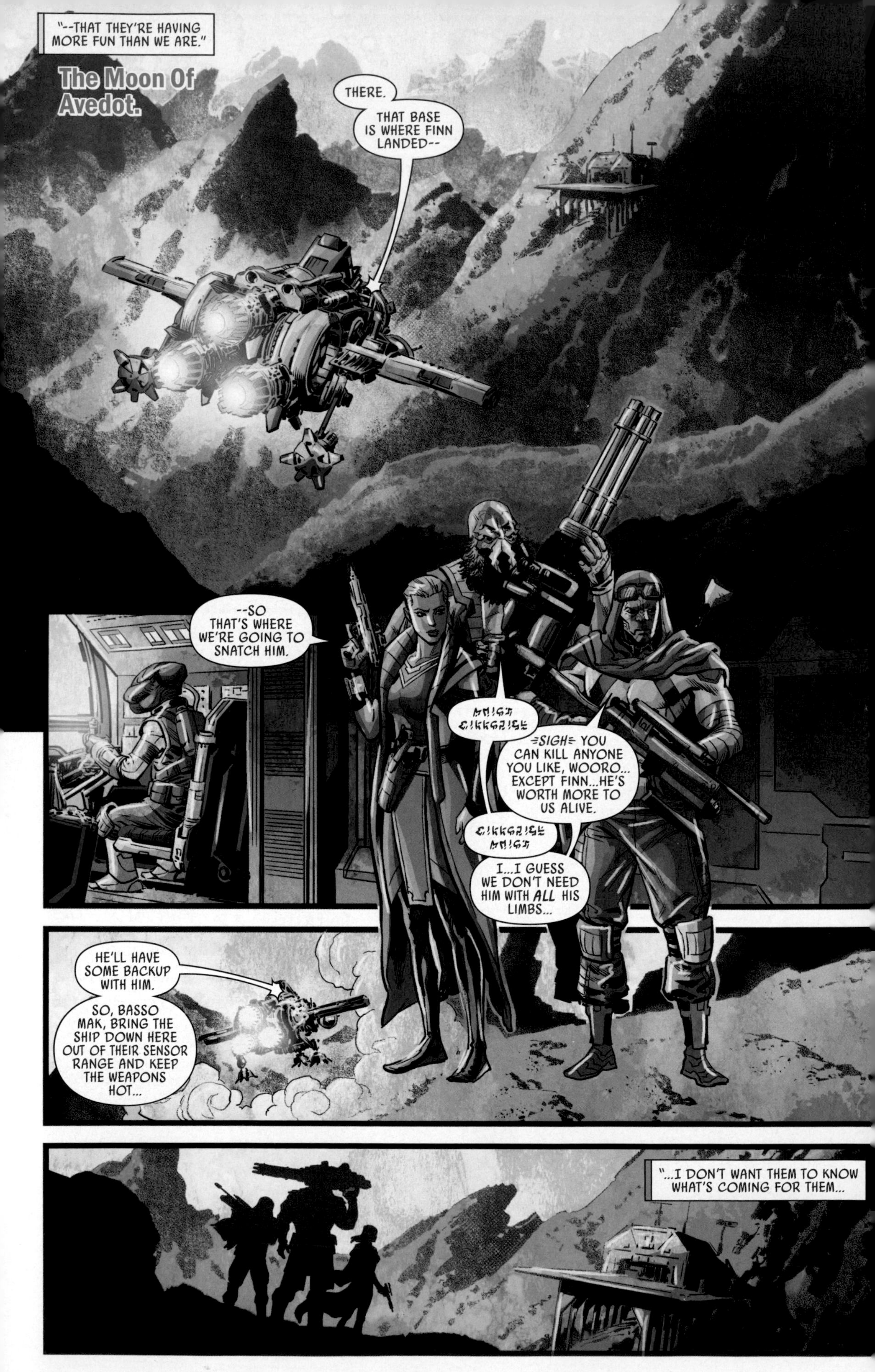
"--THAT THEY'RE HAVING MORE FUN THAN WE ARE."
The Moon Of Avedot.
THERE.
THAT BASE IS WHERE FINN LANDED--
--SO THAT'S WHERE WE'RE GOING TO SNATCH HIM.
=SIGH= YOU CAN KILL ANYONE YOU LIKE, WOORO... EXCEPT FINN...HE'S WORTH MORE TO US ALIVE.
I...I GUESS WE DON'T NEED HIM WITH ALL HIS LIMBS...
HE'LL HAVE SOME BACKUP WITH HIM.
SO, BASSO MAK, BRING THE SHIP DOWN HERE OUT OF THEIR SENSOR RANGE AND KEEP THE WEAPONS HOT...
"...I DON'T WANT THEM TO KNOW WHAT'S COMING FOR THEM...

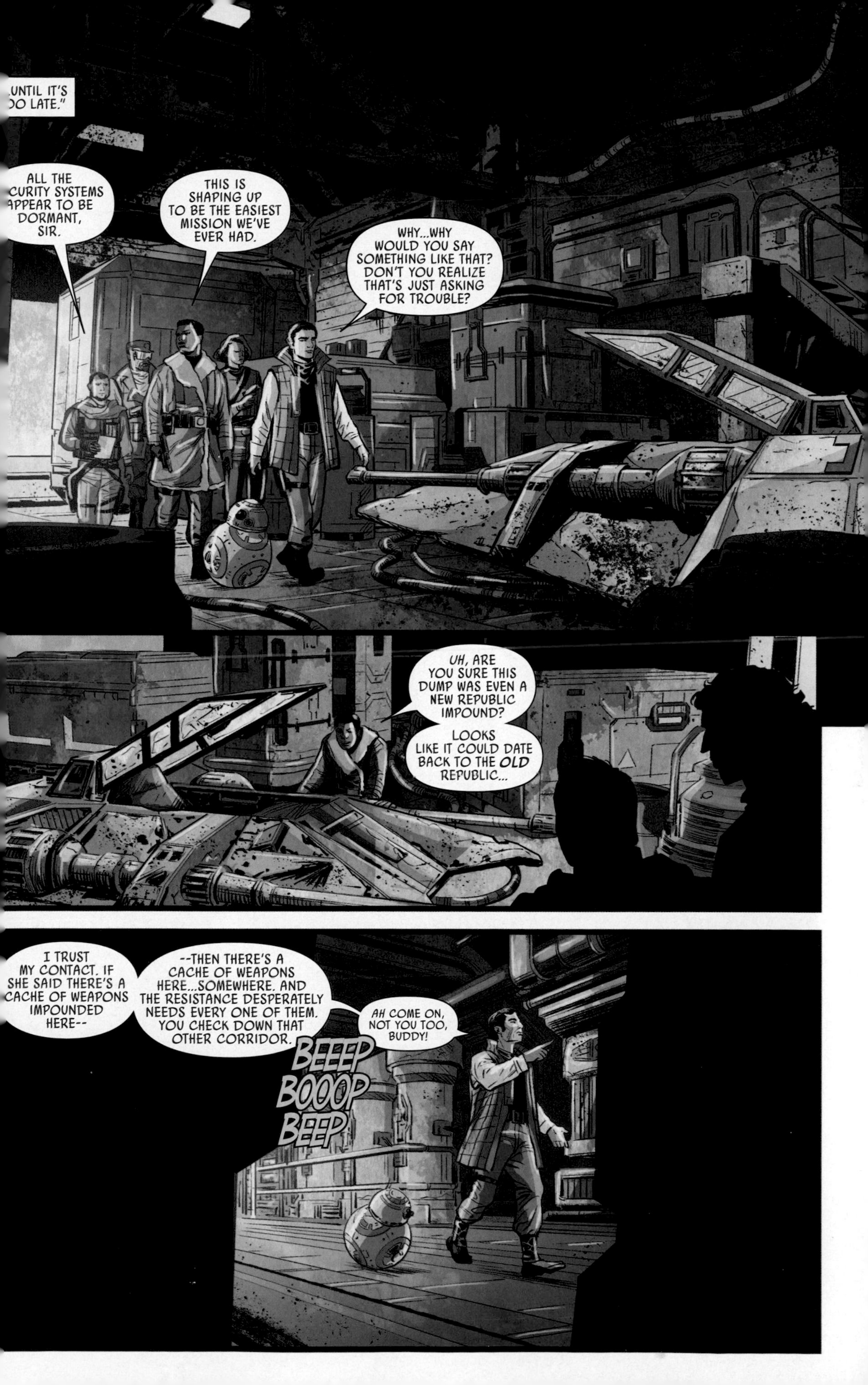

...UNTIL IT'S TOO LATE."
ALL THE SECURITY SYSTEMS APPEAR TO BE DORMANT, SIR.
THIS IS SHAPING UP TO BE THE EASIEST MISSION WE'VE EVER HAD.
WHY...WHY WOULD YOU SAY SOMETHING LIKE THAT? DON'T YOU REALIZE THAT'S JUST ASKING FOR TROUBLE?
UH, ARE YOU SURE THIS DUMP WAS EVEN A NEW REPUBLIC IMPOUND?
LOOKS LIKE IT COULD DATE BACK TO THE OLD REPUBLIC...
I TRUST MY CONTACT. IF SHE SAID THERE'S A CACHE OF WEAPONS IMPOUNDED HERE--
--THEN THERE'S A CACHE OF WEAPONS HERE...SOMEWHERE. AND THE RESISTANCE DESPERATELY NEEDS EVERY ONE OF THEM. YOU CHECK DOWN THAT OTHER CORRIDOR.
BEEEP BOOOP BEEP
AH COME ON, NOT YOU TOO, BUDDY!

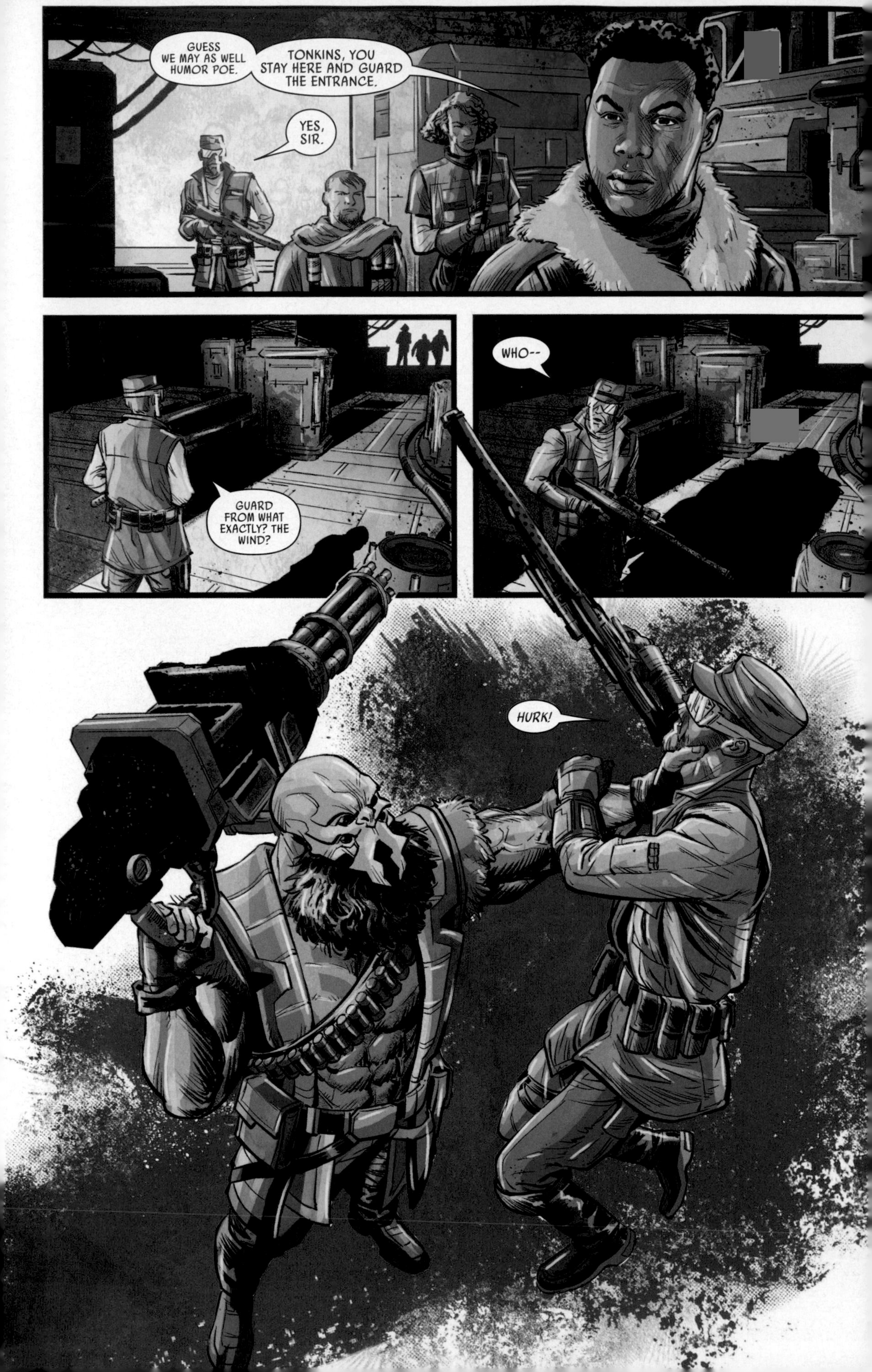
GUESS WE MAY AS WELL HUMOR POE.
TONKINS, YOU STAY HERE AND GUARD THE ENTRANCE.
YES, SIR.
GUARD FROM WHAT EXACTLY? THE WIND?
WHO--
HURK!

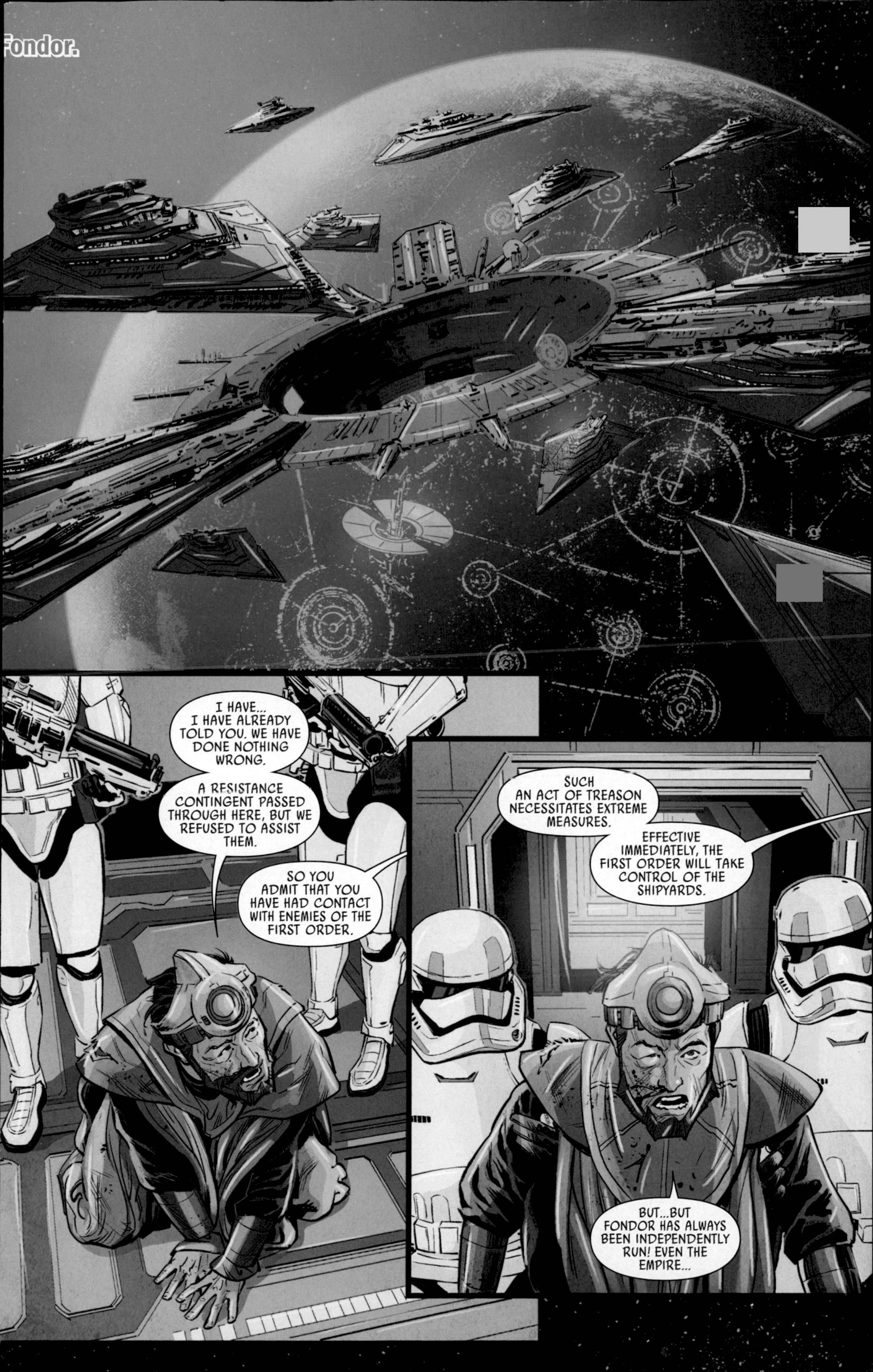
Fondor.
I HAVE... I HAVE ALREADY TOLD YOU. WE HAVE DONE NOTHING WRONG.
A RESISTANCE CONTINGENT PASSED THROUGH HERE, BUT WE REFUSED TO ASSIST THEM.
SO YOU ADMIT THAT YOU HAVE HAD CONTACT WITH ENEMIES OF THE FIRST ORDER.
SUCH AN ACT OF TREASON NECESSITATES EXTREME MEASURES.
EFFECTIVE IMMEDIATELY, THE FIRST ORDER WILL TAKE CONTROL OF THE SHIPYARDS.
BUT...BUT FONDOR HAS ALWAYS BEEN INDEPENDENTLY RUN! EVEN THE EMPIRE...

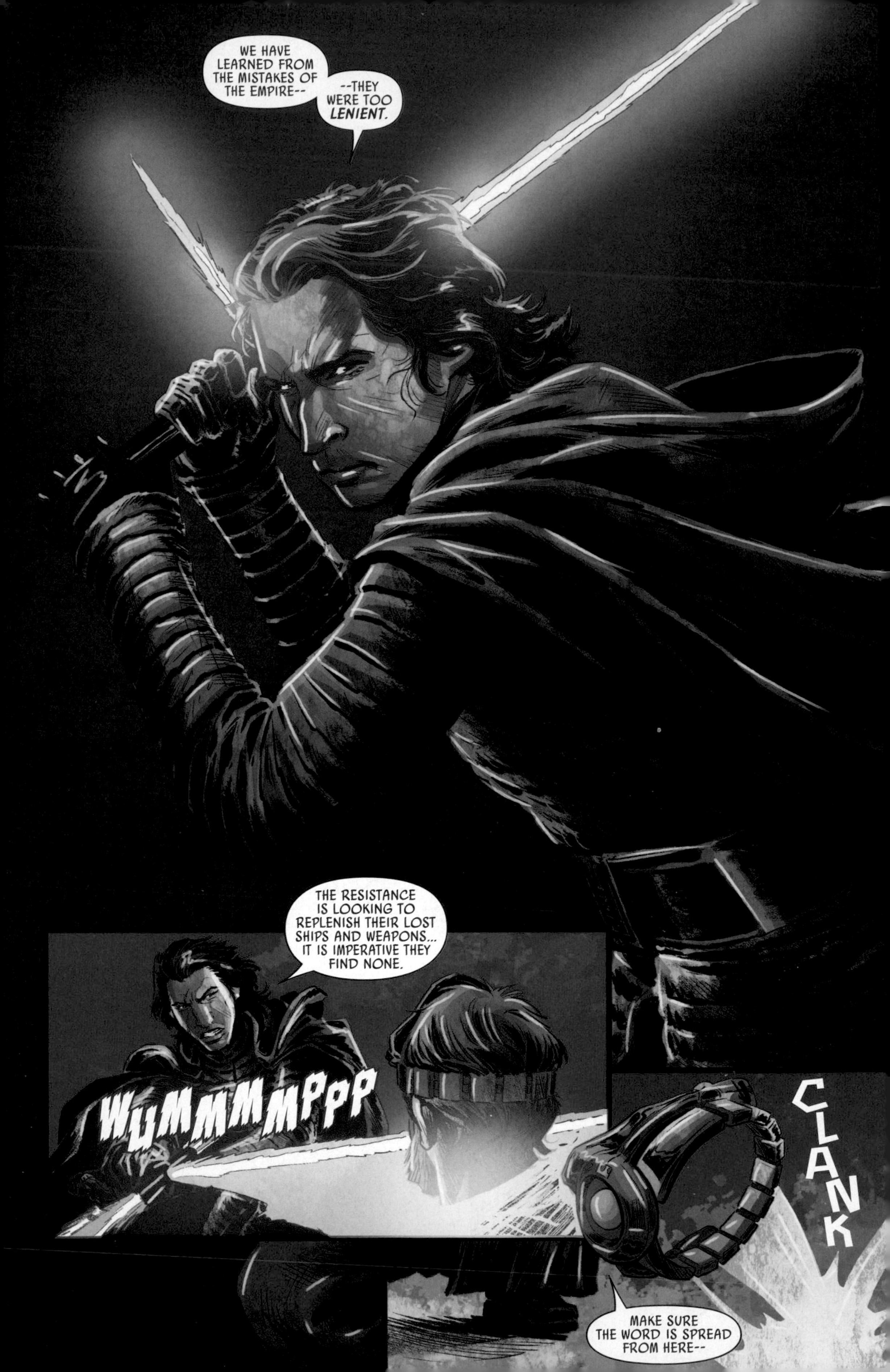
WE HAVE LEARNED FROM THE MISTAKES OF THE EMPIRE--
--THEY WERE TOO LENIENT.
THE RESISTANCE IS LOOKING TO REPLENISH THEIR LOST SHIPS AND WEAPONS... IT IS IMPERATIVE THEY FIND NONE.
WUMMMMPPP
CLANK
MAKE SURE THE WORD IS SPREAD FROM HERE--

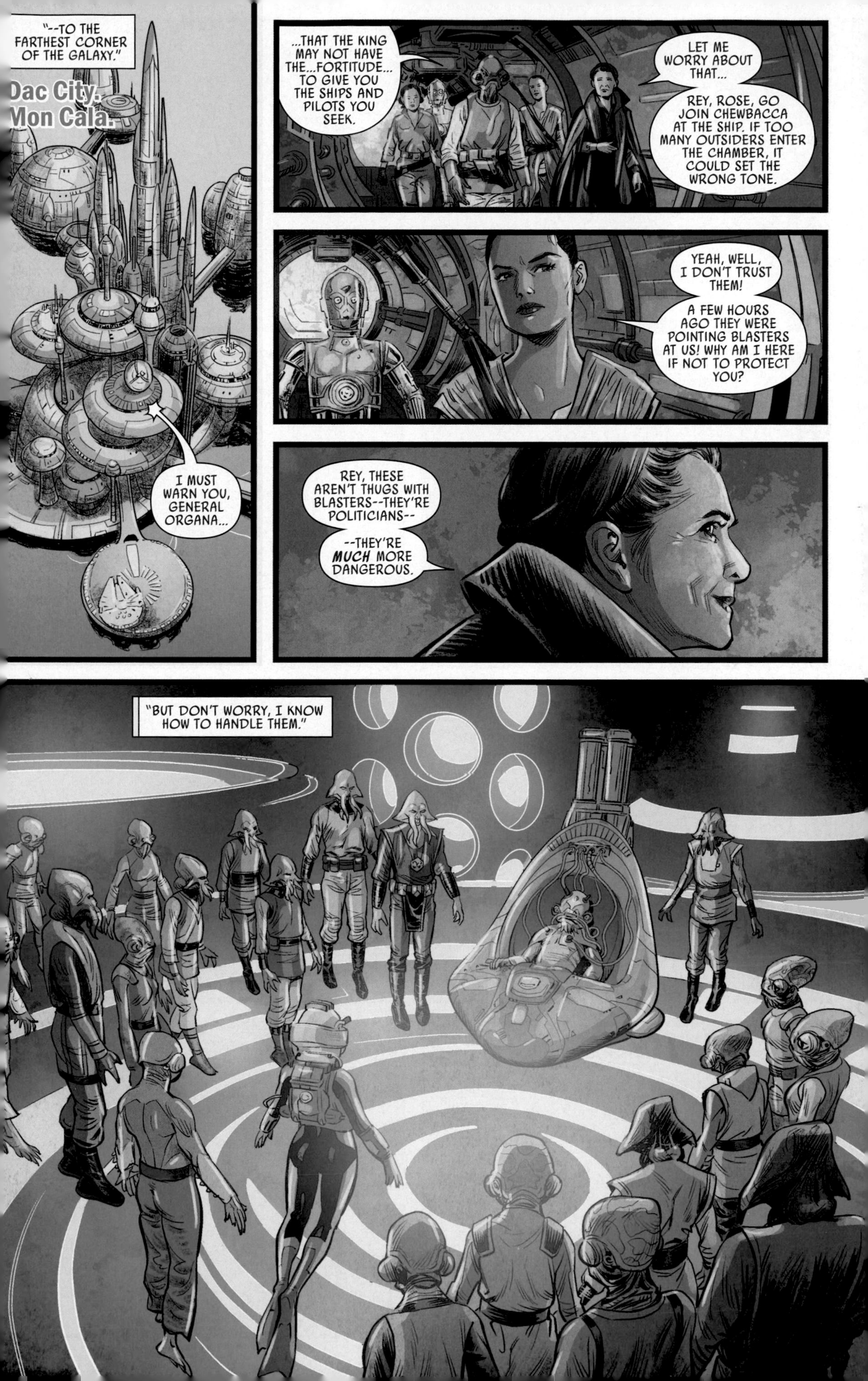

"--TO THE FARTHEST CORNER OF THE GALAXY."
Dac City. Mon Cala.
I MUST WARN YOU, GENERAL ORGANA...
...THAT THE KING MAY NOT HAVE THE...FORTITUDE... TO GIVE YOU THE SHIPS AND PILOTS YOU SEEK.
LET ME WORRY ABOUT THAT...
REY, ROSE, GO JOIN CHEWBACCA AT THE SHIP. IF TOO MANY OUTSIDERS ENTER THE CHAMBER, IT COULD SET THE WRONG TONE.
YEAH, WELL, I DON'T TRUST THEM!
A FEW HOURS AGO THEY WERE POINTING BLASTERS AT US! WHY AM I HERE IF NOT TO PROTECT YOU?
REY, THESE AREN'T THUGS WITH BLASTERS--THEY'RE POLITICIANS--
--THEY'RE MUCH MORE DANGEROUS.
"BUT DON'T WORRY, I KNOW HOW TO HANDLE THEM."

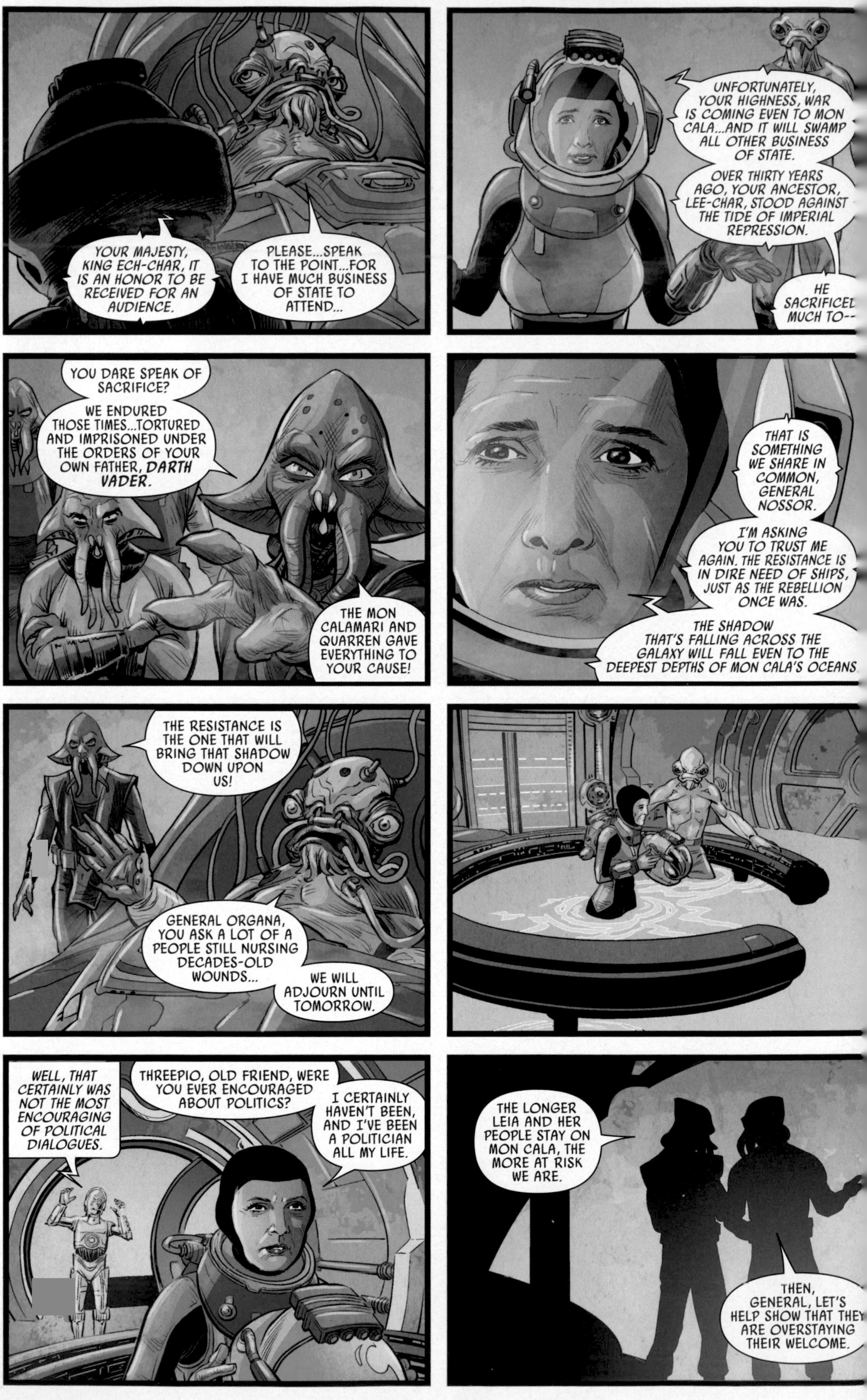
YOUR MAJESTY, KING ECH-CHAR, IT IS AN HONOR TO BE RECEIVED FOR AN AUDIENCE.
PLEASE...SPEAK TO THE POINT...FOR I HAVE MUCH BUSINESS OF STATE TO ATTEND...
UNFORTUNATELY, YOUR HIGHNESS, WAR IS COMING EVEN TO MON CALA...AND IT WILL SWAMP ALL OTHER BUSINESS OF STATE.
OVER THIRTY YEARS AGO, YOUR ANCESTOR, LEE-CHAR, STOOD AGAINST THE TIDE OF IMPERIAL REPRESSION.
HE SACRIFICED MUCH TO--
YOU DARE SPEAK OF SACRIFICE?
WE ENDURED THOSE TIMES...TORTURED AND IMPRISONED UNDER THE ORDERS OF YOUR OWN FATHER, DARTH VADER.
THE MON CALAMARI AND QUARREN GAVE EVERYTHING TO YOUR CAUSE!
THAT IS SOMETHING WE SHARE IN COMMON, GENERAL NOSSOR.
I'M ASKING YOU TO TRUST ME AGAIN. THE RESISTANCE IS IN DIRE NEED OF SHIPS, JUST AS THE REBELLION ONCE WAS.
THE SHADOW THAT'S FALLING ACROSS THE GALAXY WILL FALL EVEN TO THE DEEPEST DEPTHS OF MON CALA'S OCEANS
THE RESISTANCE IS THE ONE THAT WILL BRING THAT SHADOW DOWN UPON US!
GENERAL ORGANA, YOU ASK A LOT OF A PEOPLE STILL NURSING DECADES-OLD WOUNDS...
WE WILL ADJOURN UNTIL TOMORROW.
WELL, THAT CERTAINLY WAS NOT THE MOST ENCOURAGING OF POLITICAL DIALOGUES.
THREEPIO, OLD FRIEND, WERE YOU EVER ENCOURAGED ABOUT POLITICS?
I CERTAINLY HAVEN'T BEEN, AND I'VE BEEN A POLITICIAN ALL MY LIFE.
THE LONGER LEIA AND HER PEOPLE STAY ON MON CALA, THE MORE AT RISK WE ARE.
THEN, GENERAL, LET'S HELP SHOW THAT THEY ARE OVERSTAYING THEIR WELCOME.

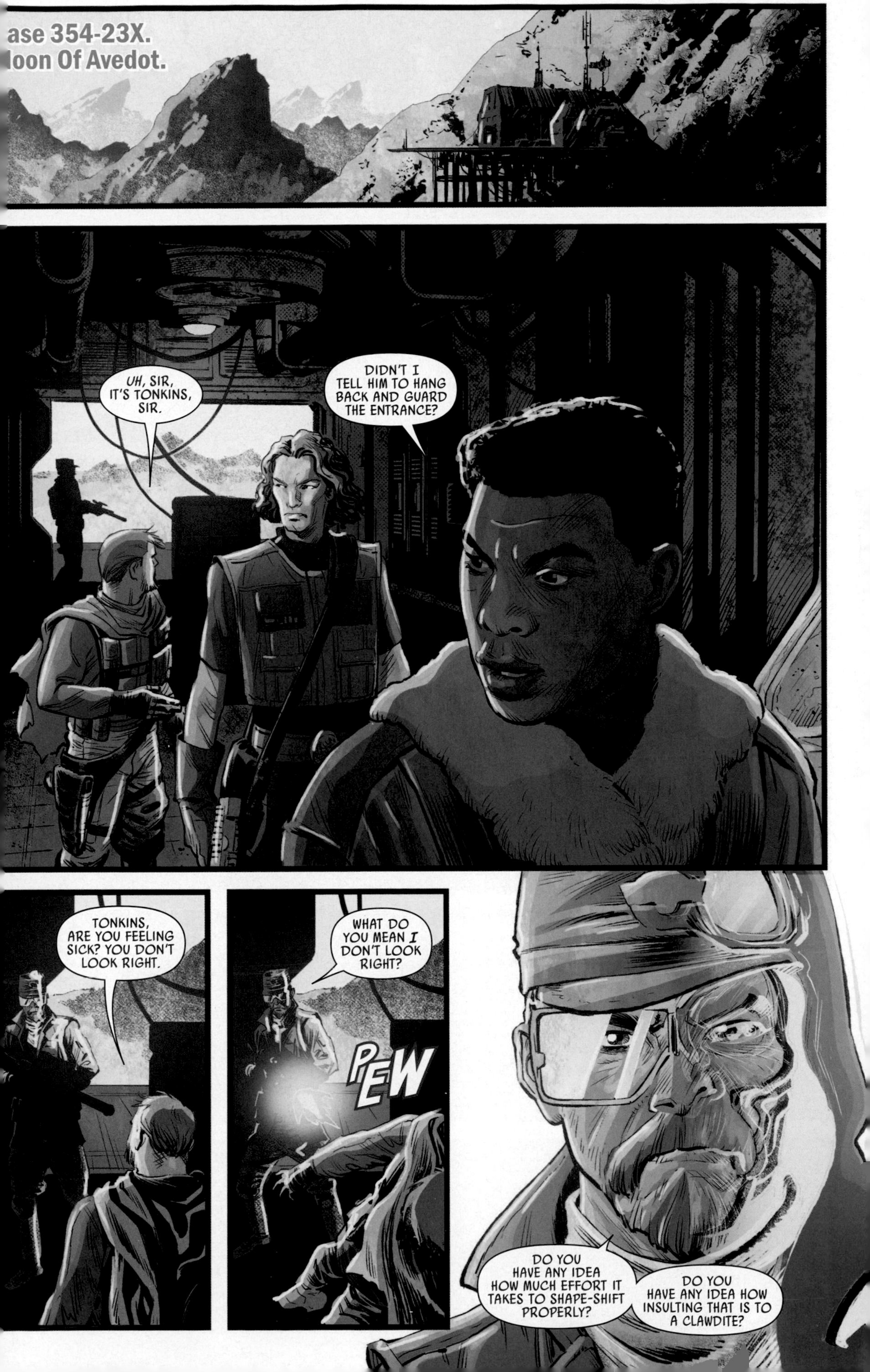
ase 354-23X.
loon Of Avedot.
UH, SIR, IT'S TONKINS, SIR.
DIDN'T I TELL HIM TO HANG BACK AND GUARD THE ENTRANCE?
TONKINS, ARE YOU FEELING SICK? YOU DON'T LOOK RIGHT.
WHAT DO YOU MEAN *I* DON'T LOOK RIGHT?
PEW
DO YOU HAVE ANY IDEA HOW MUCH EFFORT IT TAKES TO SHAPE-SHIFT PROPERLY?
DO YOU HAVE ANY IDEA HOW INSULTING THAT IS TO A CLAWDITE?

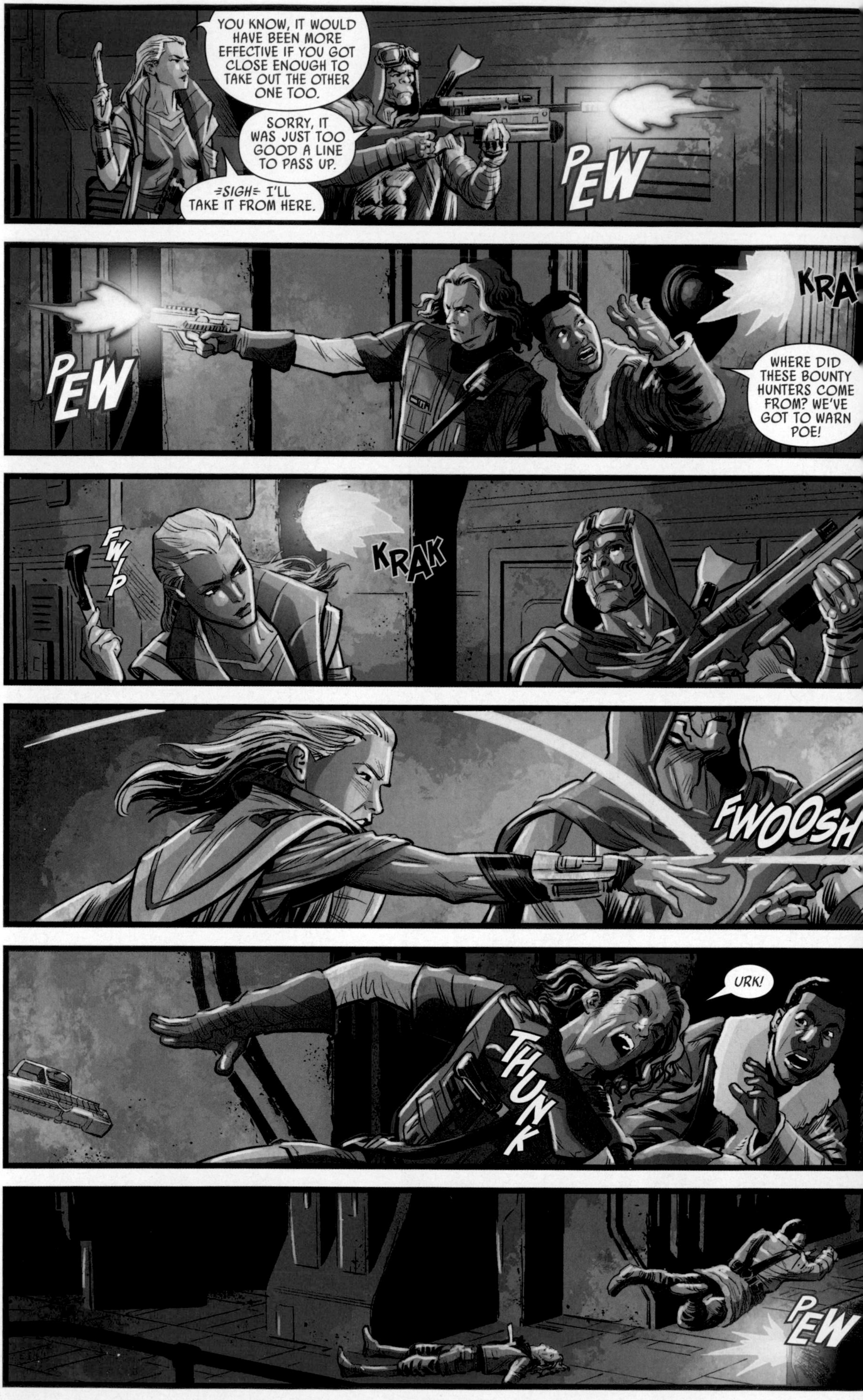
YOU KNOW, IT WOULD HAVE BEEN MORE EFFECTIVE IF YOU GOT CLOSE ENOUGH TO TAKE OUT THE OTHER ONE TOO.
SORRY, IT WAS JUST TOO GOOD A LINE TO PASS UP.
PEW
=SIGH= I'LL TAKE IT FROM HERE.
PEW
KRAK
WHERE DID THESE BOUNTY HUNTERS COME FROM? WE'VE GOT TO WARN POE!
FWIP
KRAK
FWOOSH
URK!
THUNK
PEW

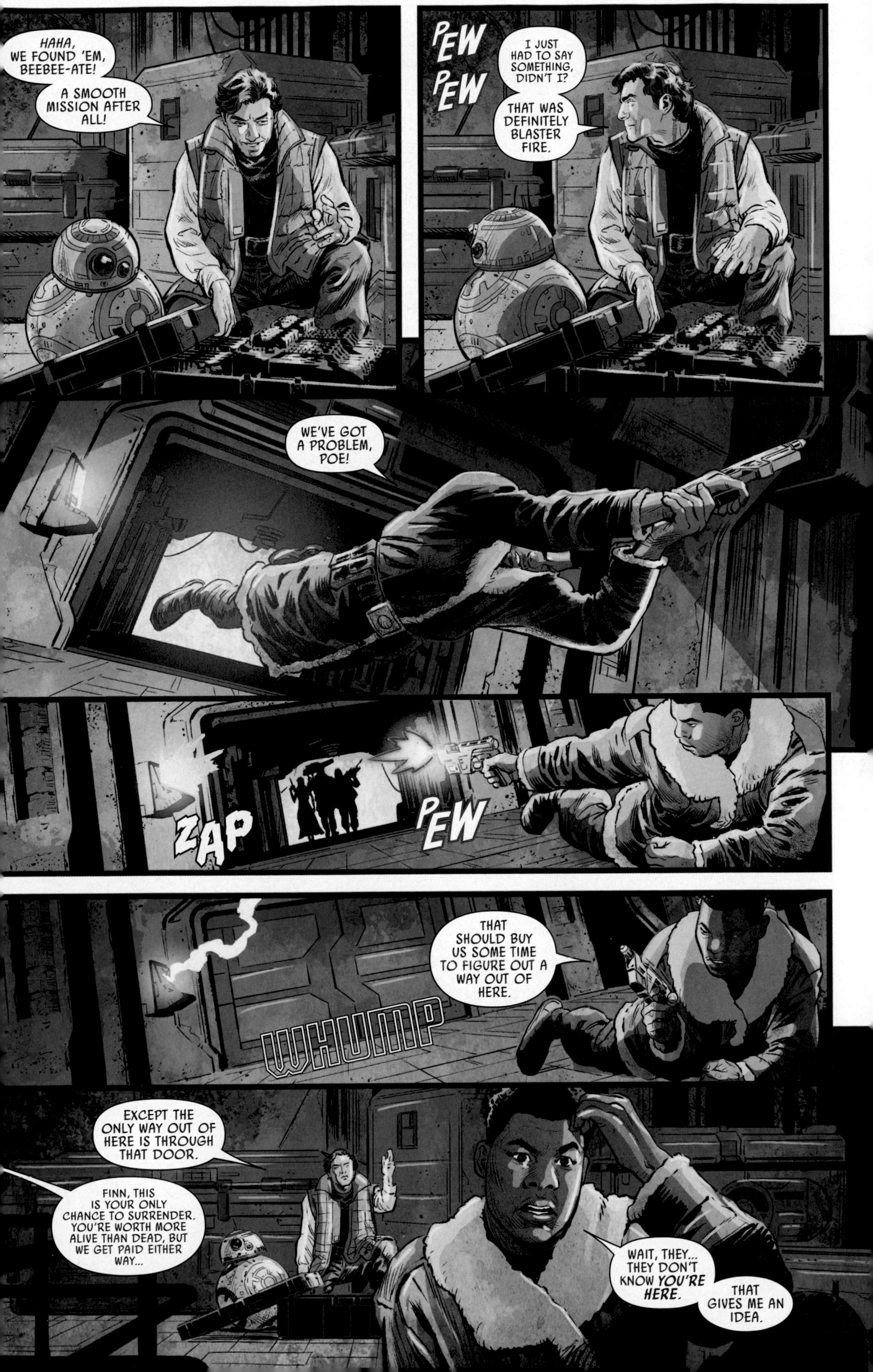
HAHA, WE FOUND 'EM, BEEBEE-ATE!
A SMOOTH MISSION AFTER ALL!
PEW
PEW
I JUST HAD TO SAY SOMETHING, DIDN'T I?
THAT WAS DEFINITELY BLASTER FIRE.
WE'VE GOT A PROBLEM, POE!
ZAP
PEW
THAT SHOULD BUY US SOME TIME TO FIGURE OUT A WAY OUT OF HERE.
WHUMP
EXCEPT THE ONLY WAY OUT OF HERE IS THROUGH THAT DOOR.
FINN, THIS IS YOUR ONLY CHANCE TO SURRENDER. YOU'RE WORTH MORE ALIVE THAN DEAD, BUT WE GET PAID EITHER WAY...
WAIT, THEY... THEY DON'T KNOW *YOU'RE HERE.*
THAT GIVES ME AN IDEA.

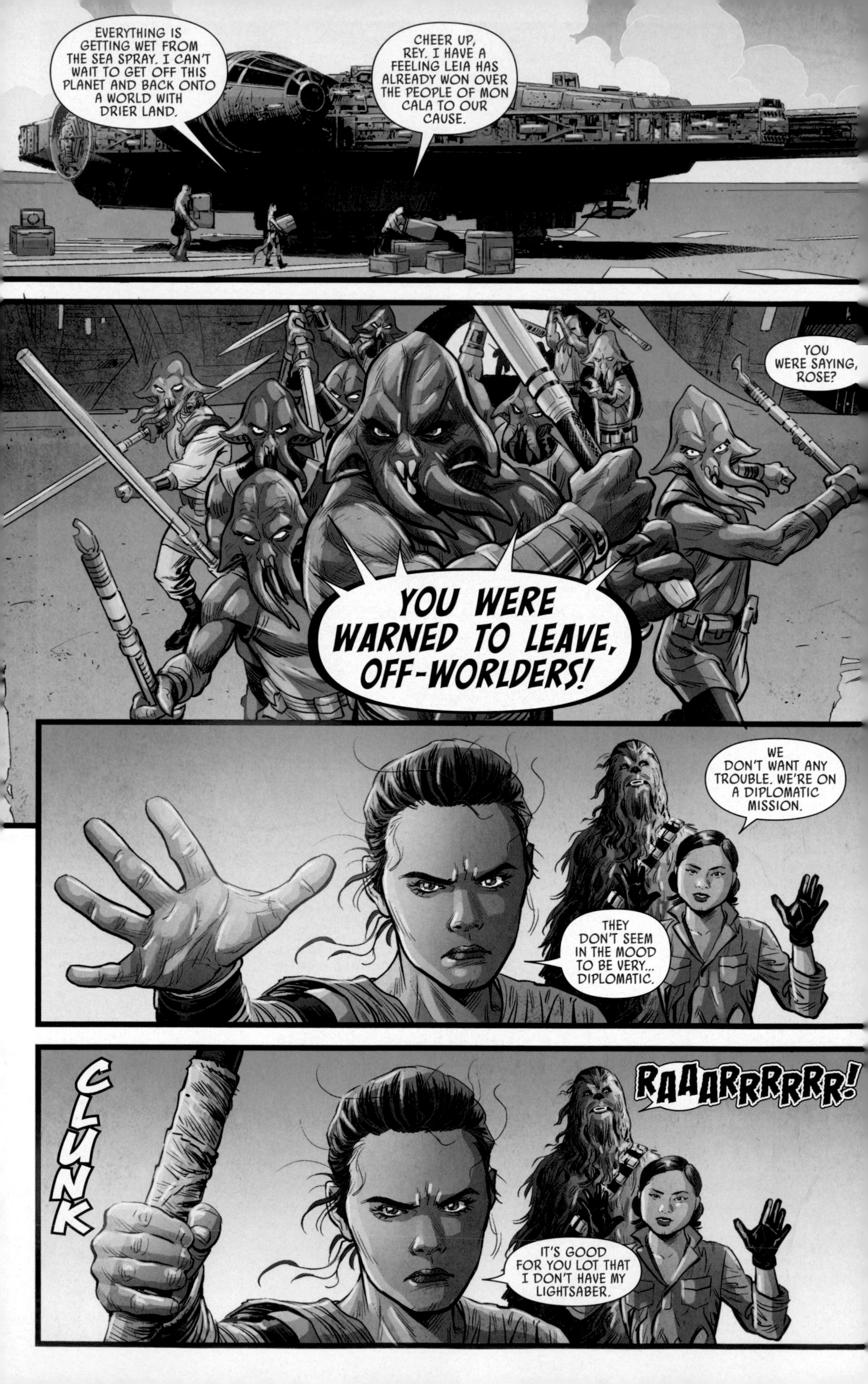
EVERYTHING IS GETTING WET FROM THE SEA SPRAY. I CAN'T WAIT TO GET OFF THIS PLANET AND BACK ONTO A WORLD WITH DRIER LAND.
CHEER UP, REY. I HAVE A FEELING LEIA HAS ALREADY WON OVER THE PEOPLE OF MON CALA TO OUR CAUSE.
YOU WERE SAYING, ROSE?
YOU WERE WARNED TO LEAVE, OFF-WORLDERS!
WE DON'T WANT ANY TROUBLE. WE'RE ON A DIPLOMATIC MISSION.
THEY DON'T SEEM IN THE MOOD TO BE VERY... DIPLOMATIC.
CLUNK
RAAARRRRRR!
IT'S GOOD FOR YOU LOT THAT I DON'T HAVE MY LIGHTSABER.

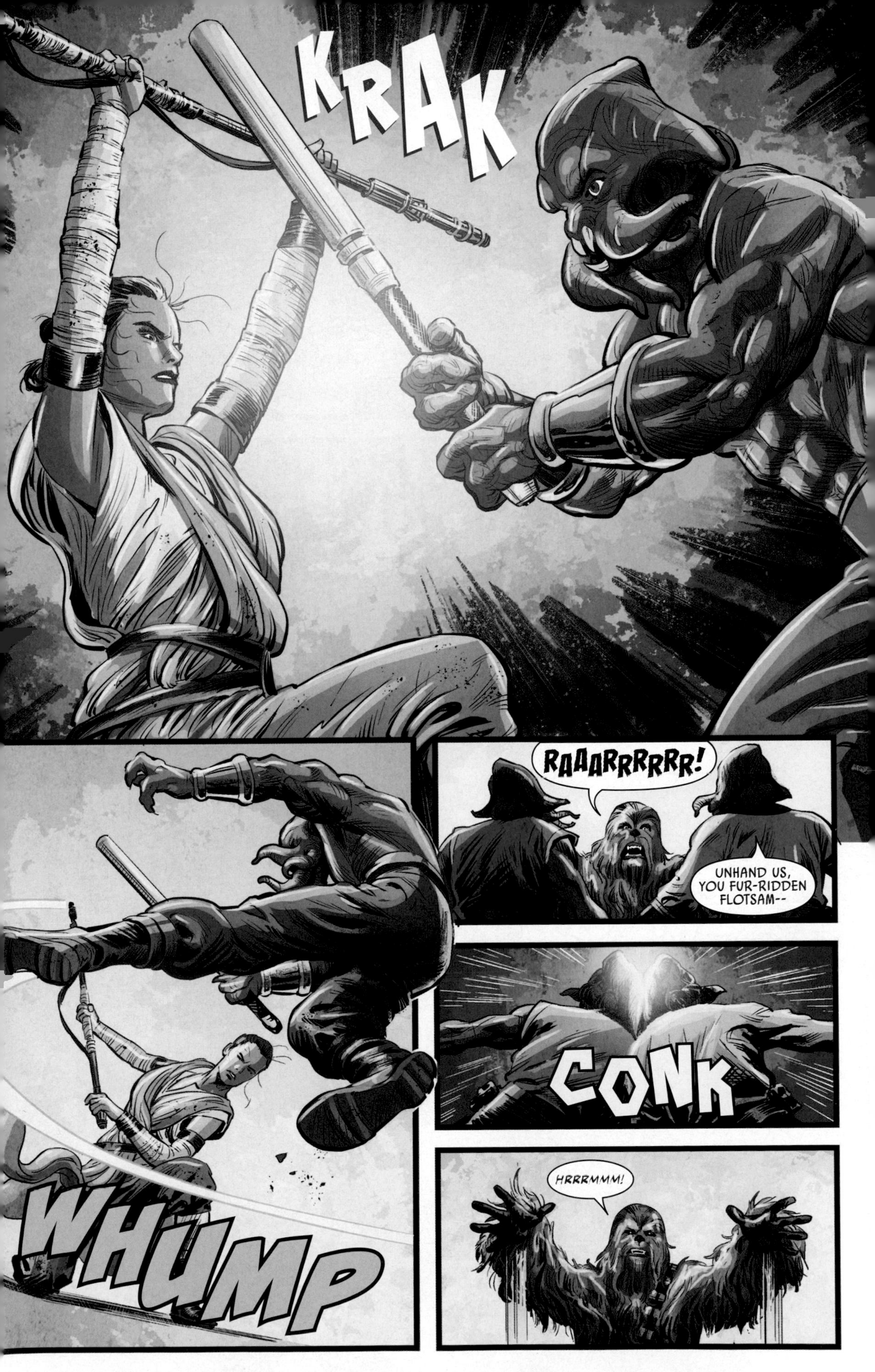
KRAK
WHUMP
RAAARRRRRR!
UNHAND US, YOU FUR-RIDDEN FLOTSAM--
CONK
HRRRMMM!

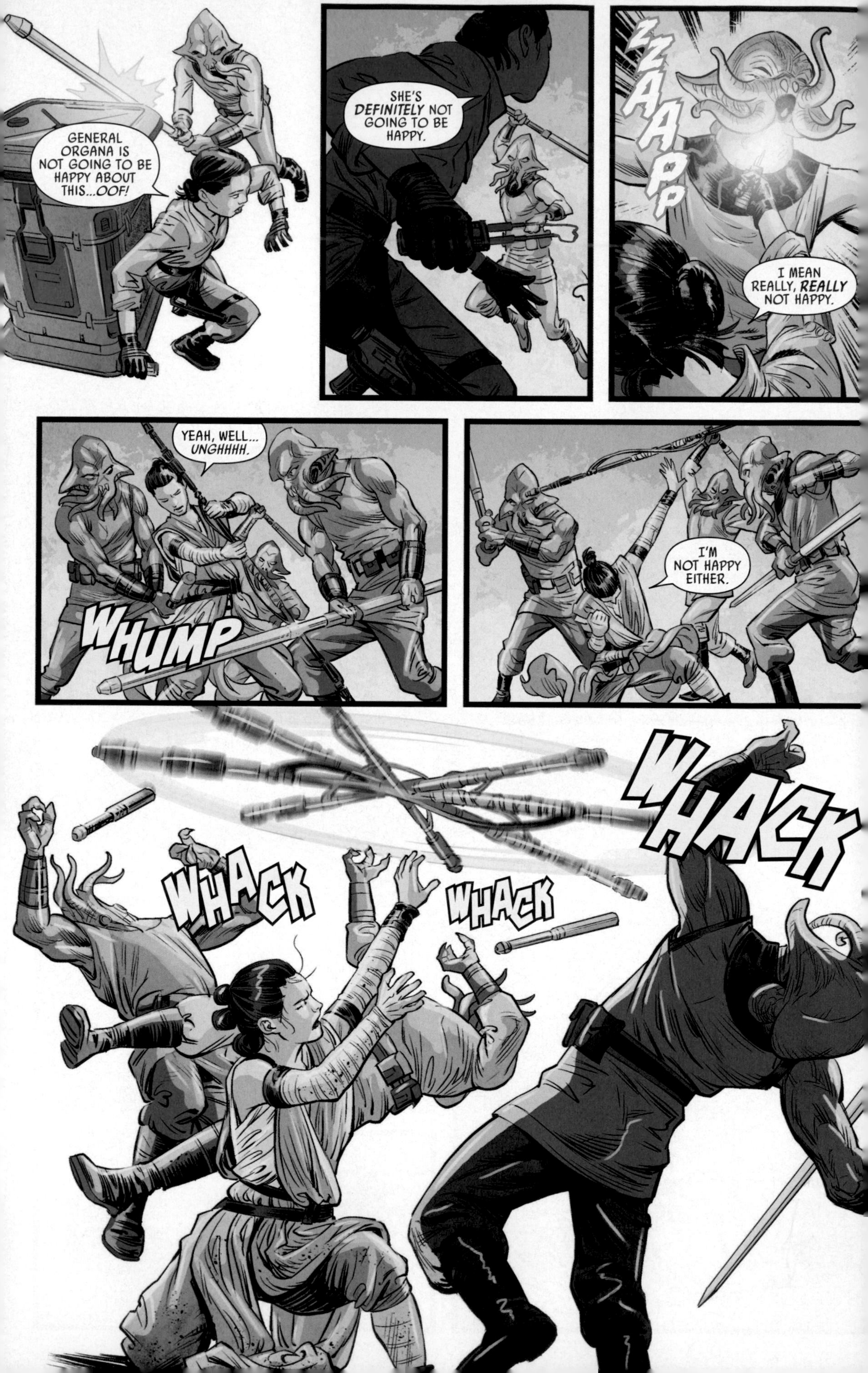
GENERAL ORGANA IS NOT GOING TO BE HAPPY ABOUT THIS...OOF!
SHE'S DEFINITELY NOT GOING TO BE HAPPY.
ZZAAAPP
I MEAN REALLY, REALLY NOT HAPPY.
YEAH, WELL... UNGHHHH.
WHUMP
I'M NOT HAPPY EITHER.
WHACK
WHACK
WHACK

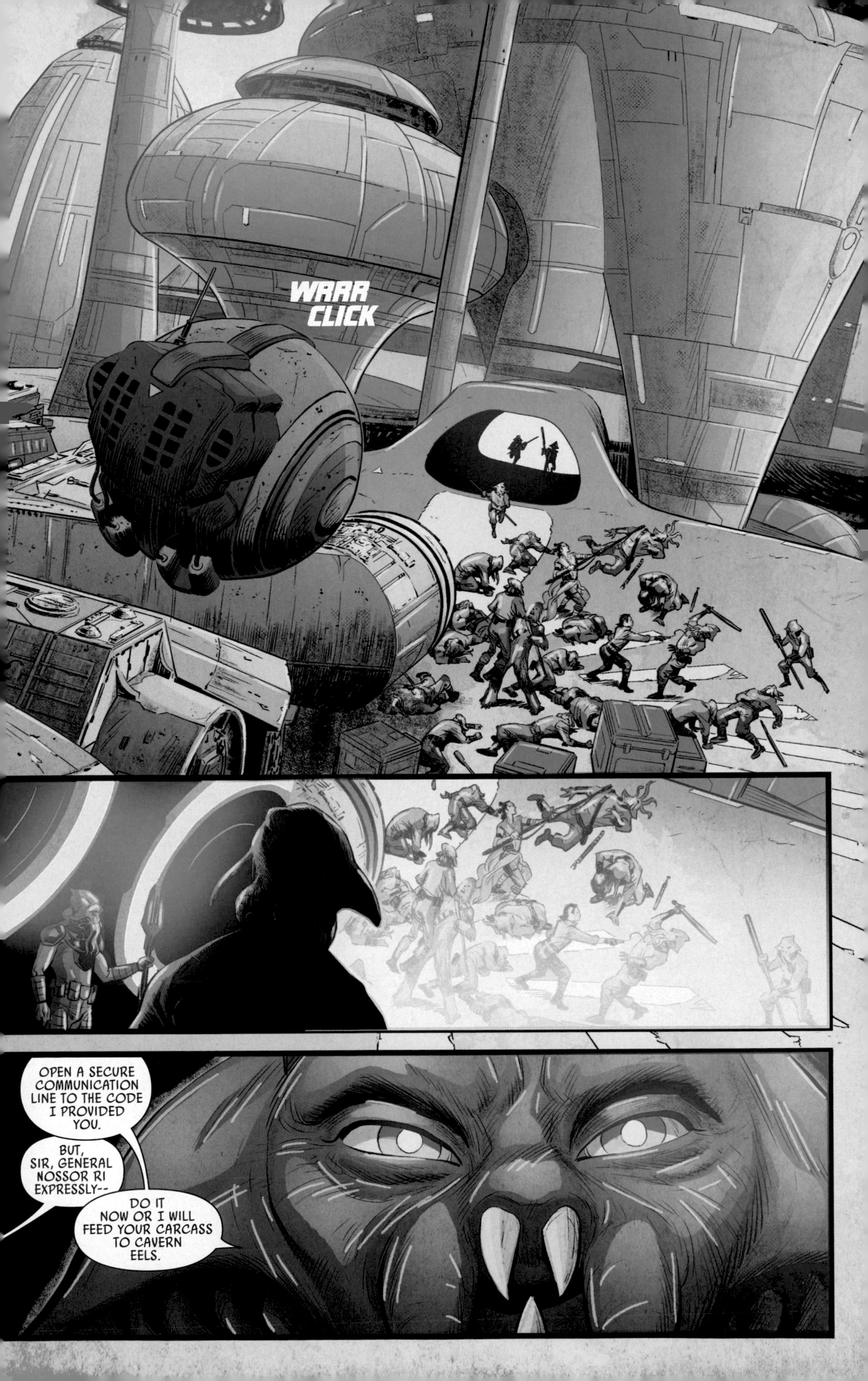
WRRR
CLICK
OPEN A SECURE COMMUNICATION LINE TO THE CODE I PROVIDED YOU.
BUT, SIR, GENERAL NOSSOR RI EXPRESSLY--
DO IT NOW OR I WILL FEED YOUR CARCASS TO CAVERN EELS.

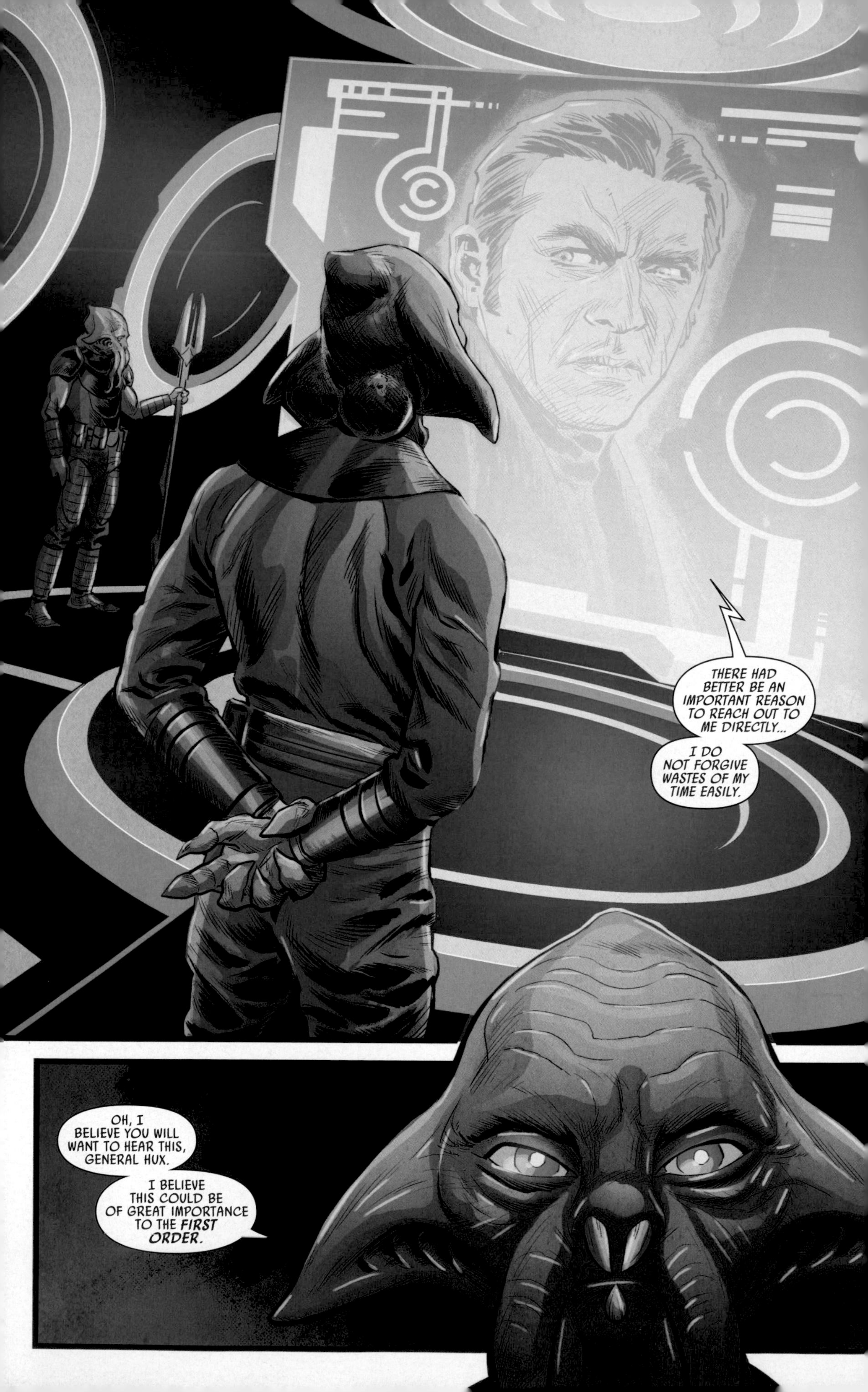
THERE HAD BETTER BE AN IMPORTANT REASON TO REACH OUT TO ME DIRECTLY...
I DO NOT FORGIVE WASTES OF MY TIME EASILY.
OH, I BELIEVE YOU WILL WANT TO HEAR THIS, GENERAL HUX.
I BELIEVE THIS COULD BE OF GREAT IMPORTANCE TO THE FIRST ORDER.

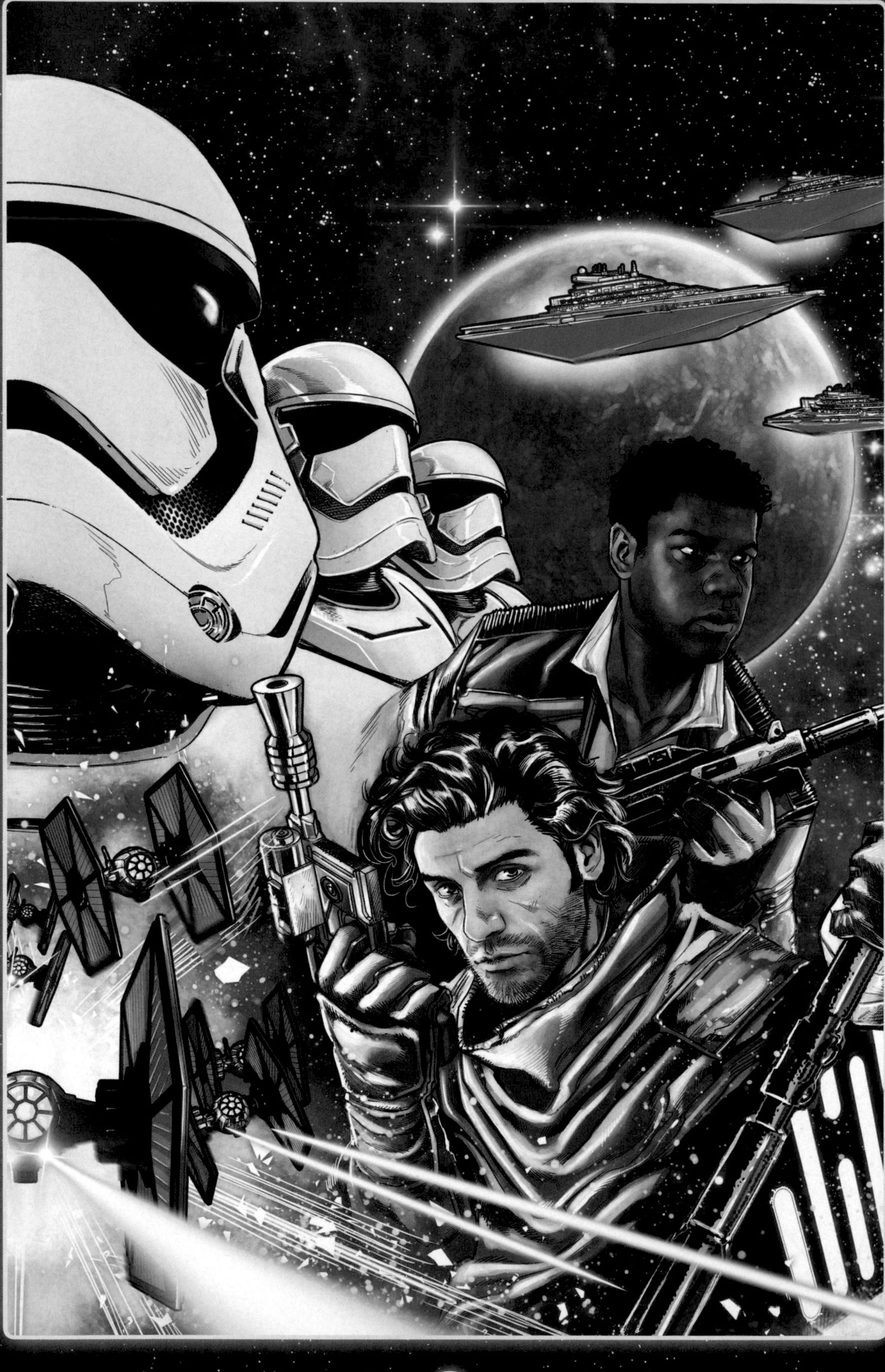

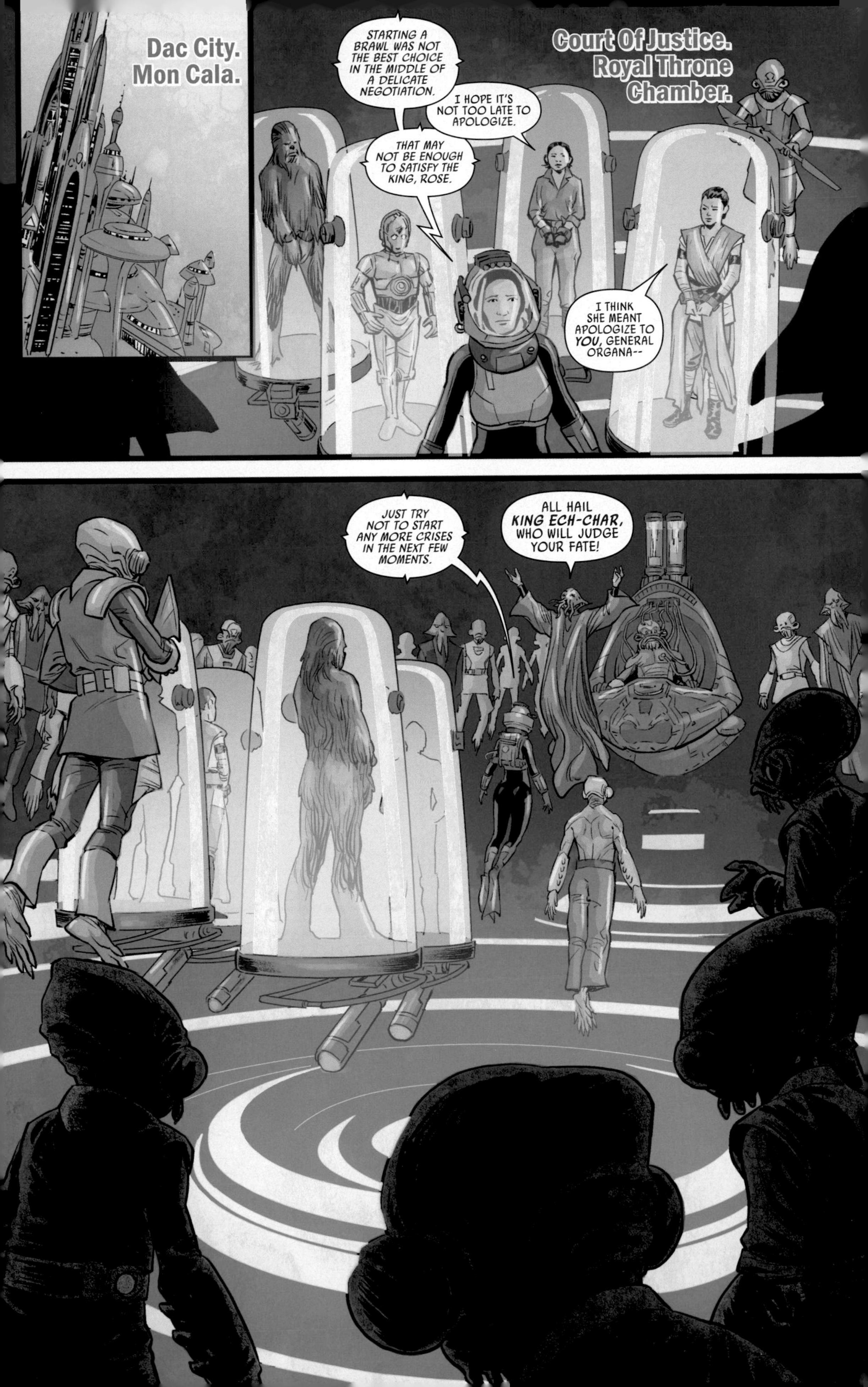
Dac City. Mon Cala.
Court Of Justice. Royal Throne Chamber.
STARTING A BRAWL WAS NOT THE BEST CHOICE IN THE MIDDLE OF A DELICATE NEGOTIATION.
I HOPE IT'S NOT TOO LATE TO APOLOGIZE.
THAT MAY NOT BE ENOUGH TO SATISFY THE KING, ROSE.
I THINK SHE MEANT APOLOGIZE TO YOU, GENERAL ORGANA--
JUST TRY NOT TO START ANY MORE CRISES IN THE NEXT FEW MOMENTS.
ALL HAIL KING ECH-CHAR, WHO WILL JUDGE YOUR FATE!

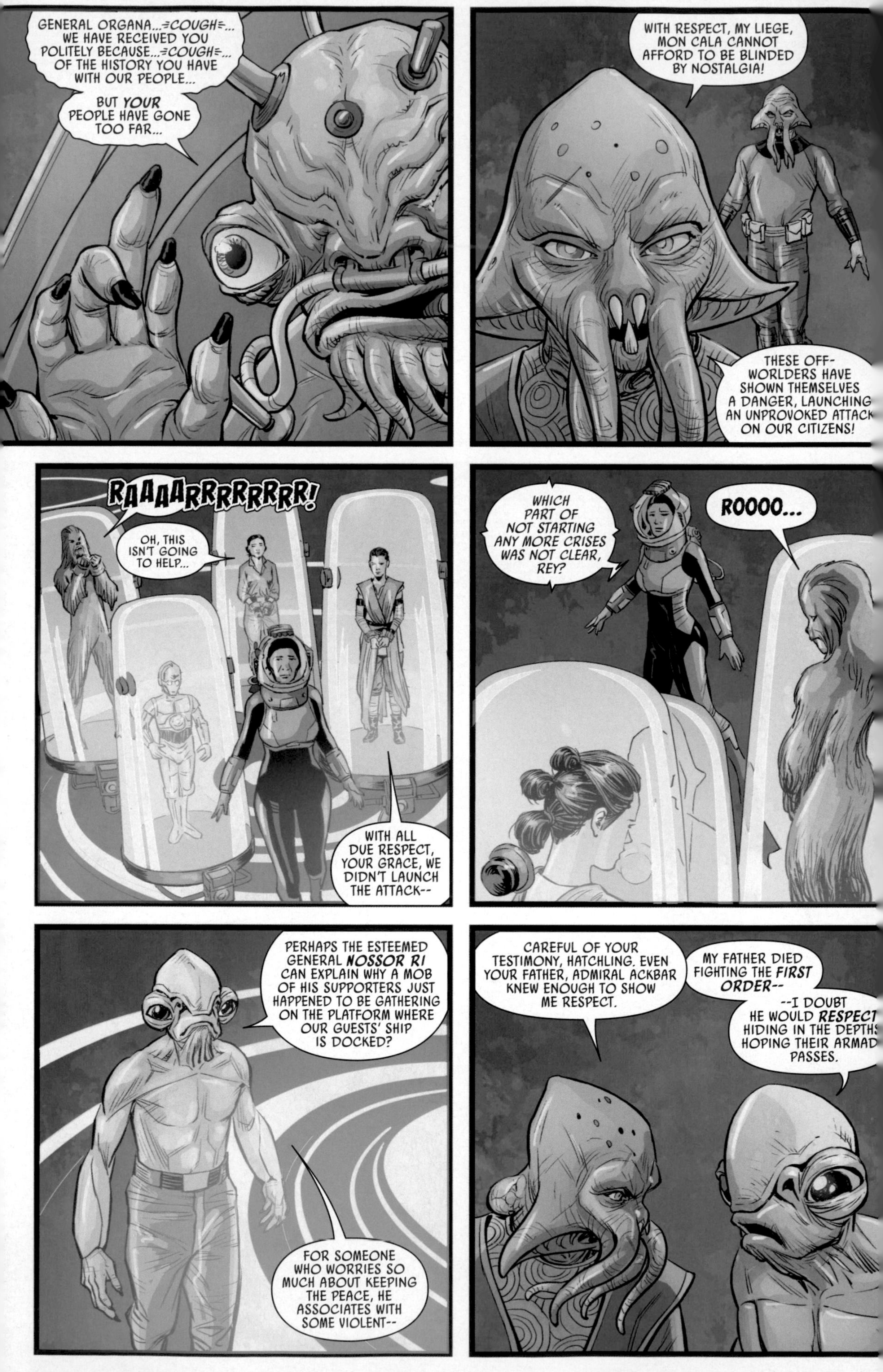
GENERAL ORGANA... COUGH... WE HAVE RECEIVED YOU POLITELY BECAUSE... COUGH... OF THE HISTORY YOU HAVE WITH OUR PEOPLE...
BUT YOUR PEOPLE HAVE GONE TOO FAR...
WITH RESPECT, MY LIEGE, MON CALA CANNOT AFFORD TO BE BLINDED BY NOSTALGIA!
THESE OFF-WORLDERS HAVE SHOWN THEMSELVES A DANGER, LAUNCHING AN UNPROVOKED ATTACK ON OUR CITIZENS!
RAAAARRRRRRRR!
OH, THIS ISN'T GOING TO HELP...
WITH ALL DUE RESPECT, YOUR GRACE, WE DIDN'T LAUNCH THE ATTACK--
WHICH PART OF NOT STARTING ANY MORE CRISES WAS NOT CLEAR, REY?
ROOOO...
PERHAPS THE ESTEEMED GENERAL NOSSOR RI CAN EXPLAIN WHY A MOB OF HIS SUPPORTERS JUST HAPPENED TO BE GATHERING ON THE PLATFORM WHERE OUR GUESTS' SHIP IS DOCKED?
FOR SOMEONE WHO WORRIES SO MUCH ABOUT KEEPING THE PEACE, HE ASSOCIATES WITH SOME VIOLENT--
CAREFUL OF YOUR TESTIMONY, HATCHLING. EVEN YOUR FATHER, ADMIRAL ACKBAR KNEW ENOUGH TO SHOW ME RESPECT.
MY FATHER DIED FIGHTING THE FIRST ORDER--
--I DOUBT HE WOULD RESPECT HIDING IN THE DEPTHS HOPING THEIR ARMADA PASSES.

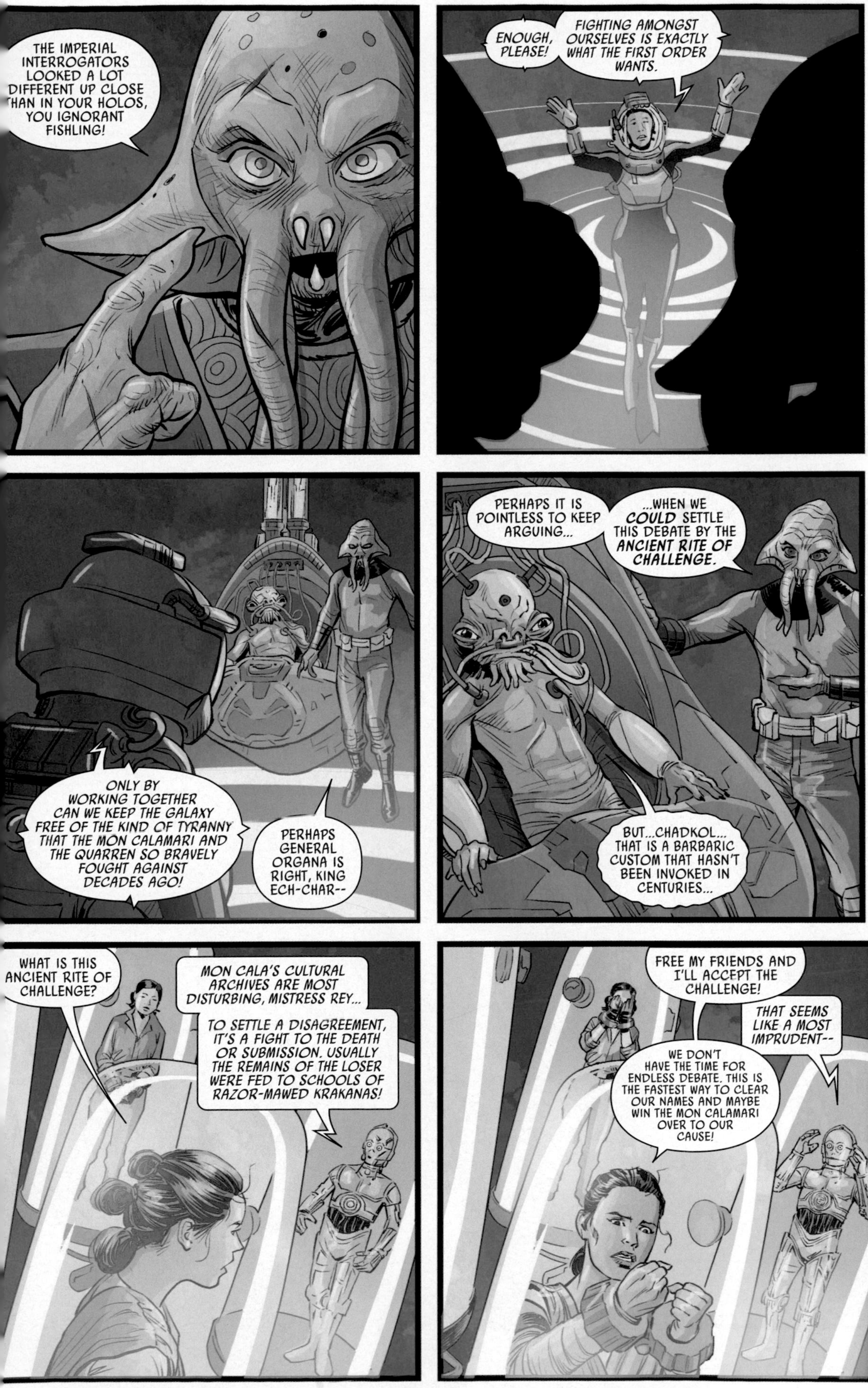
THE IMPERIAL INTERROGATORS LOOKED A LOT DIFFERENT UP CLOSE THAN IN YOUR HOLOS, YOU IGNORANT FISHLING!
ENOUGH, PLEASE!
FIGHTING AMONGST OURSELVES IS EXACTLY WHAT THE FIRST ORDER WANTS.
ONLY BY WORKING TOGETHER CAN WE KEEP THE GALAXY FREE OF THE KIND OF TYRANNY THAT THE MON CALAMARI AND THE QUARREN SO BRAVELY FOUGHT AGAINST DECADES AGO!
PERHAPS GENERAL ORGANA IS RIGHT, KING ECH-CHAR--
PERHAPS IT IS POINTLESS TO KEEP ARGUING...
...WHEN WE COULD SETTLE THIS DEBATE BY THE ANCIENT RITE OF CHALLENGE.
BUT...CHADKOL... THAT IS A BARBARIC CUSTOM THAT HASN'T BEEN INVOKED IN CENTURIES...
WHAT IS THIS ANCIENT RITE OF CHALLENGE?
MON CALA'S CULTURAL ARCHIVES ARE MOST DISTURBING, MISTRESS REY...
TO SETTLE A DISAGREEMENT, IT'S A FIGHT TO THE DEATH OR SUBMISSION. USUALLY THE REMAINS OF THE LOSER WERE FED TO SCHOOLS OF RAZOR-MAWED KRAKANAS!
FREE MY FRIENDS AND I'LL ACCEPT THE CHALLENGE!
THAT SEEMS LIKE A MOST IMPRUDENT--
WE DON'T HAVE THE TIME FOR ENDLESS DEBATE. THIS IS THE FASTEST WAY TO CLEAR OUR NAMES AND MAYBE WIN THE MON CALAMARI OVER TO OUR CAUSE!

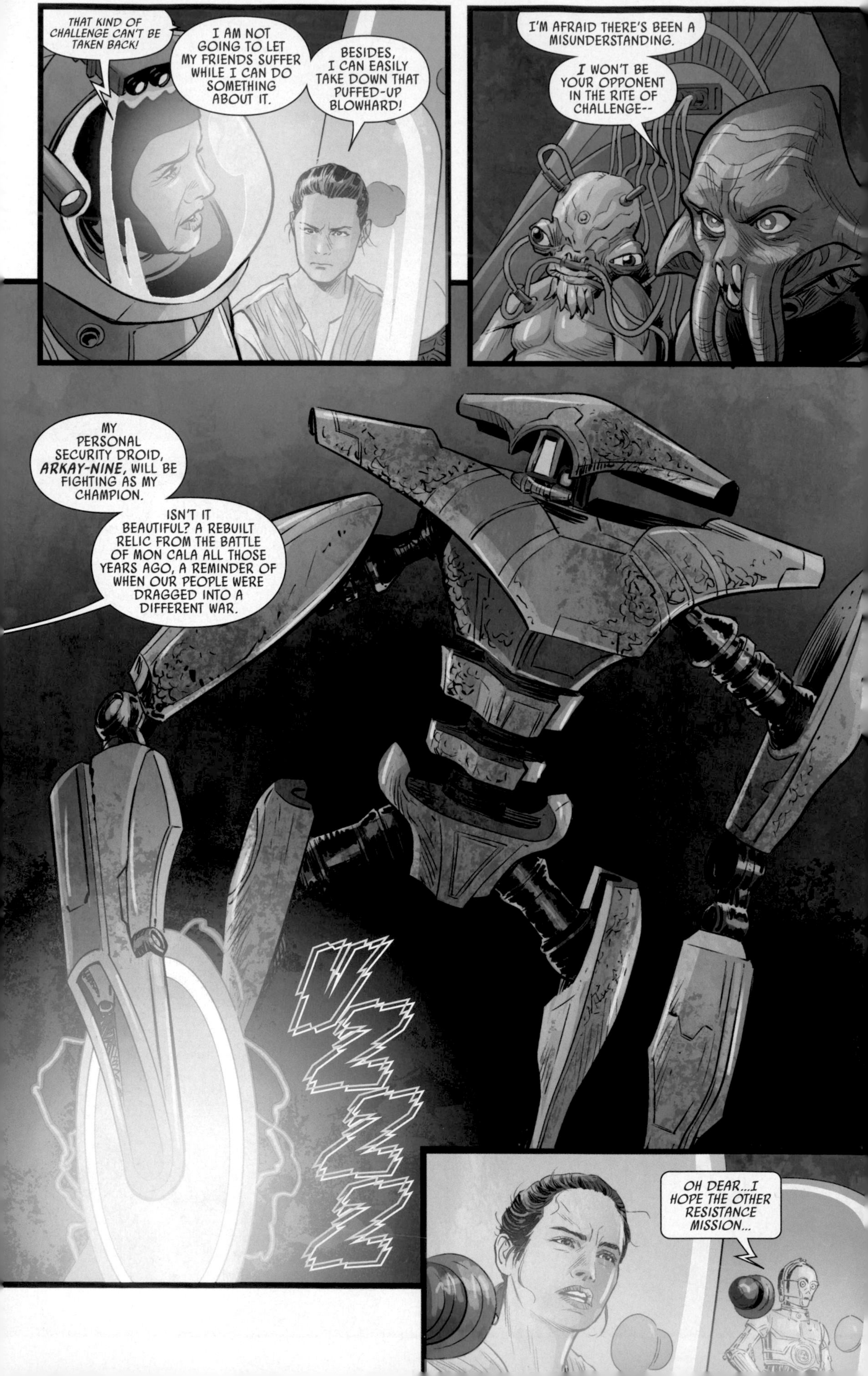

THAT KIND OF CHALLENGE CAN'T BE TAKEN BACK!
I AM NOT GOING TO LET MY FRIENDS SUFFER WHILE I CAN DO SOMETHING ABOUT IT.
BESIDES, I CAN EASILY TAKE DOWN THAT PUFFED-UP BLOWHARD!
I'M AFRAID THERE'S BEEN A MISUNDERSTANDING.
I WON'T BE YOUR OPPONENT IN THE RITE OF CHALLENGE--
MY PERSONAL SECURITY DROID, ARKAY-NINE, WILL BE FIGHTING AS MY CHAMPION.
ISN'T IT BEAUTIFUL? A REBUILT RELIC FROM THE BATTLE OF MON CALA ALL THOSE YEARS AGO, A REMINDER OF WHEN OUR PEOPLE WERE DRAGGED INTO A DIFFERENT WAR.
VZZZ
OH DEAR...I HOPE THE OTHER RESISTANCE MISSION...

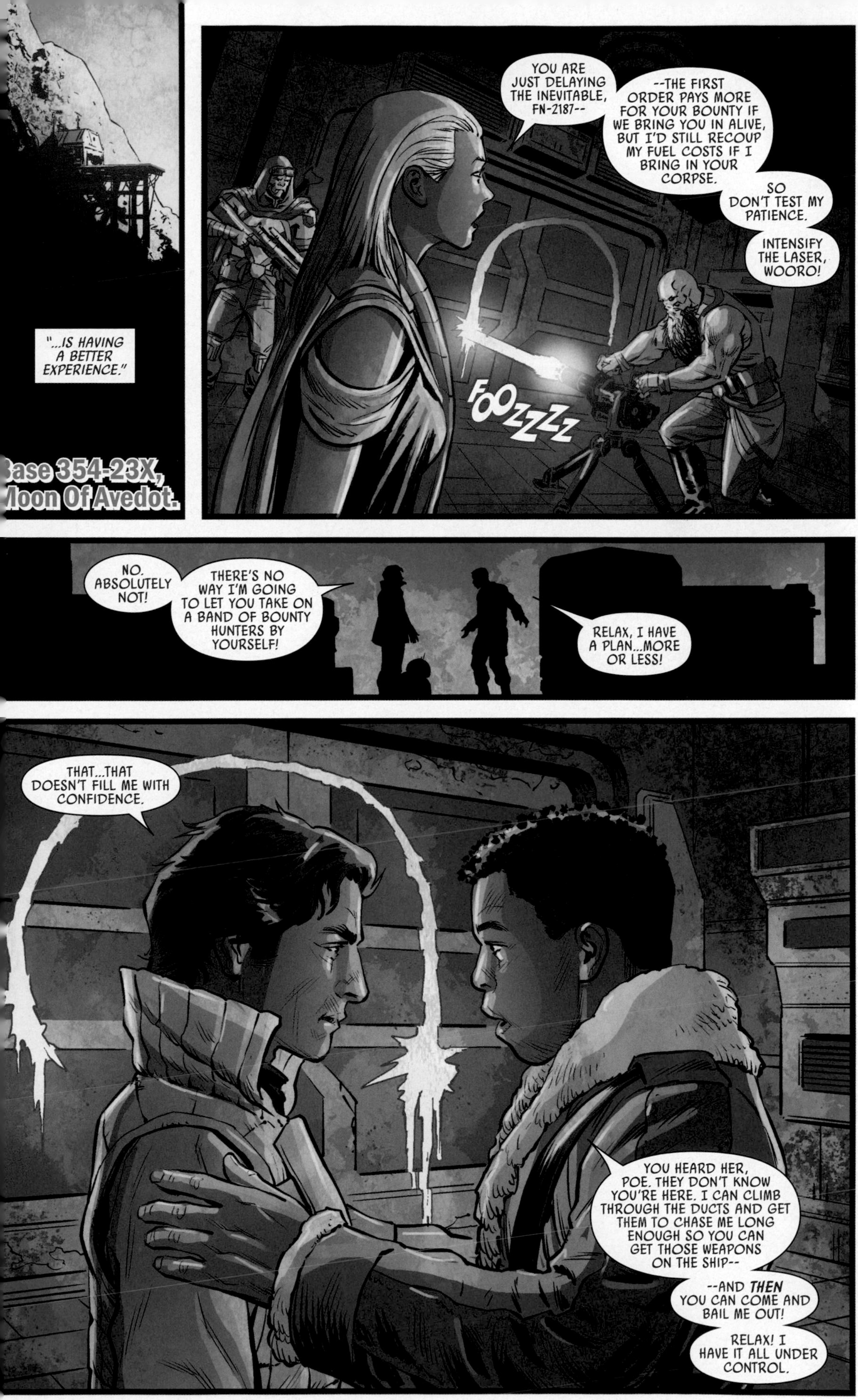
"...IS HAVING A BETTER EXPERIENCE."
Base 354-23X, Moon Of Avedot.
YOU ARE JUST DELAYING THE INEVITABLE, FN-2187--
--THE FIRST ORDER PAYS MORE FOR YOUR BOUNTY IF WE BRING YOU IN ALIVE, BUT I'D STILL RECOUP MY FUEL COSTS IF I BRING IN YOUR CORPSE.
SO DON'T TEST MY PATIENCE.
INTENSIFY THE LASER, WOORO!
FOOZZZZ
NO. ABSOLUTELY NOT!
THERE'S NO WAY I'M GOING TO LET YOU TAKE ON A BAND OF BOUNTY HUNTERS BY YOURSELF!
RELAX, I HAVE A PLAN...MORE OR LESS!
THAT...THAT DOESN'T FILL ME WITH CONFIDENCE.
YOU HEARD HER, POE. THEY DON'T KNOW YOU'RE HERE. I CAN CLIMB THROUGH THE DUCTS AND GET THEM TO CHASE ME LONG ENOUGH SO YOU CAN GET THOSE WEAPONS ON THE SHIP--
--AND *THEN* YOU CAN COME AND BAIL ME OUT!
RELAX! I HAVE IT ALL UNDER CONTROL.

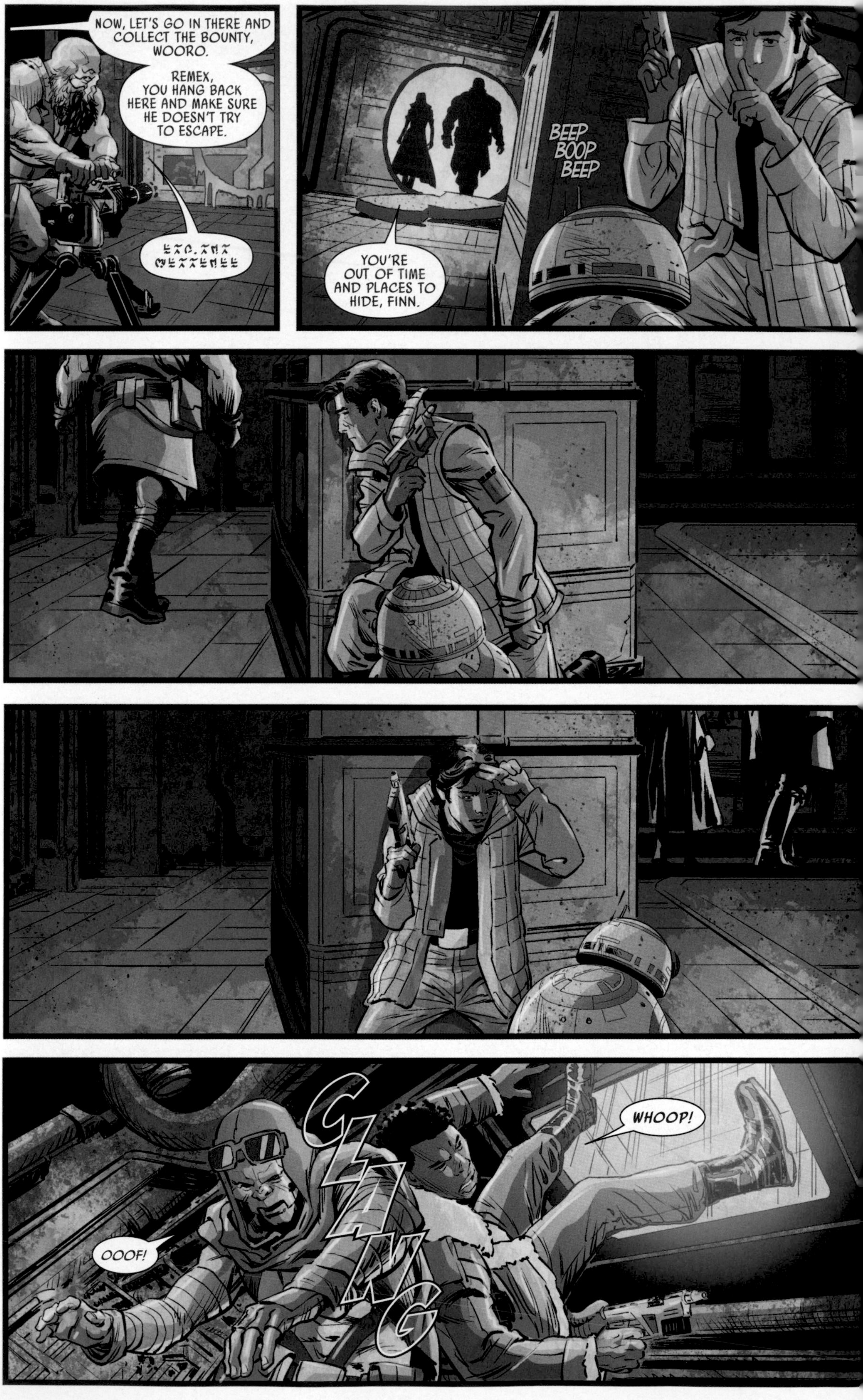
NOW, LET'S GO IN THERE AND COLLECT THE BOUNTY, WOORO.
REMEX, YOU HANG BACK HERE AND MAKE SURE HE DOESN'T TRY TO ESCAPE.
YOU'RE OUT OF TIME AND PLACES TO HIDE, FINN.
BEEP BOOP BEEP
CLANG
WHOOP!
OOOF!

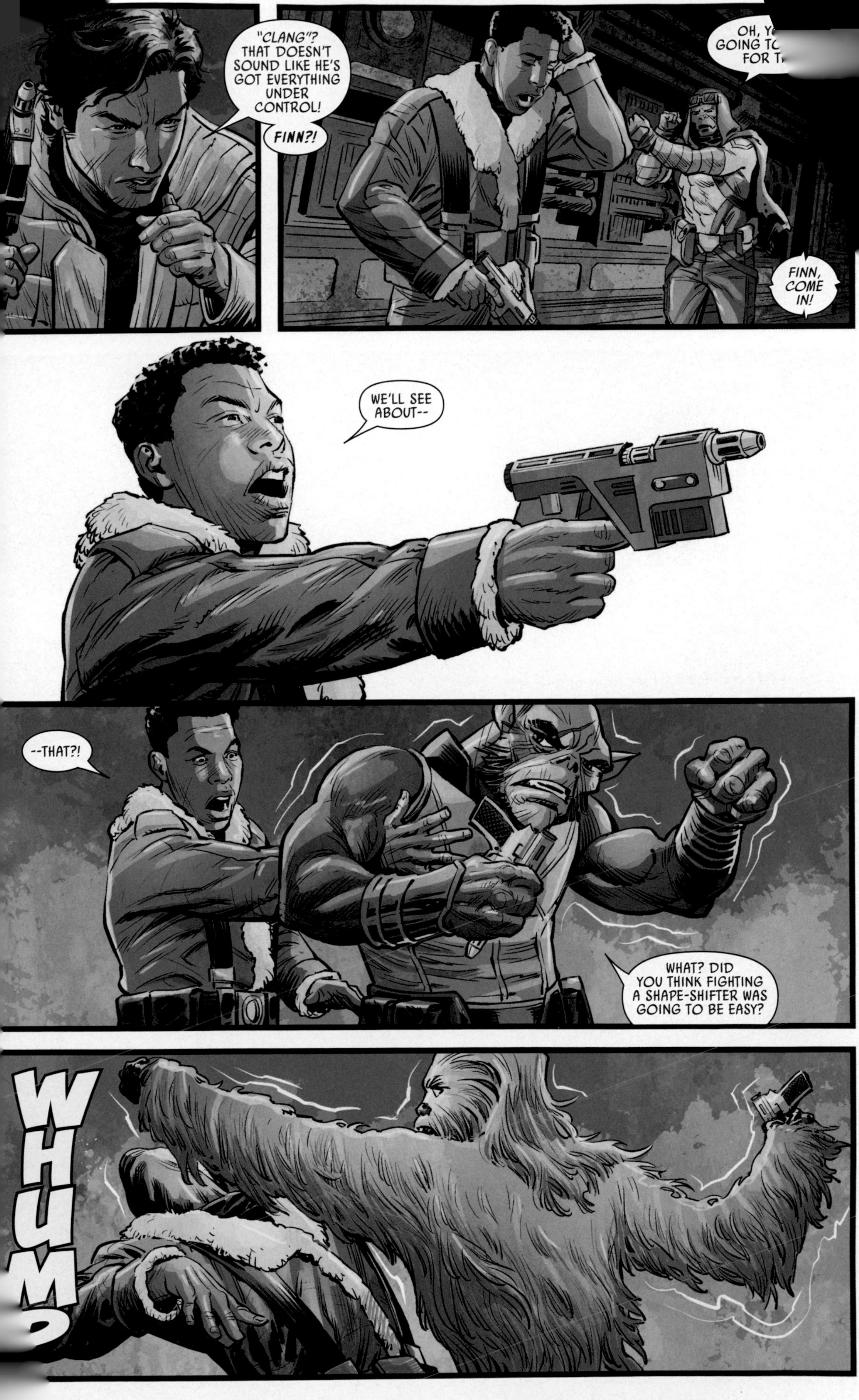
"CLANG"? THAT DOESN'T SOUND LIKE HE'S GOT EVERYTHING UNDER CONTROL!
FINN?!
FINN, COME IN!
WE'LL SEE ABOUT--
--THAT?!
WHAT? DID YOU THINK FIGHTING A SHAPE-SHIFTER WAS GOING TO BE EASY?
WHUM

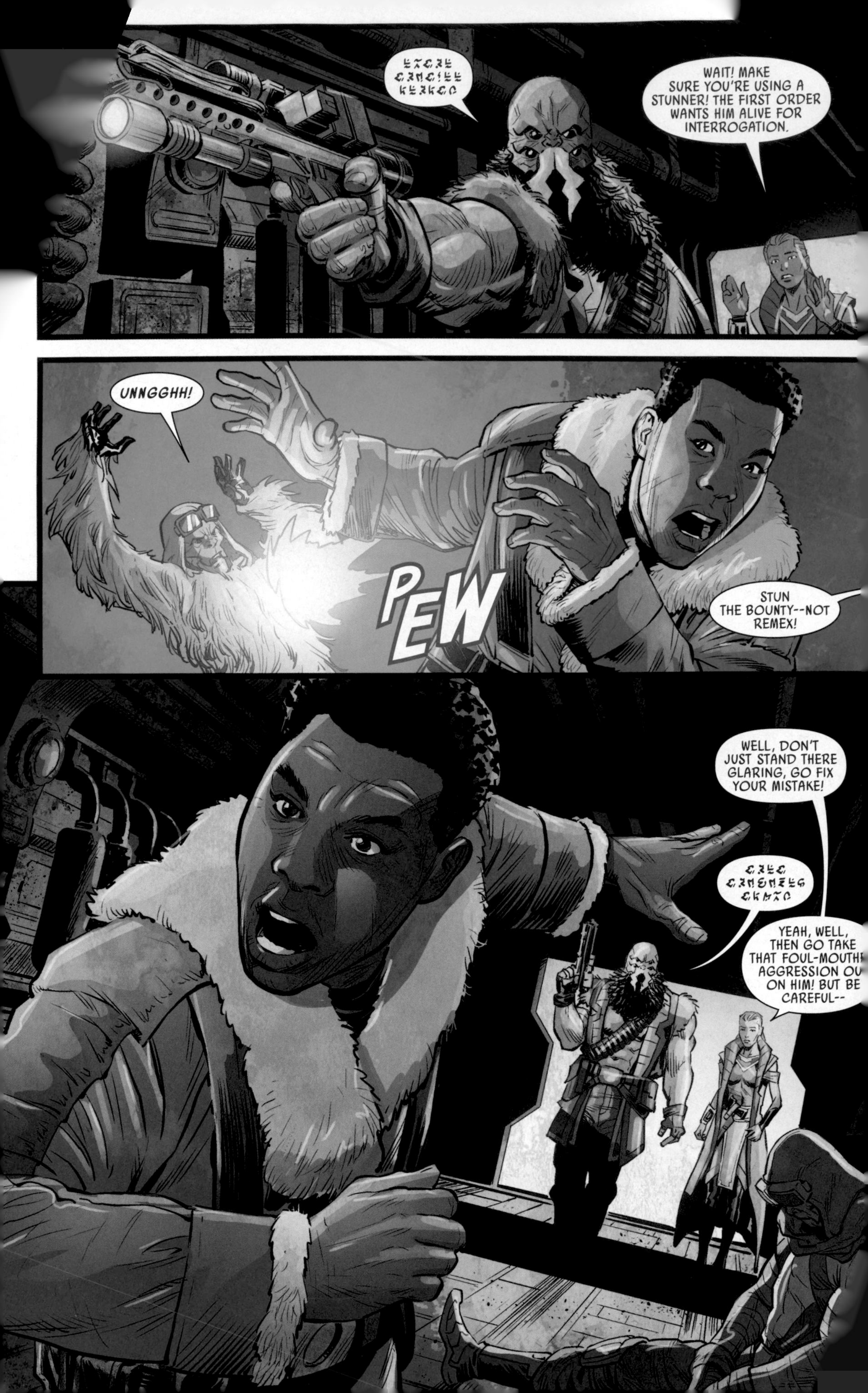
WAIT! MAKE SURE YOU'RE USING A STUNNER! THE FIRST ORDER WANTS HIM ALIVE FOR INTERROGATION.
UNNGGHH!
PEW
STUN THE BOUNTY--NOT REMEX!
WELL, DON'T JUST STAND THERE GLARING, GO FIX YOUR MISTAKE!
YEAH, WELL, THEN GO TAKE THAT FOUL-MOUTH AGGRESSION OU ON HIM! BUT BE CAREFUL--

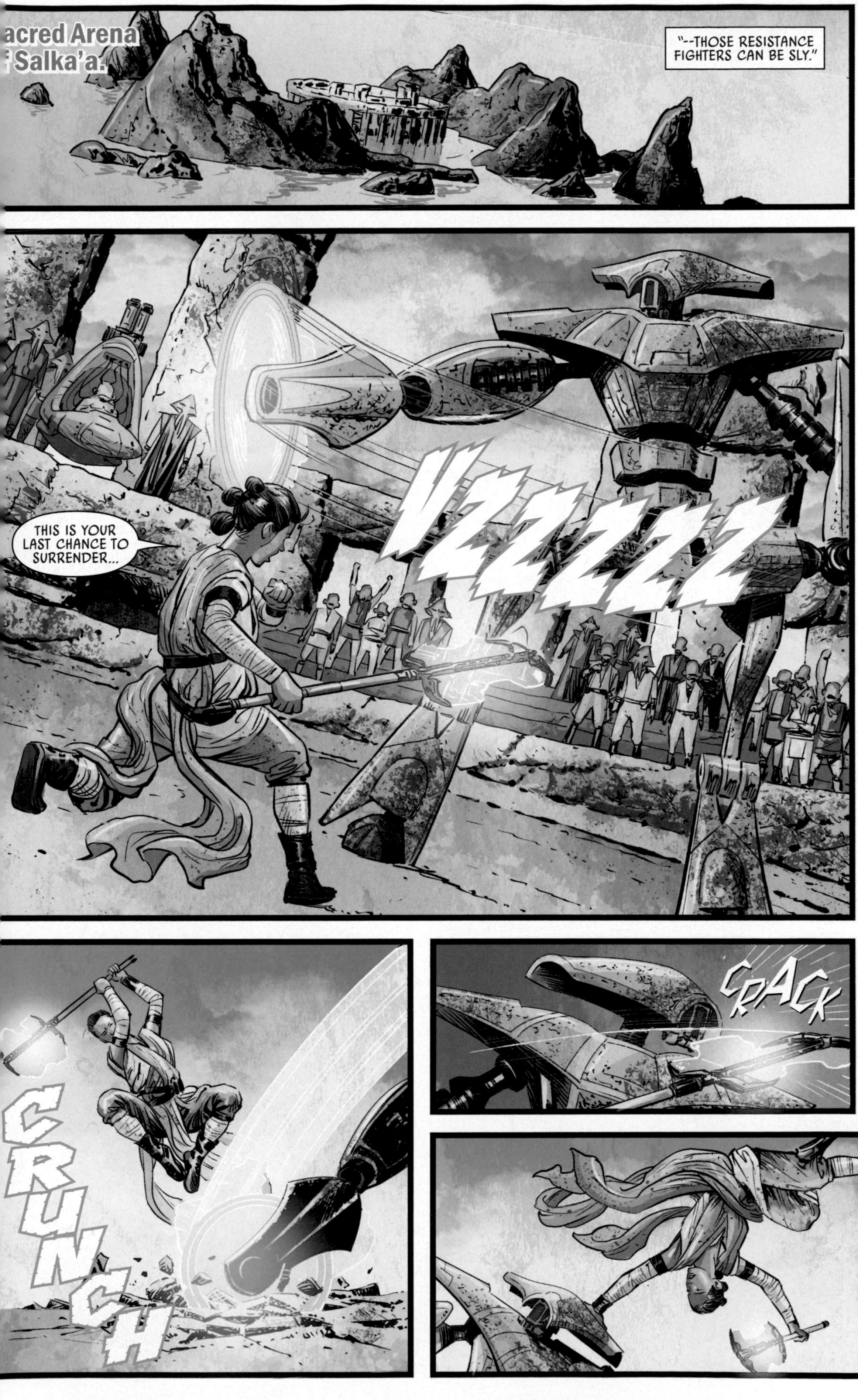

acred Arena
f Salka'a.
"--THOSE RESISTANCE FIGHTERS CAN BE SLY."
THIS IS YOUR LAST CHANCE TO SURRENDER...
VZZZZZ
CRUNCH
CRACK

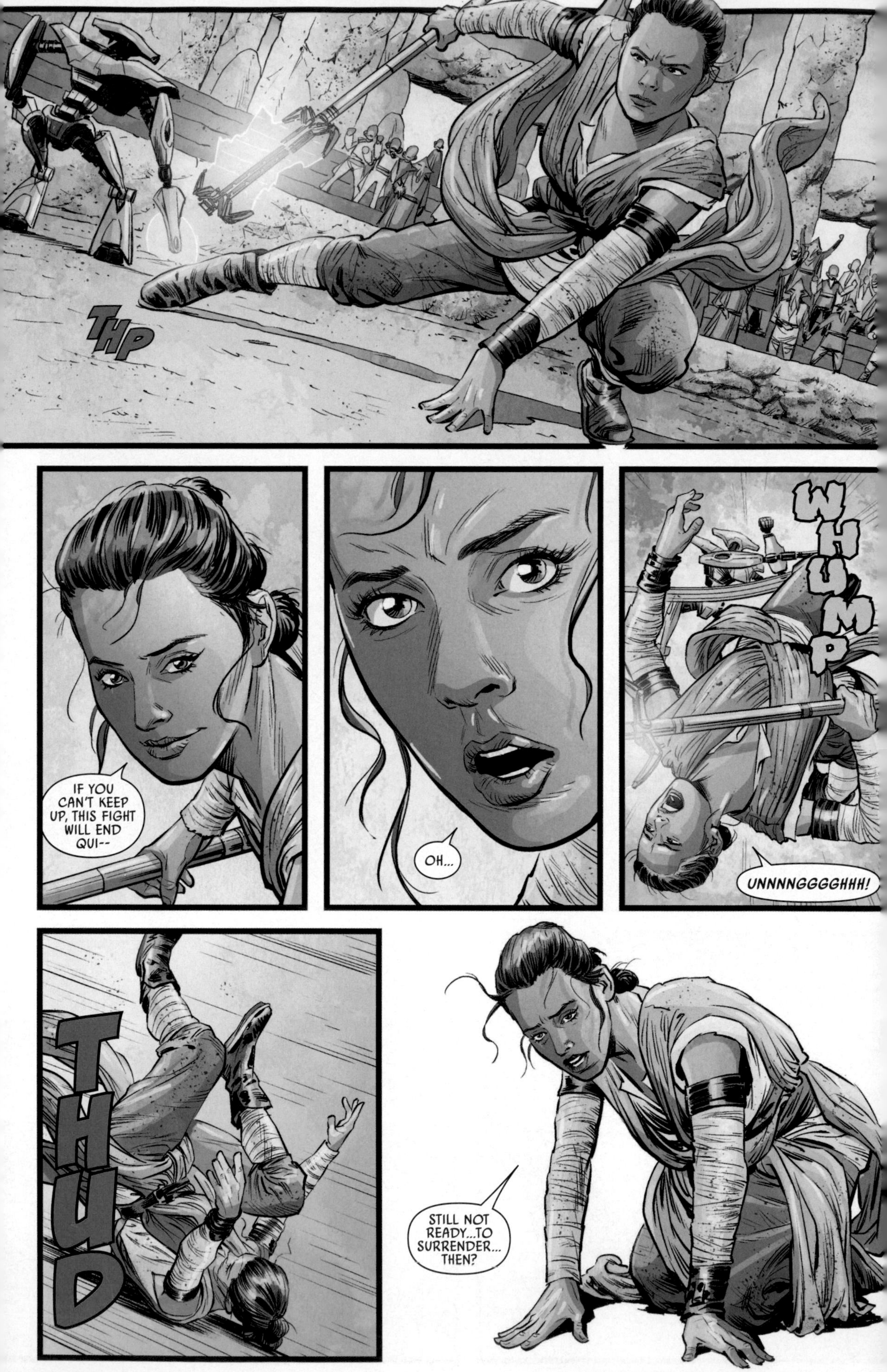
THP
IF YOU CAN'T KEEP UP, THIS FIGHT WILL END QUI--
OH...
WHUMP
UNNNNGGGGHHH!
THUD
STILL NOT READY...TO SURRENDER... THEN?

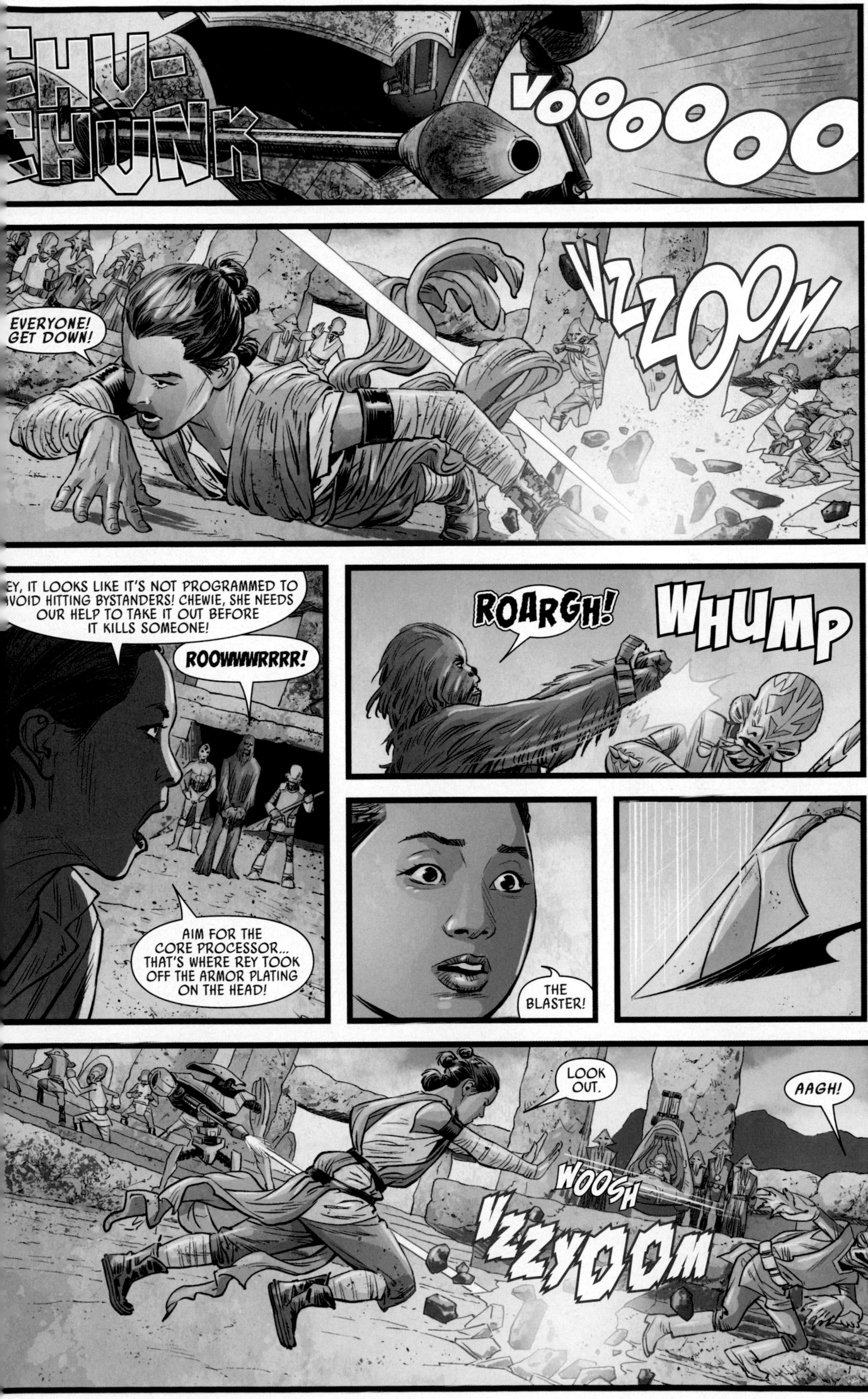
CHU-CHUNK
VOOOOOO
EVERYONE! GET DOWN!
VZZOOM
EY, IT LOOKS LIKE IT'S NOT PROGRAMMED TO VOID HITTING BYSTANDERS! CHEWIE, SHE NEEDS OUR HELP TO TAKE IT OUT BEFORE IT KILLS SOMEONE!
ROOWWWRRRR!
AIM FOR THE CORE PROCESSOR... THAT'S WHERE REY TOOK OFF THE ARMOR PLATING ON THE HEAD!
ROARGH!
WHUMP
THE BLASTER!
LOOK OUT.
AAGH!
WOOSH
VZZYOOM

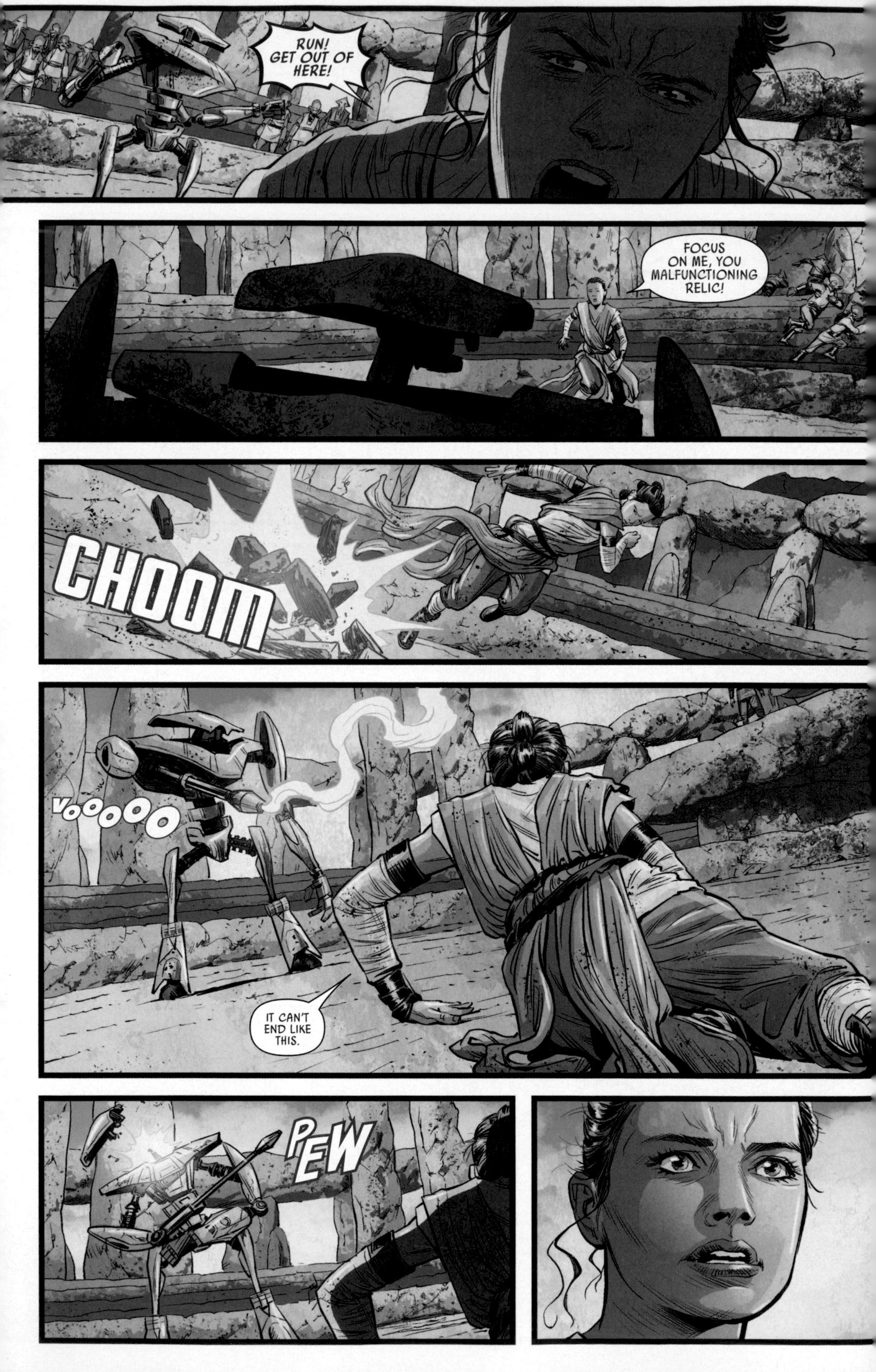
RUN! GET OUT OF HERE!
FOCUS ON ME, YOU MALFUNCTIONING RELIC!
CHOOM
VOOOOO
IT CAN'T END LIKE THIS.
PEW

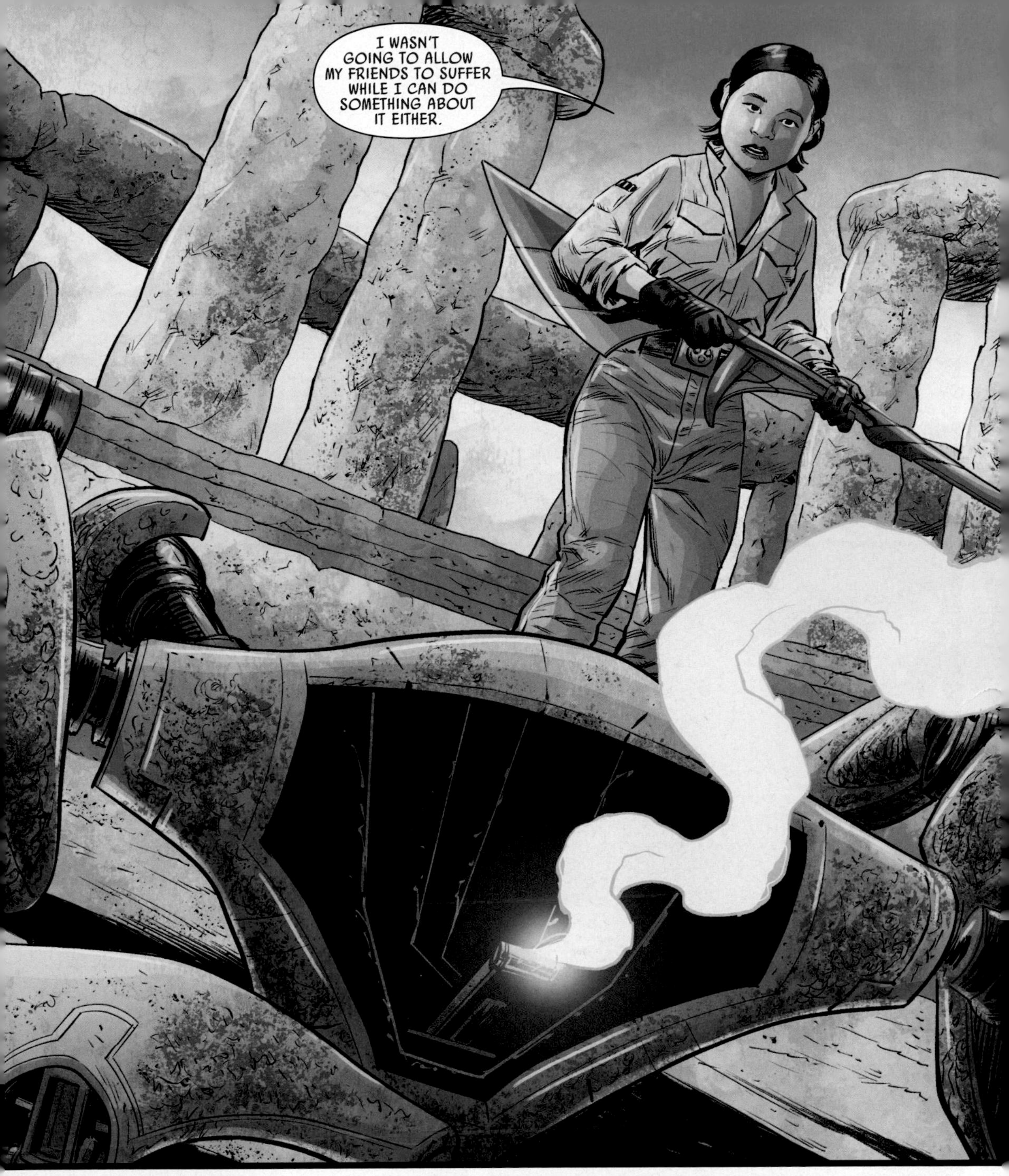
I WASN'T GOING TO ALLOW MY FRIENDS TO SUFFER WHILE I CAN DO SOMETHING ABOUT IT EITHER.

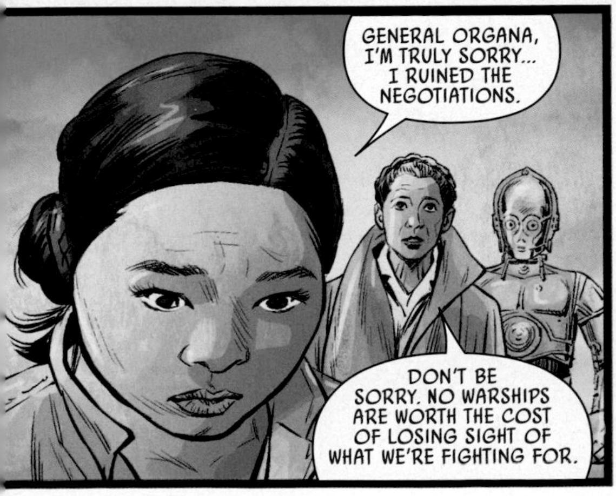
GENERAL ORGANA, I'M TRULY SORRY... I RUINED THE NEGOTIATIONS.
DON'T BE SORRY. NO WARSHIPS ARE WORTH THE COST OF LOSING SIGHT OF WHAT WE'RE FIGHTING FOR.

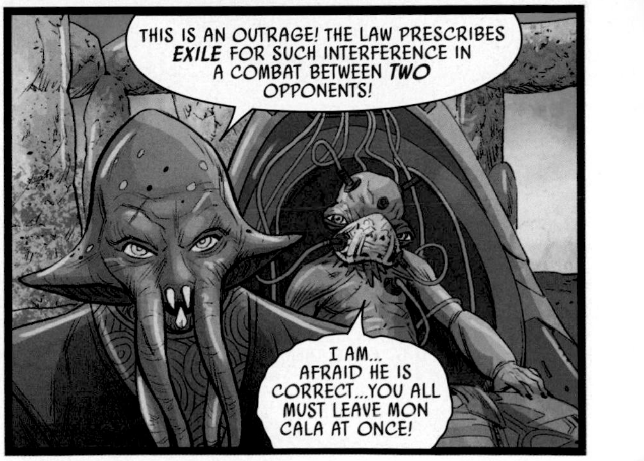
THIS IS AN OUTRAGE! THE LAW PRESCRIBES EXILE FOR SUCH INTERFERENCE IN A COMBAT BETWEEN TWO OPPONENTS!
I AM... AFRAID HE IS CORRECT...YOU ALL MUST LEAVE MON CALA AT ONCE!

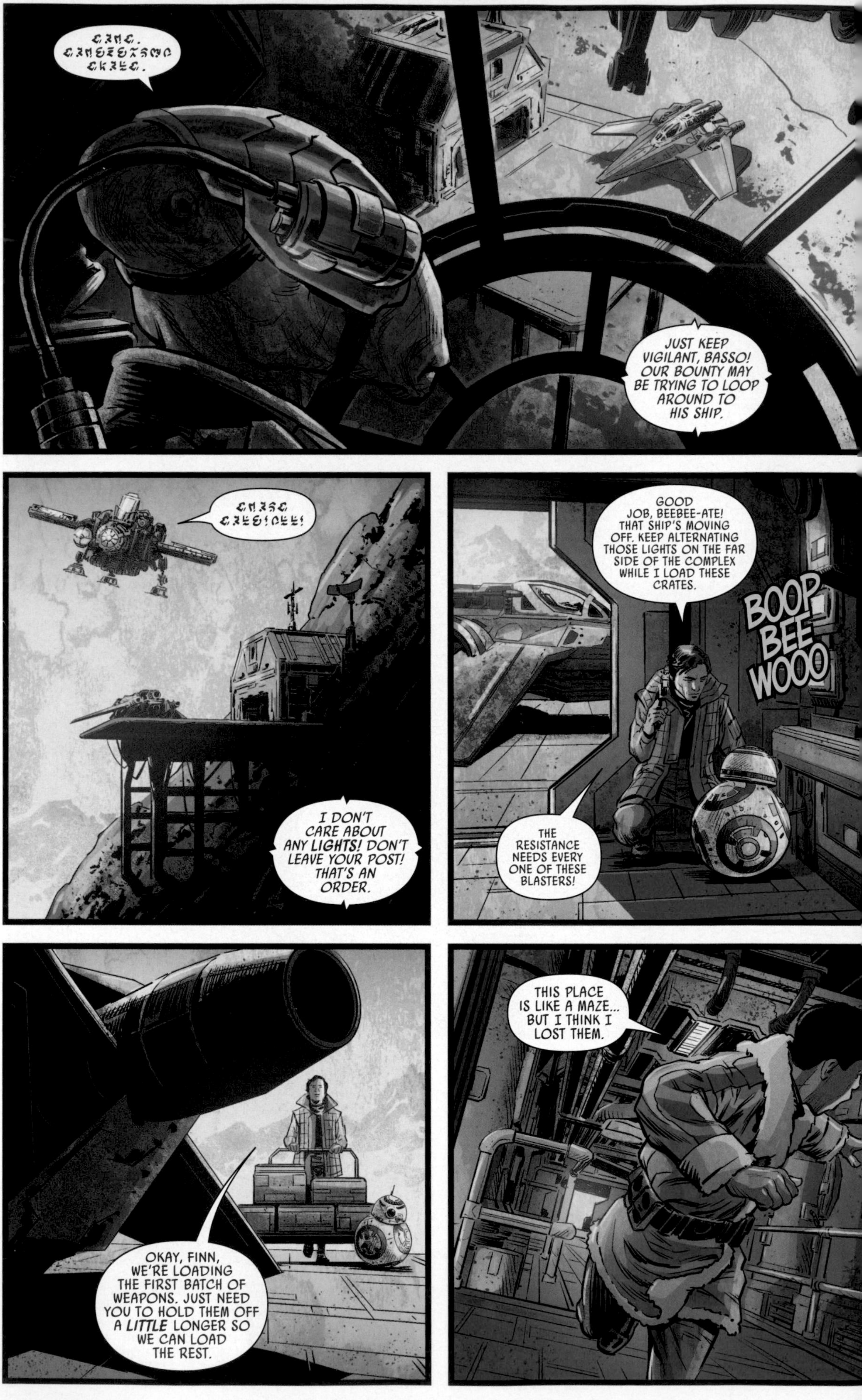
JUST KEEP VIGILANT, BASSO! OUR BOUNTY MAY BE TRYING TO LOOP AROUND TO HIS SHIP.
I DON'T CARE ABOUT ANY LIGHTS! DON'T LEAVE YOUR POST! THAT'S AN ORDER.
GOOD JOB, BEEBEE-ATE! THAT SHIP'S MOVING OFF. KEEP ALTERNATING THOSE LIGHTS ON THE FAR SIDE OF THE COMPLEX WHILE I LOAD THESE CRATES.
BOOP BEE WOOO
THE RESISTANCE NEEDS EVERY ONE OF THESE BLASTERS!
OKAY, FINN, WE'RE LOADING THE FIRST BATCH OF WEAPONS. JUST NEED YOU TO HOLD THEM OFF A LITTLE LONGER SO WE CAN LOAD THE REST.
THIS PLACE IS LIKE A MAZE... BUT I THINK I LOST THEM.

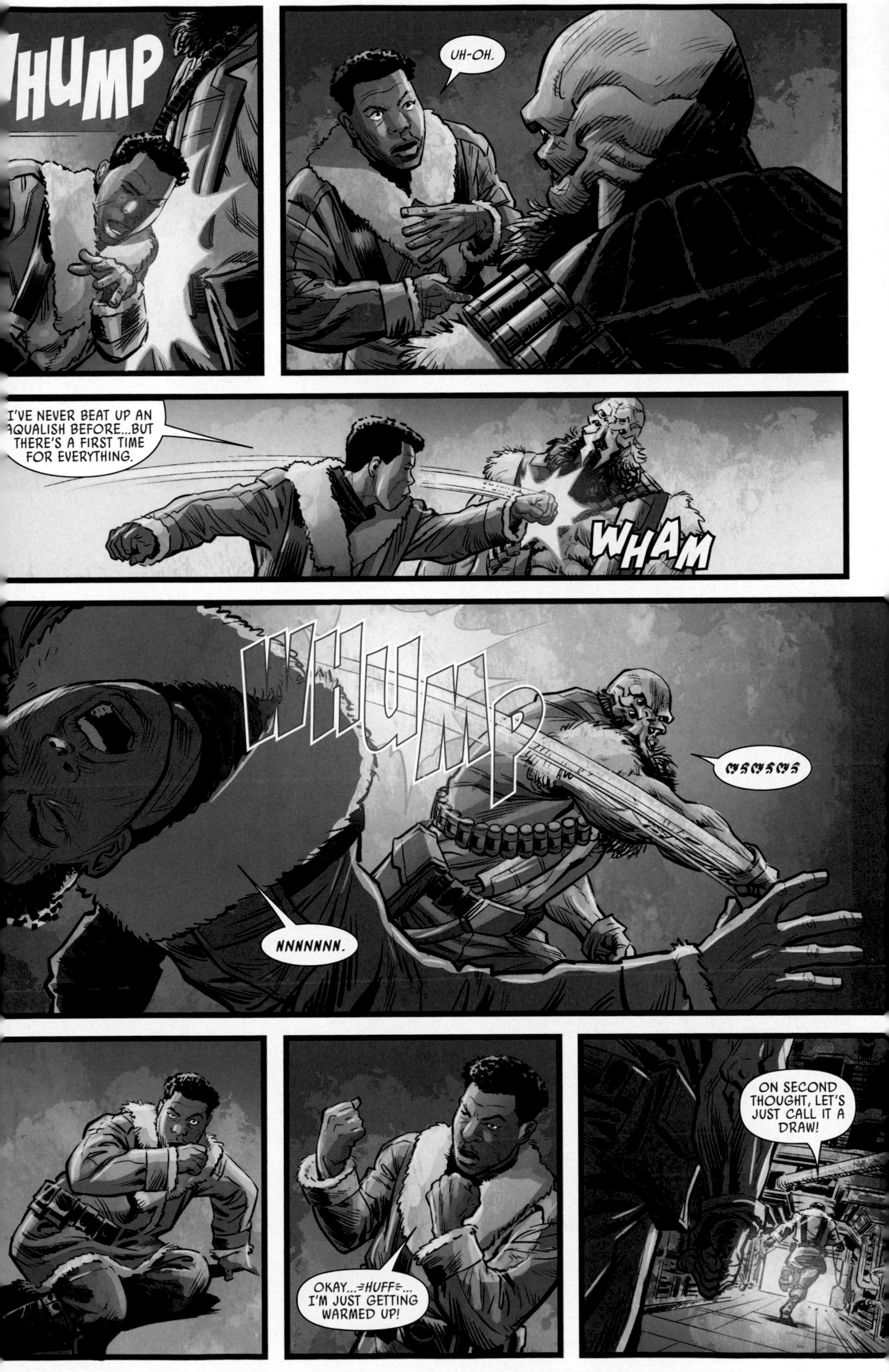

WHUMP
UH-OH.
I'VE NEVER BEAT UP AN AQUALISH BEFORE...BUT THERE'S A FIRST TIME FOR EVERYTHING.
WHAM
WHUMP
NNNNNNN.
OKAY... HUFF... I'M JUST GETTING WARMED UP!
ON SECOND THOUGHT, LET'S JUST CALL IT A DRAW!

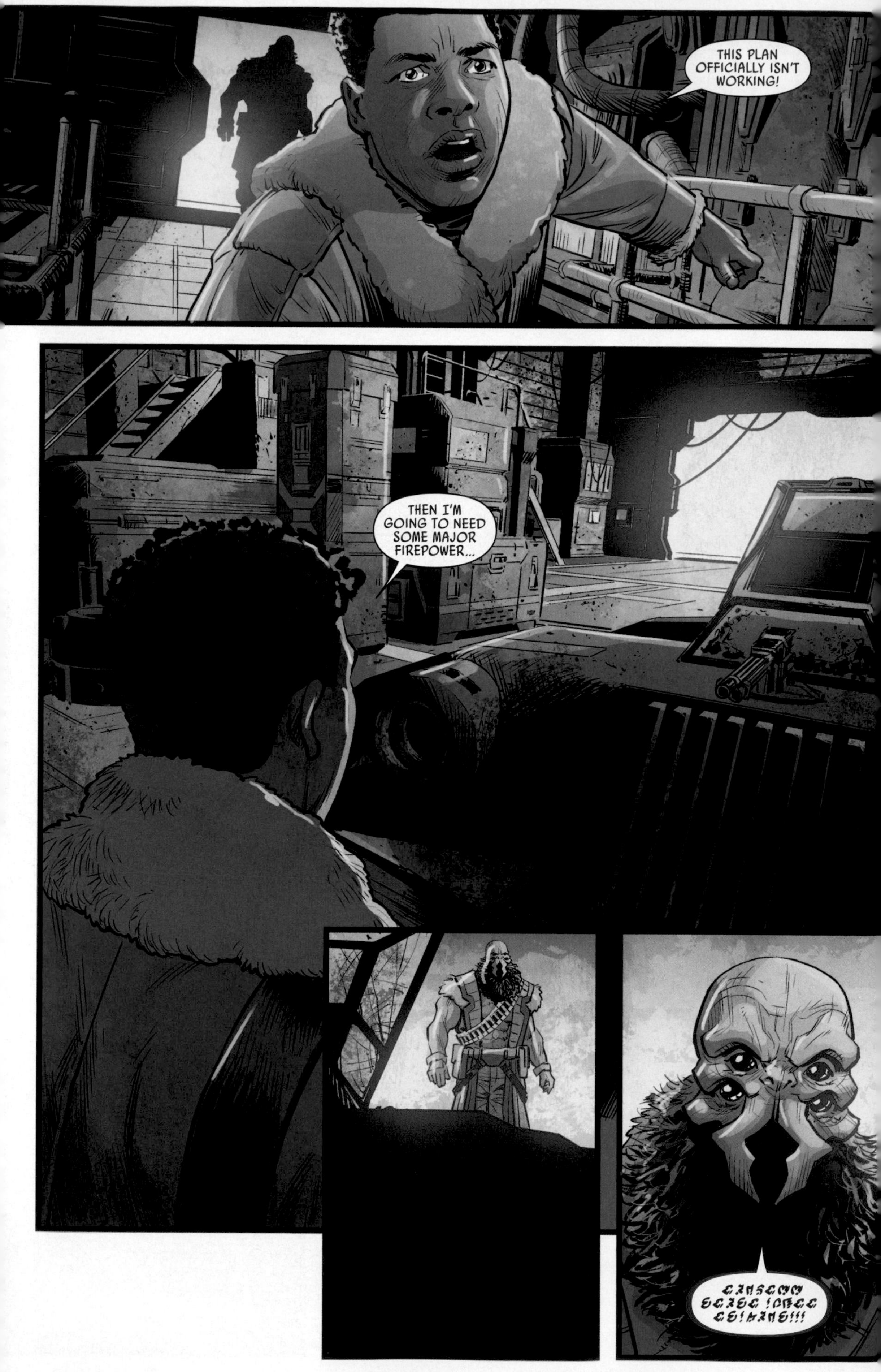
THIS PLAN OFFICIALLY ISN'T WORKING!
THEN I'M GOING TO NEED SOME MAJOR FIREPOWER...

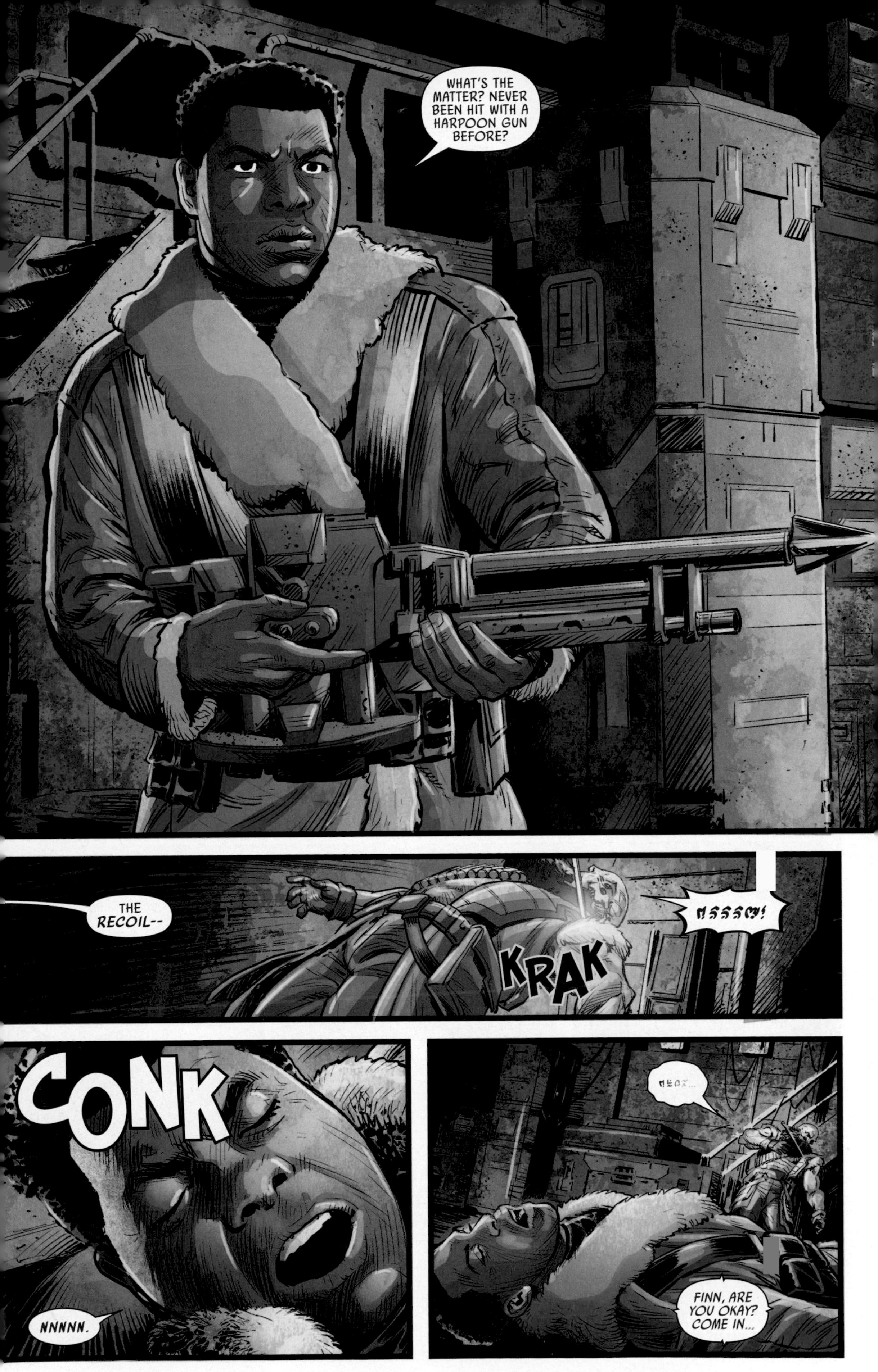
WHAT'S THE MATTER? NEVER BEEN HIT WITH A HARPOON GUN BEFORE?
THE RECOIL--
KRAK
CONK
NNNNN.
FINN, ARE YOU OKAY? COME IN...

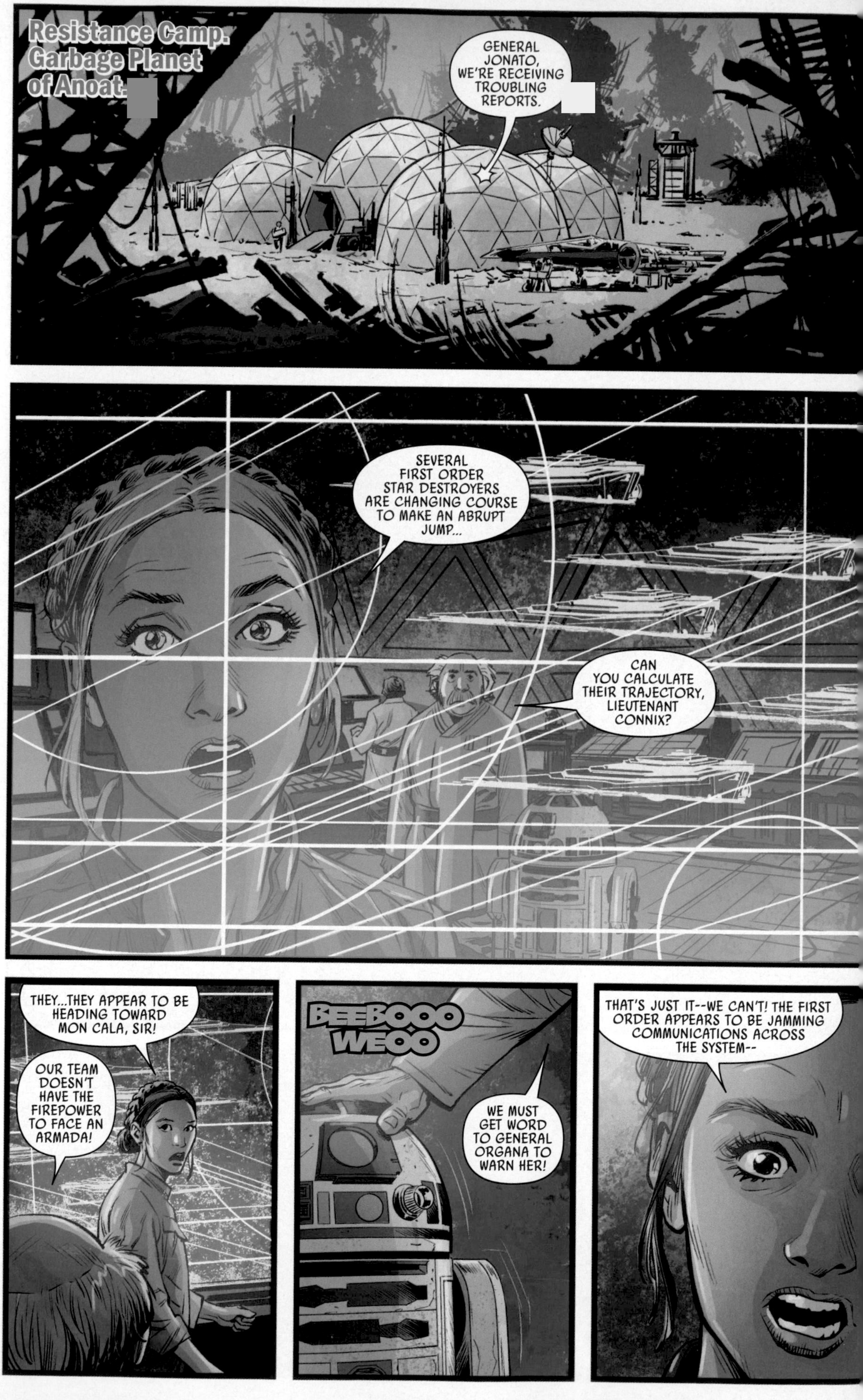
Resistance Camp. Garbage Planet of Anoat.
GENERAL JONATO, WE'RE RECEIVING TROUBLING REPORTS.
SEVERAL FIRST ORDER STAR DESTROYERS ARE CHANGING COURSE TO MAKE AN ABRUPT JUMP...
CAN YOU CALCULATE THEIR TRAJECTORY, LIEUTENANT CONNIX?
THEY...THEY APPEAR TO BE HEADING TOWARD MON CALA, SIR!
OUR TEAM DOESN'T HAVE THE FIREPOWER TO FACE AN ARMADA!
BEEBOOO WEOO
WE MUST GET WORD TO GENERAL ORGANA TO WARN HER!
THAT'S JUST IT--WE CAN'T! THE FIRST ORDER APPEARS TO BE JAMMING COMMUNICATIONS ACROSS THE SYSTEM--

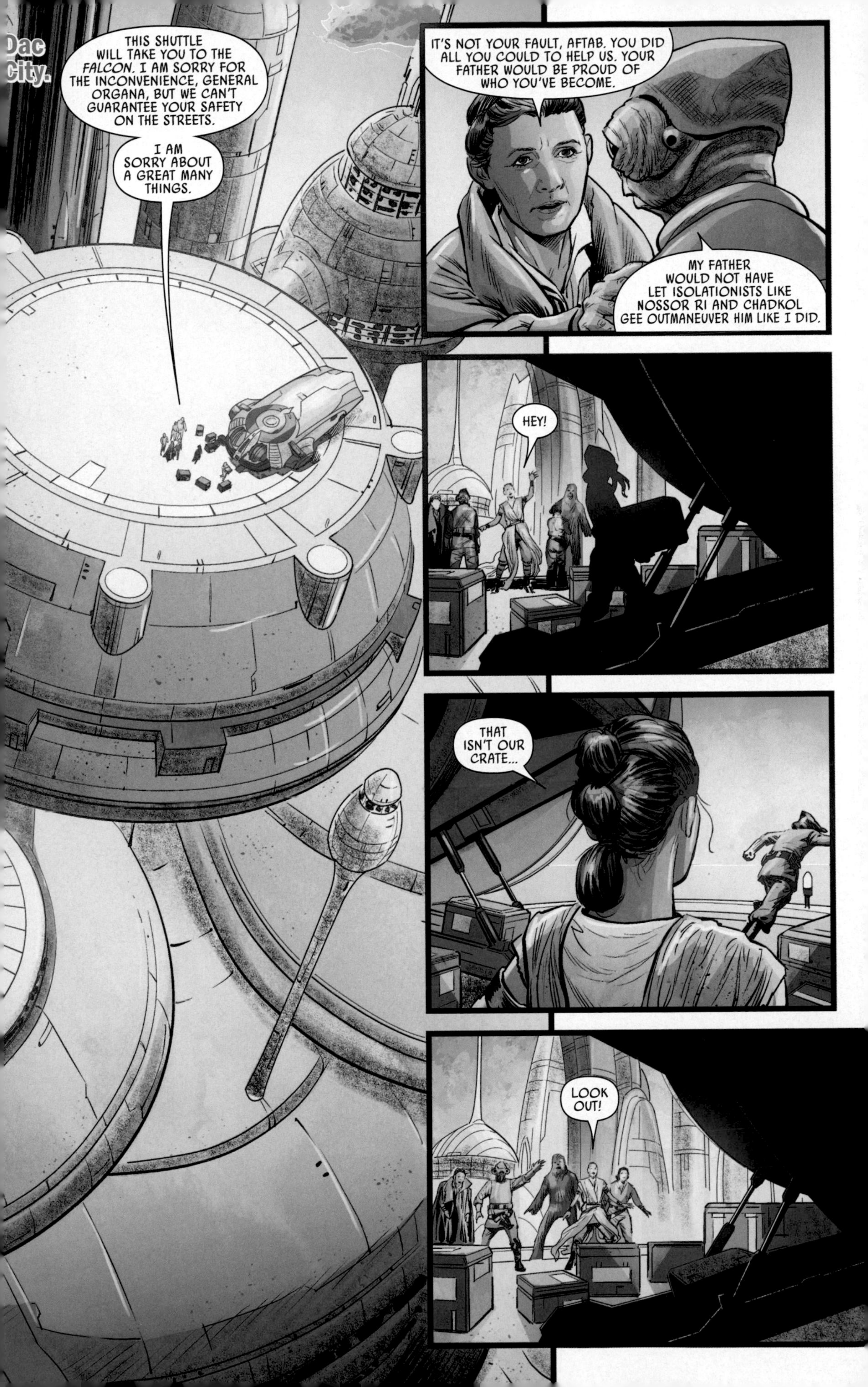
Dac City.
THIS SHUTTLE WILL TAKE YOU TO THE FALCON. I AM SORRY FOR THE INCONVENIENCE, GENERAL ORGANA, BUT WE CAN'T GUARANTEE YOUR SAFETY ON THE STREETS.
I AM SORRY ABOUT A GREAT MANY THINGS.
IT'S NOT YOUR FAULT, AFTAB. YOU DID ALL YOU COULD TO HELP US. YOUR FATHER WOULD BE PROUD OF WHO YOU'VE BECOME.
MY FATHER WOULD NOT HAVE LET ISOLATIONISTS LIKE NOSSOR RI AND CHADKOL GEE OUTMANEUVER HIM LIKE I DID.
HEY!
THAT ISN'T OUR CRATE...
LOOK OUT!

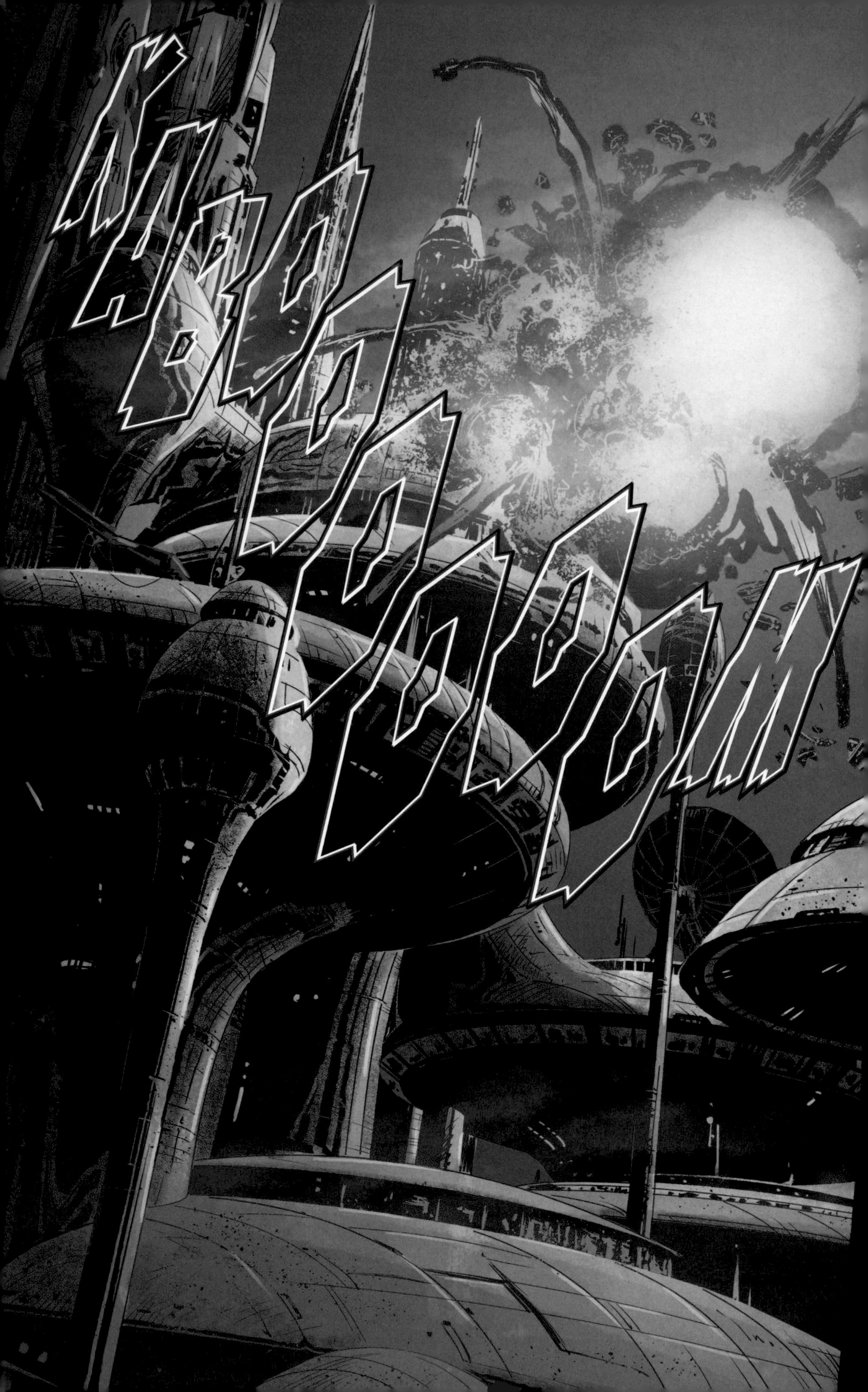
KBOOOOOOM

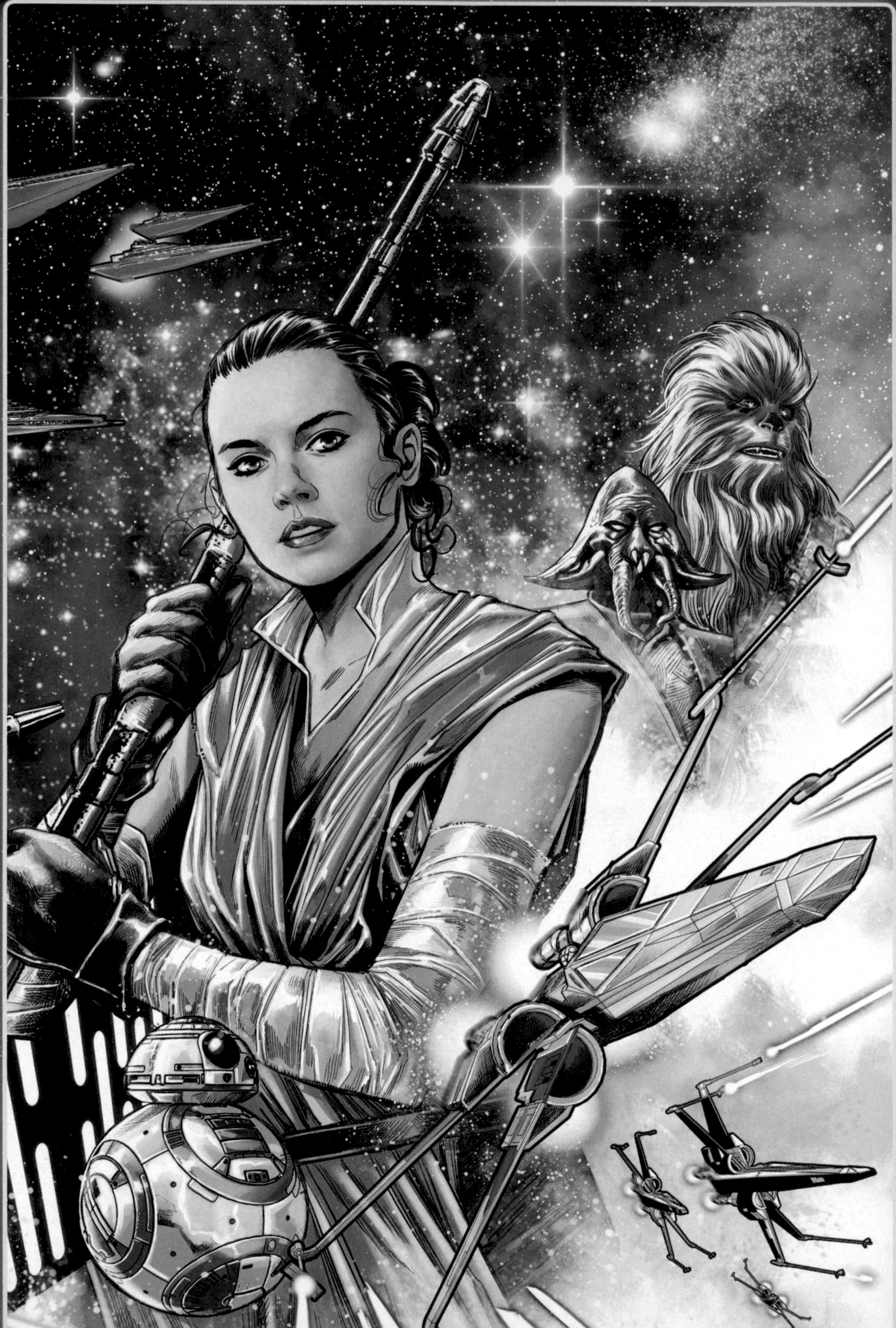

4

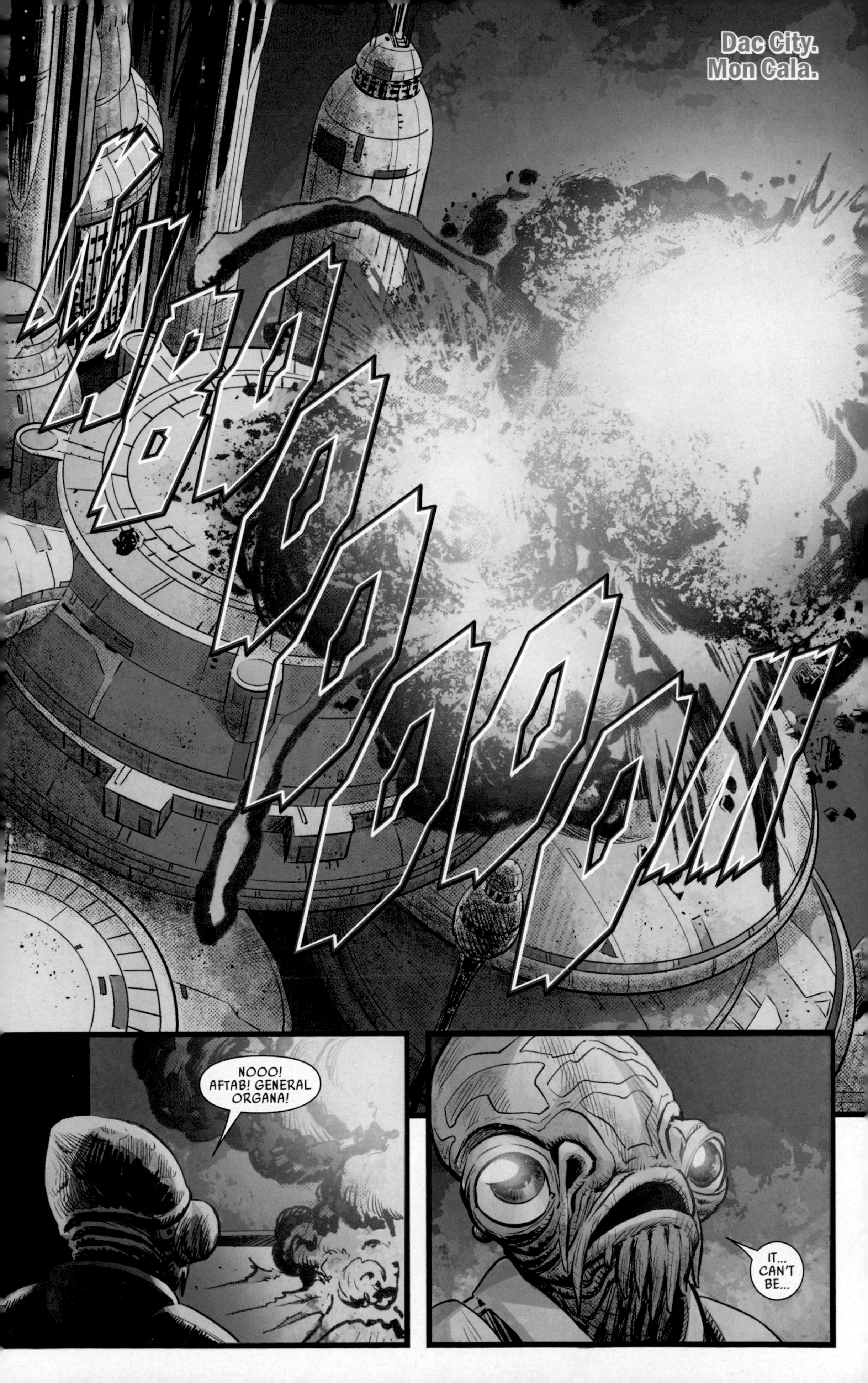
Dac City.
Mon Cala.
NOOO! AFTAB! GENERAL ORGANA!
IT... CAN'T BE...

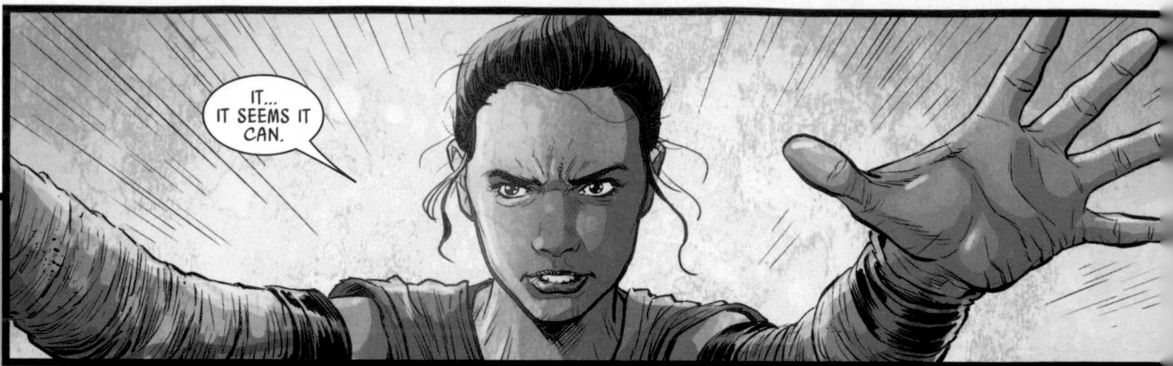
IT... IT SEEMS IT CAN.

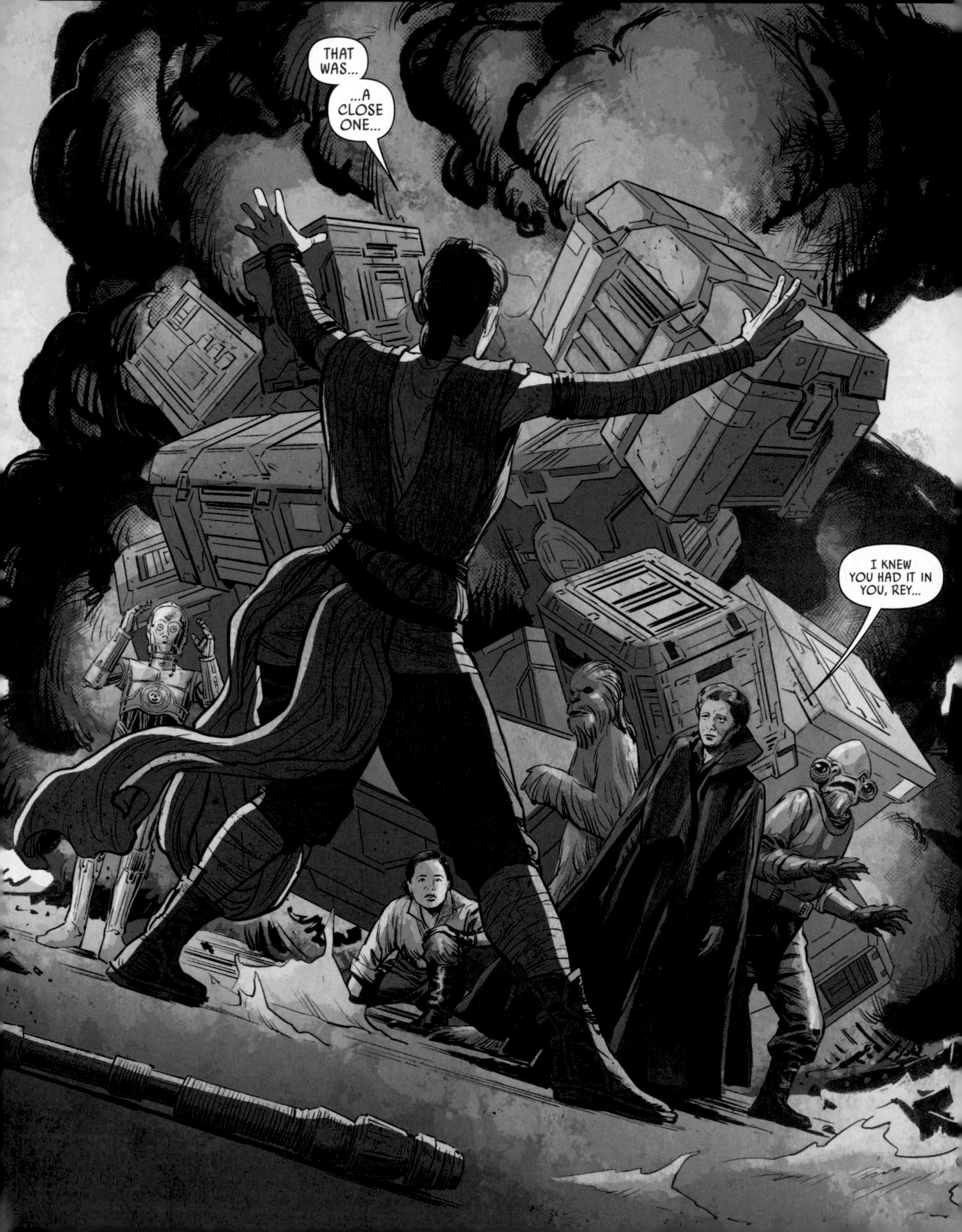
THAT WAS...
...A CLOSE ONE...
I KNEW YOU HAD IT IN YOU, REY...

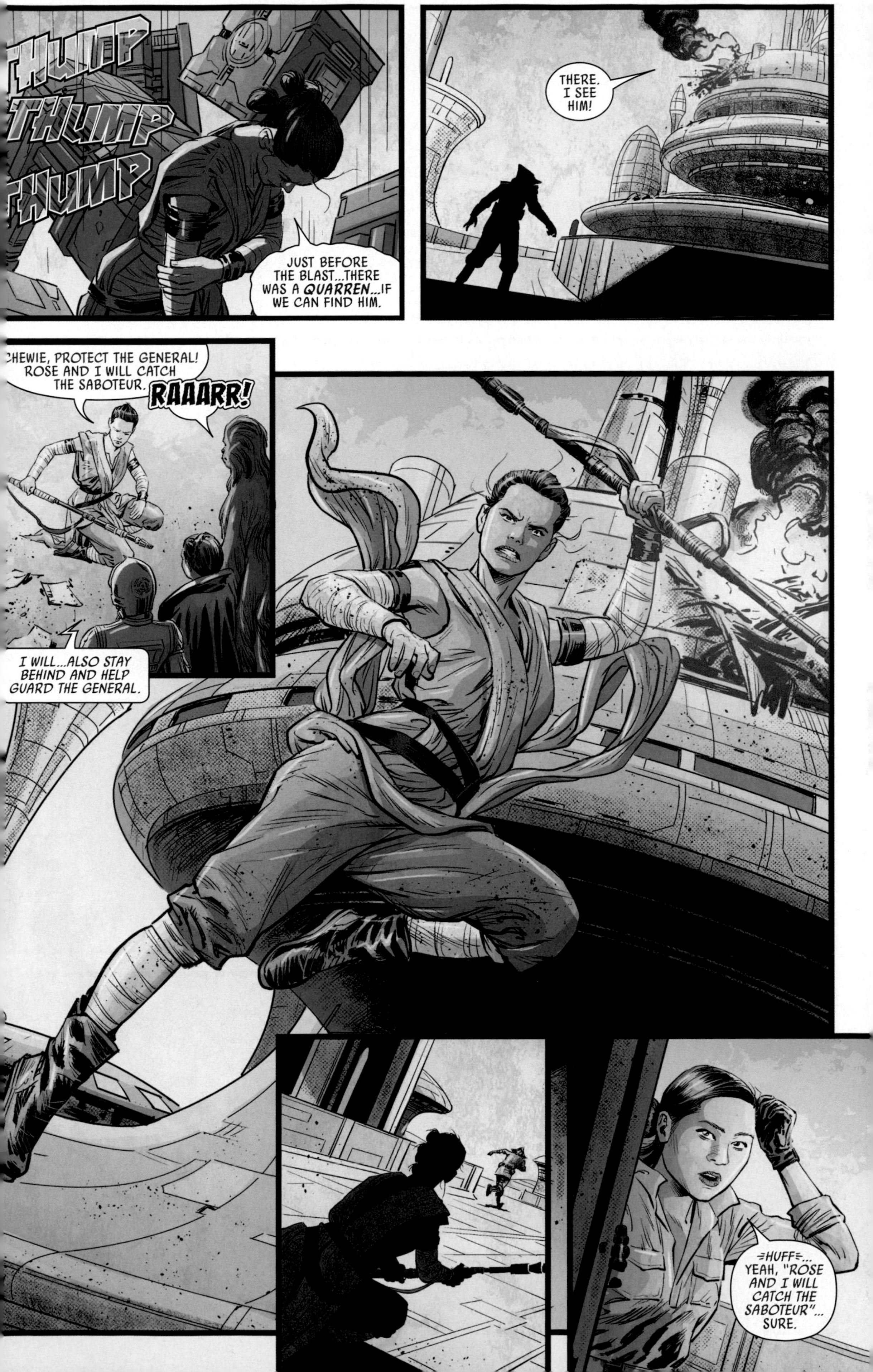
THUMP
THUMP
THUMP
JUST BEFORE THE BLAST...THERE WAS A QUARREN...IF WE CAN FIND HIM.
THERE. I SEE HIM!
CHEWIE, PROTECT THE GENERAL! ROSE AND I WILL CATCH THE SABOTEUR.
RAAARR!
I WILL...ALSO STAY BEHIND AND HELP GUARD THE GENERAL.
HUFF... YEAH, "ROSE AND I WILL CATCH THE SABOTEUR"... SURE.

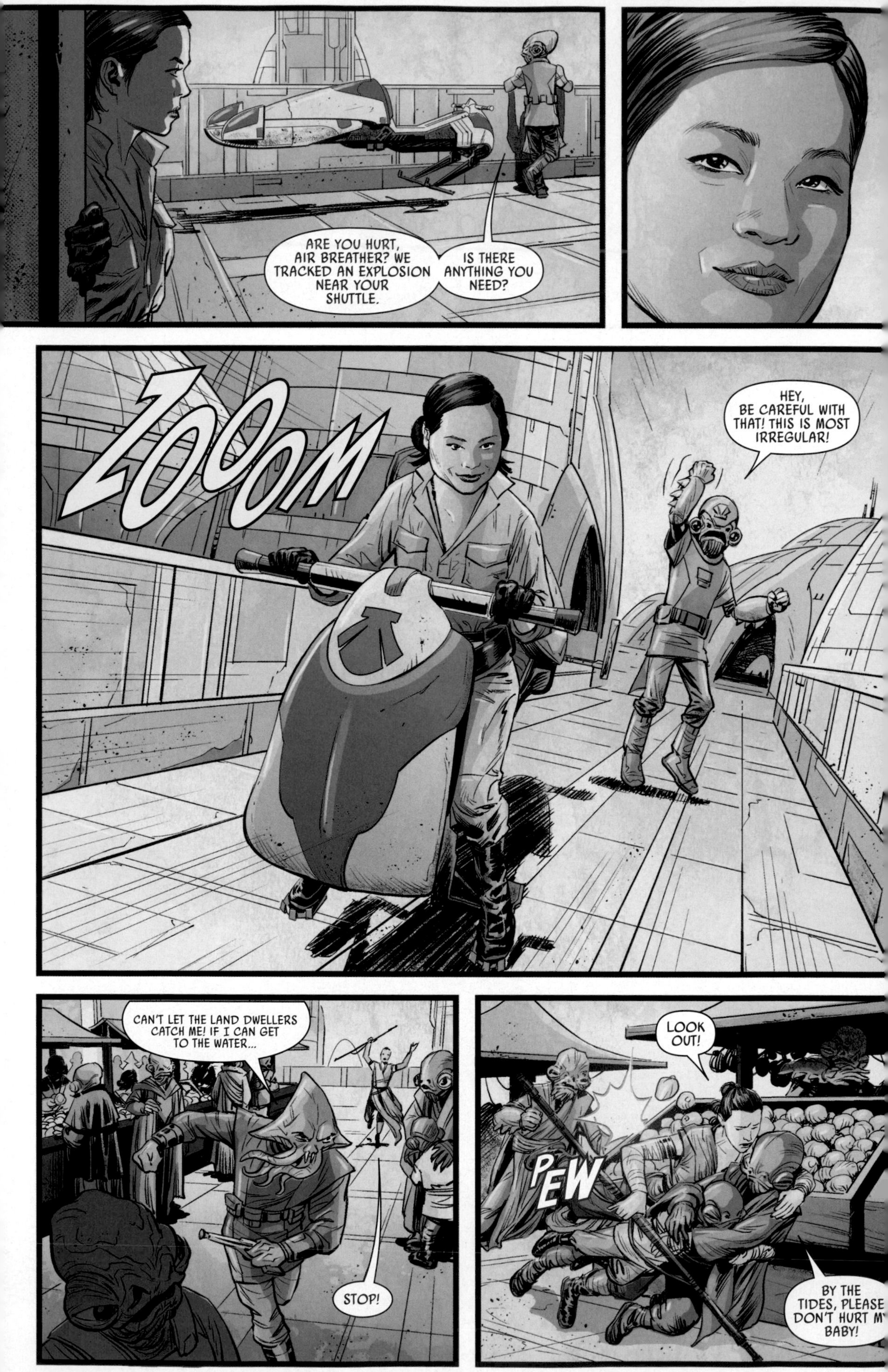
ARE YOU HURT, AIR BREATHER? WE TRACKED AN EXPLOSION NEAR YOUR SHUTTLE.
IS THERE ANYTHING YOU NEED?
ZOOOOM
HEY, BE CAREFUL WITH THAT! THIS IS MOST IRREGULAR!
CAN'T LET THE LAND DWELLERS CATCH ME! IF I CAN GET TO THE WATER...
STOP!
LOOK OUT!
PEW
BY THE TIDES, PLEASE DON'T HURT M BABY!

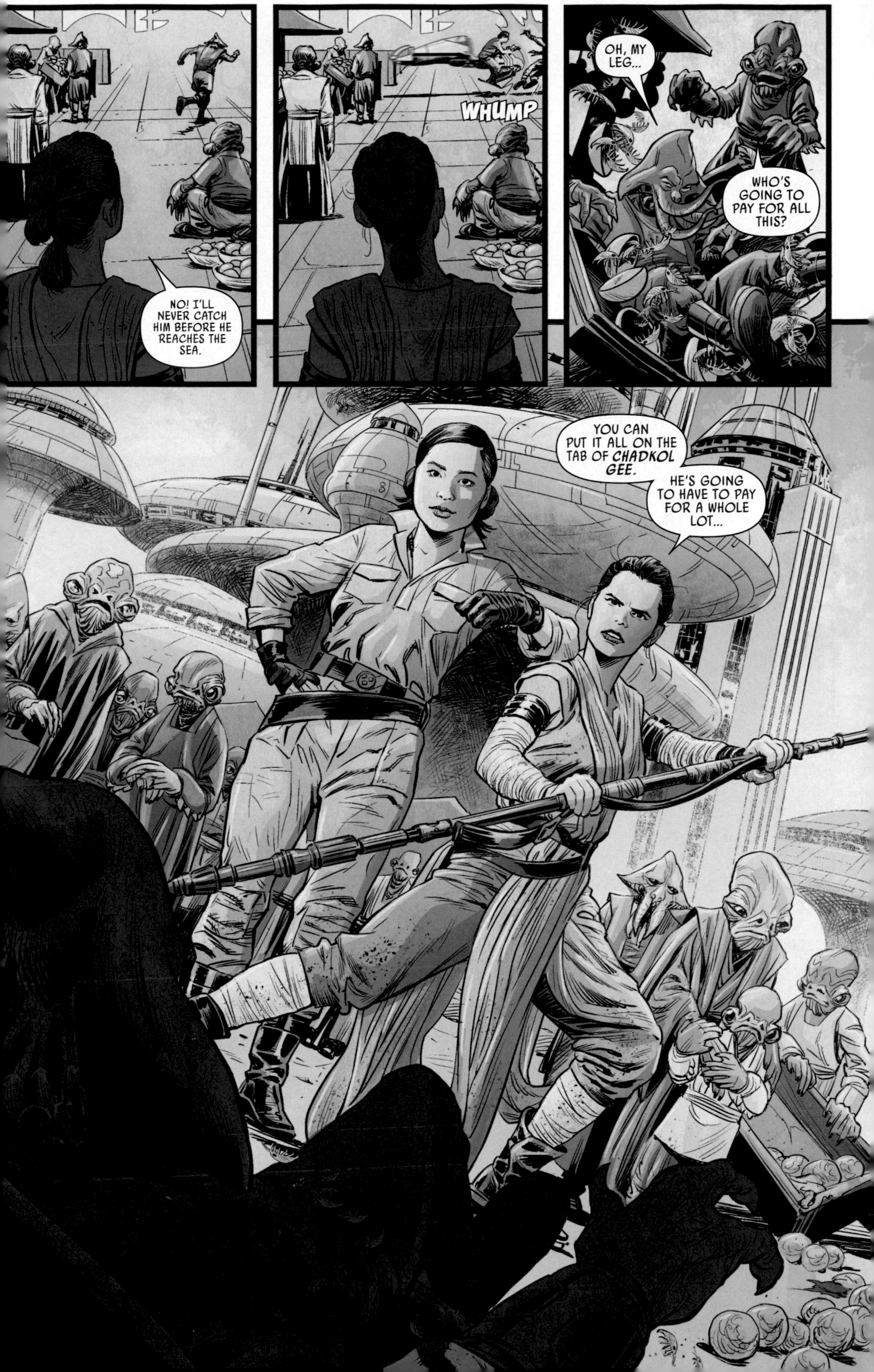
NO! I'LL NEVER CATCH HIM BEFORE HE REACHES THE SEA.
WHUMP
OH, MY LEG...
WHO'S GOING TO PAY FOR ALL THIS?
YOU CAN PUT IT ALL ON THE TAB OF CHADKOL GEE.
HE'S GOING TO HAVE TO PAY FOR A WHOLE LOT...

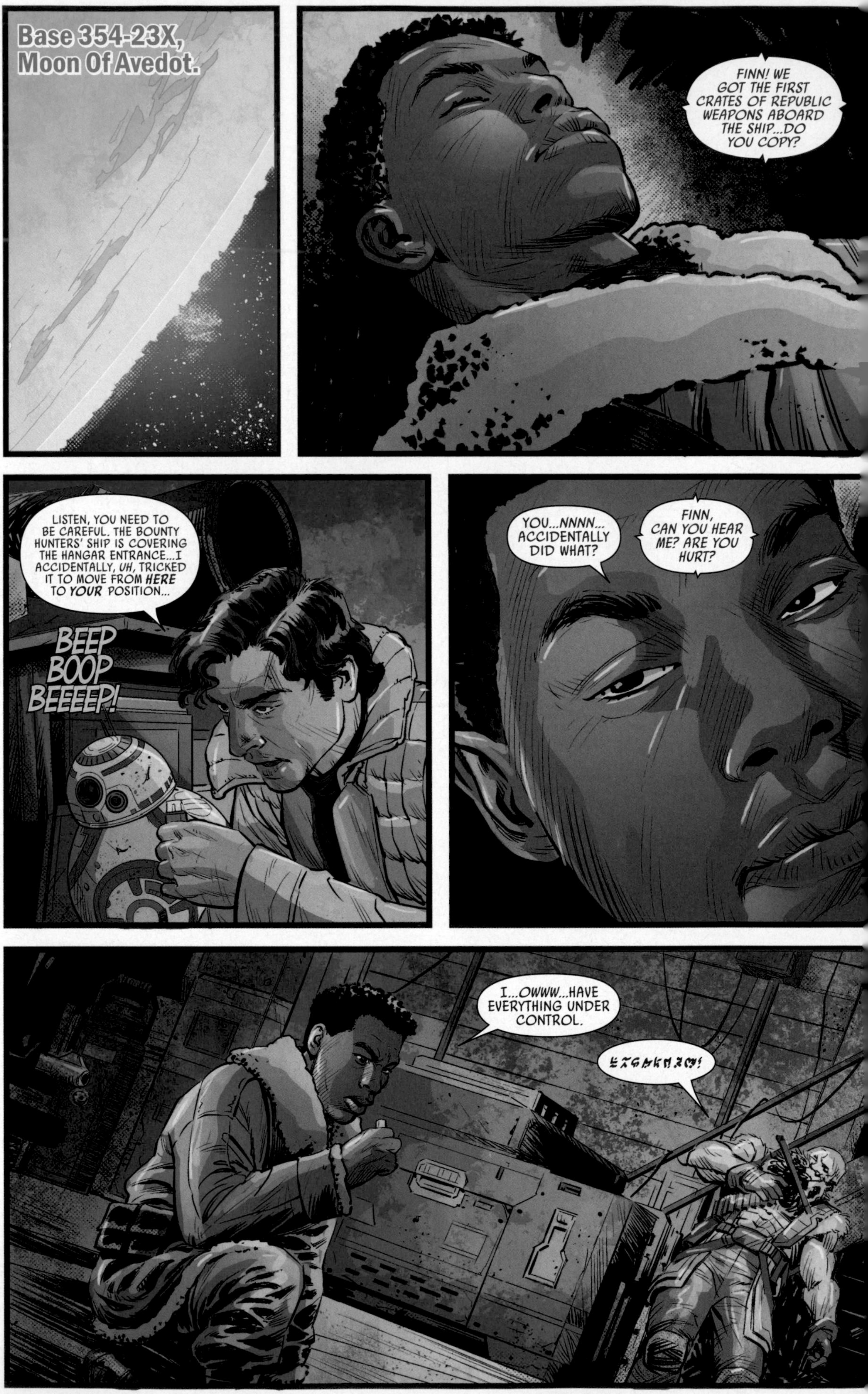
Base 354-23X, Moon Of Avedot.
FINN! WE GOT THE FIRST CRATES OF REPUBLIC WEAPONS ABOARD THE SHIP...DO YOU COPY?
LISTEN, YOU NEED TO BE CAREFUL. THE BOUNTY HUNTERS' SHIP IS COVERING THE HANGAR ENTRANCE...I ACCIDENTALLY, UH, TRICKED IT TO MOVE FROM HERE TO YOUR POSITION...
BEEP BOOP BEEEEP!
FINN, CAN YOU HEAR ME? ARE YOU HURT?
YOU...NNNN... ACCIDENTALLY DID WHAT?
I...OWWW...HAVE EVERYTHING UNDER CONTROL.

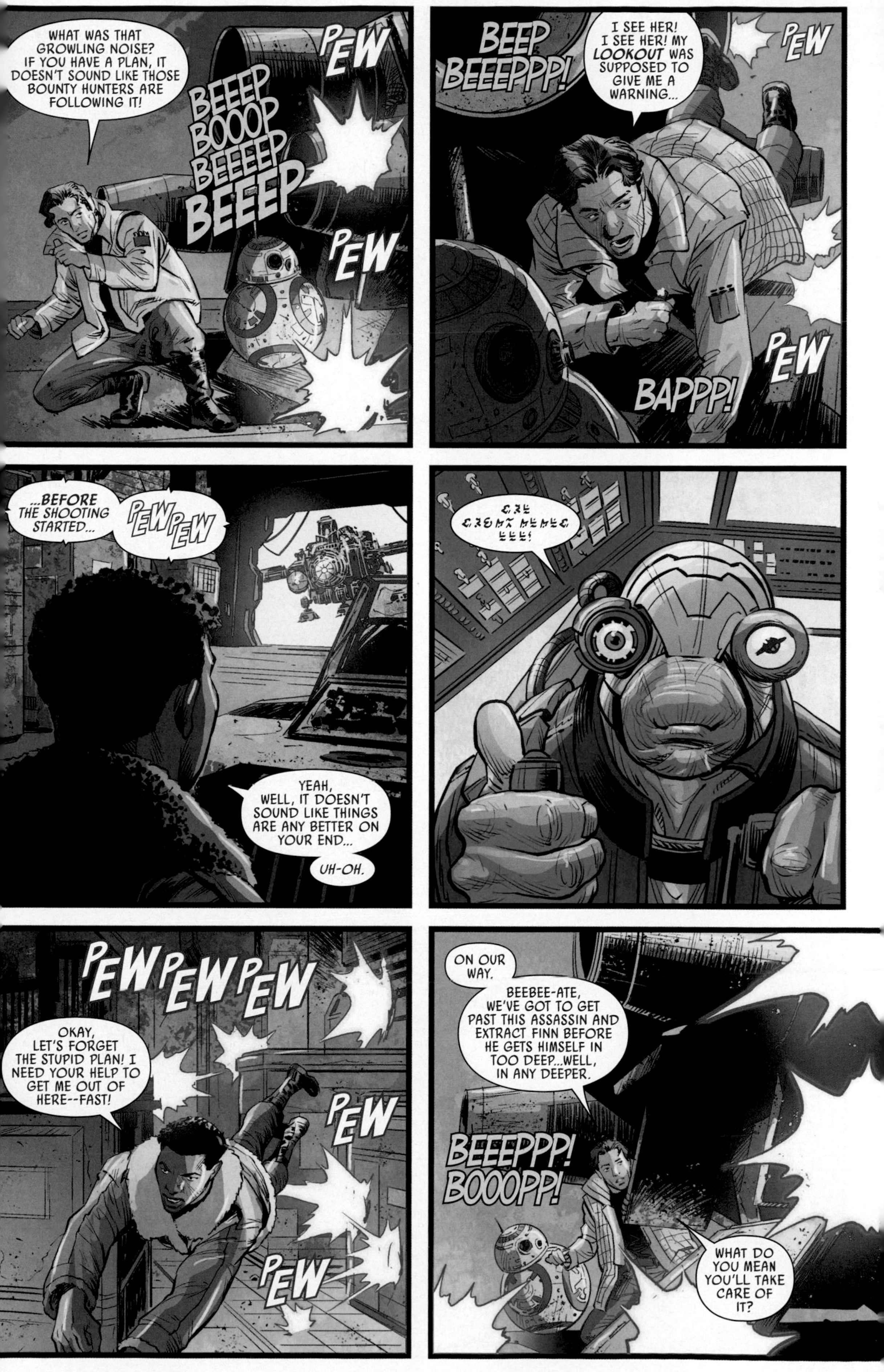

WHAT WAS THAT GROWLING NOISE? IF YOU HAVE A PLAN, IT DOESN'T SOUND LIKE THOSE BOUNTY HUNTERS ARE FOLLOWING IT!
PEW
BEEEP BOOOP BEEEEP BEEEP
PEW
BEEP BEEEPPP!
I SEE HER! I SEE HER! MY LOOKOUT WAS SUPPOSED TO GIVE ME A WARNING...
PEW
PEW
BAPPP!
...BEFORE THE SHOOTING STARTED...
PEWPEW
YEAH, WELL, IT DOESN'T SOUND LIKE THINGS ARE ANY BETTER ON YOUR END...
UH-OH.
PEWPEWPEW
OKAY, LET'S FORGET THE STUPID PLAN! I NEED YOUR HELP TO GET ME OUT OF HERE--FAST!
PEW
PEW
ON OUR WAY.
BEEBEE-ATE, WE'VE GOT TO GET PAST THIS ASSASSIN AND EXTRACT FINN BEFORE HE GETS HIMSELF IN TOO DEEP...WELL, IN ANY DEEPER.
BEEEPPP! BOOOPP!
WHAT DO YOU MEAN YOU'LL TAKE CARE OF IT?

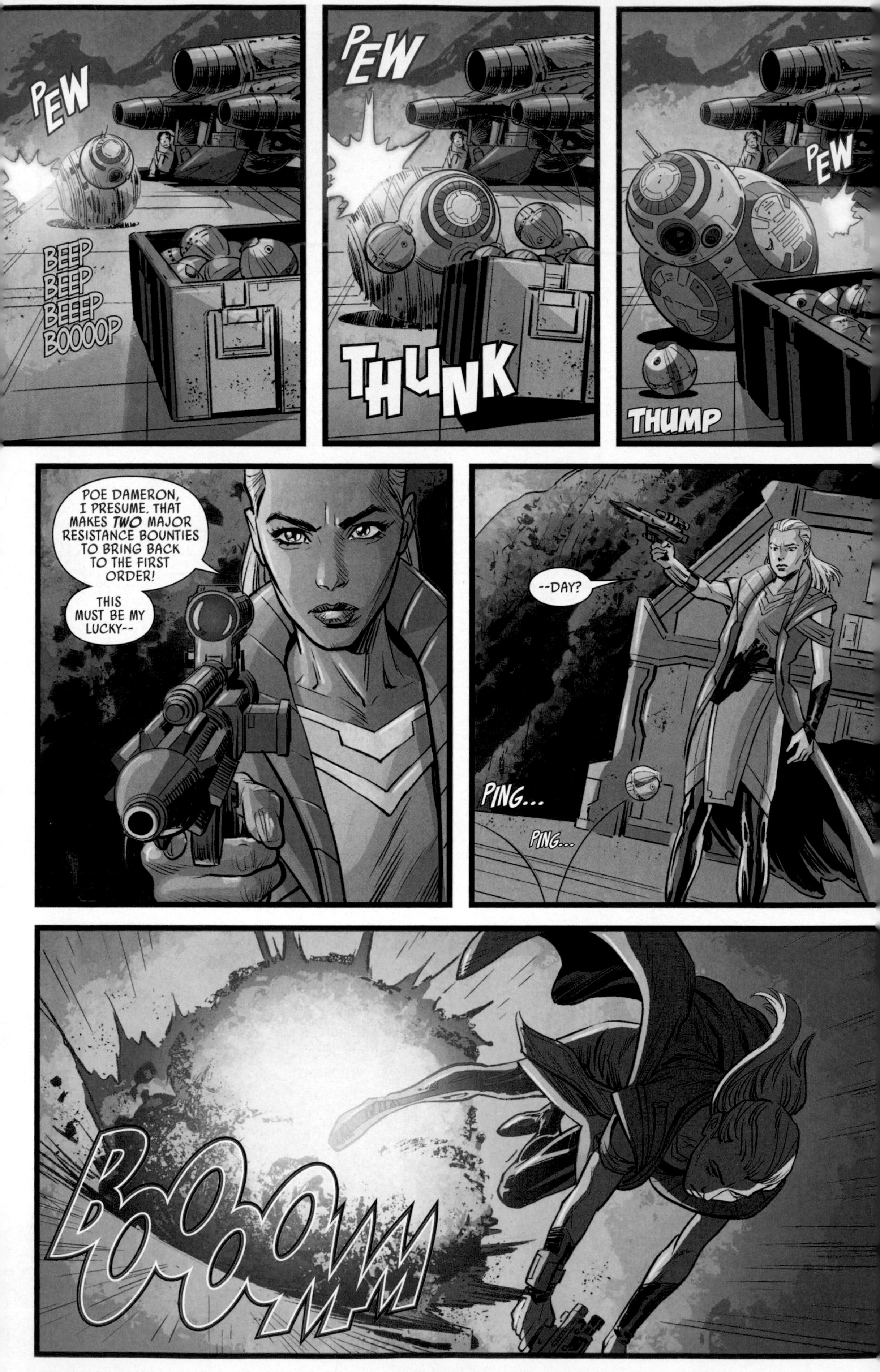
PEW
BEEP BEEP BEEEP BOOOOP
PEW
THUNK
PEW
THUMP
POE DAMERON, I PRESUME. THAT MAKES TWO MAJOR RESISTANCE BOUNTIES TO BRING BACK TO THE FIRST ORDER!
THIS MUST BE MY LUCKY--
--DAY?
PING...
PING...
BOOOOM

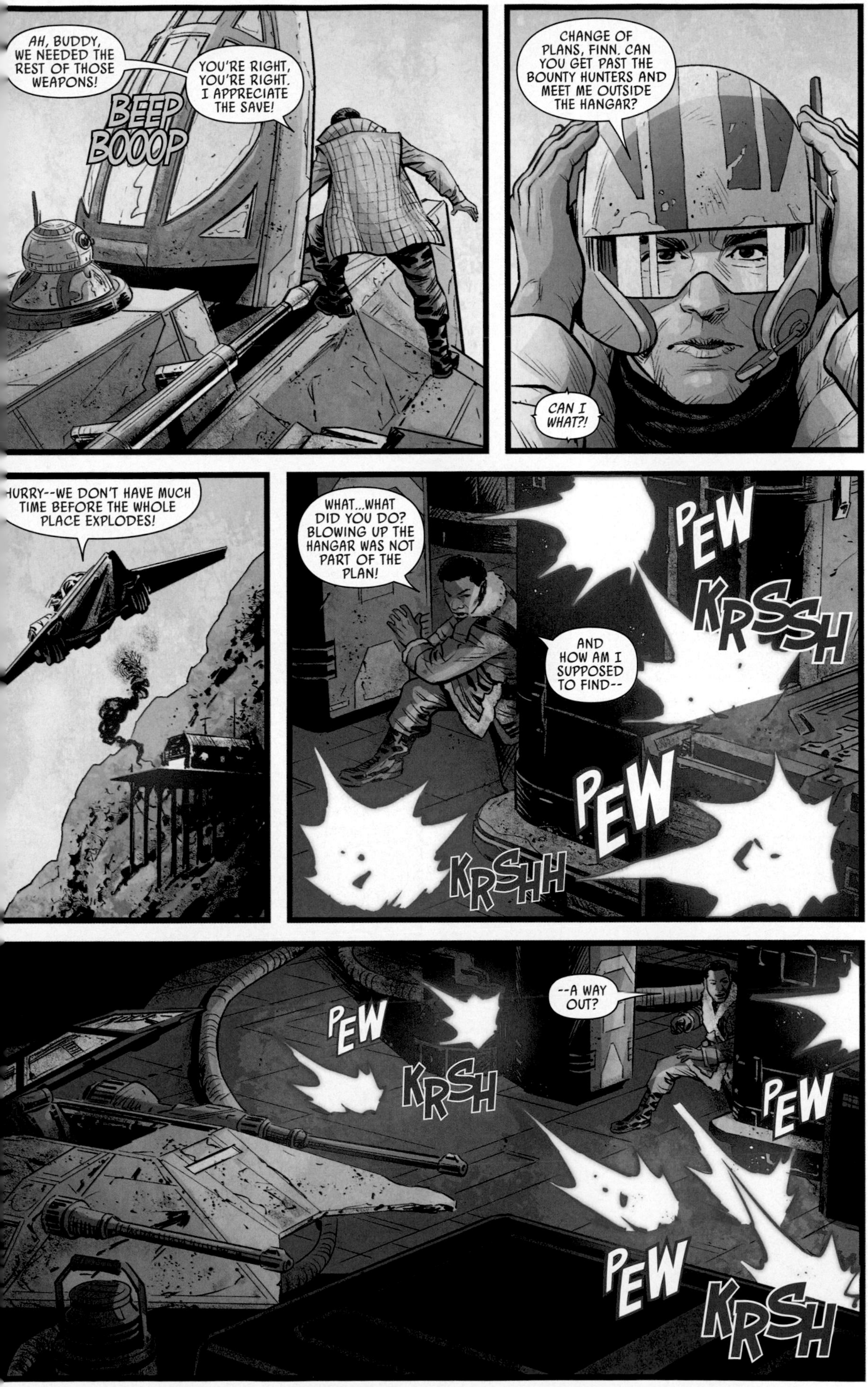
AH, BUDDY, WE NEEDED THE REST OF THOSE WEAPONS!
BEEP BOOOP
YOU'RE RIGHT, YOU'RE RIGHT. I APPRECIATE THE SAVE!
CHANGE OF PLANS, FINN. CAN YOU GET PAST THE BOUNTY HUNTERS AND MEET ME OUTSIDE THE HANGAR?
CAN I WHAT?!
HURRY--WE DON'T HAVE MUCH TIME BEFORE THE WHOLE PLACE EXPLODES!
WHAT...WHAT DID YOU DO? BLOWING UP THE HANGAR WAS NOT PART OF THE PLAN!
PEW
KRSSSH
AND HOW AM I SUPPOSED TO FIND--
PEW
KRSHH
--A WAY OUT?
PEW
KRSH
PEW
PEW
KRSH

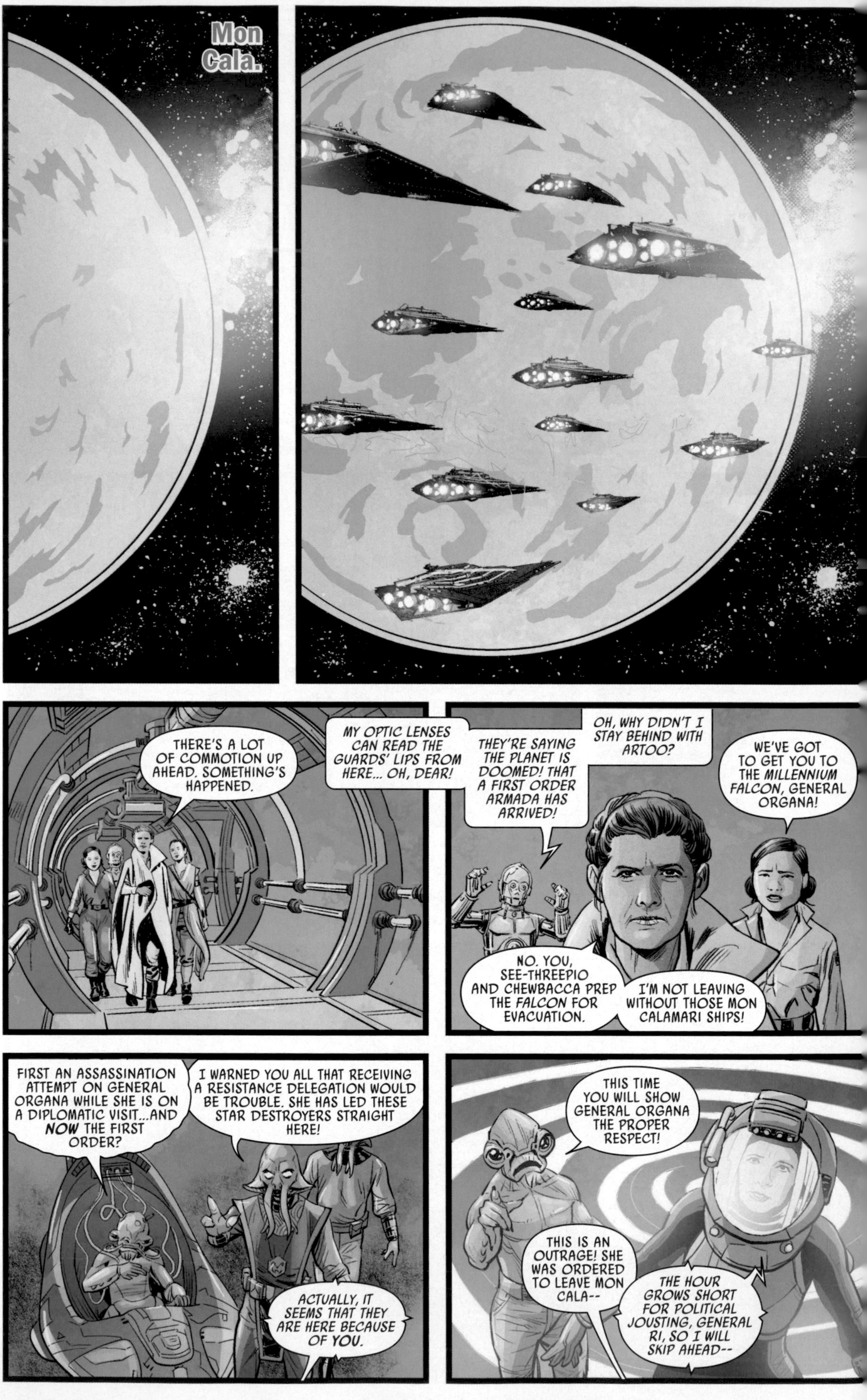

Mon Cala.
THERE'S A LOT OF COMMOTION UP AHEAD. SOMETHING'S HAPPENED.
MY OPTIC LENSES CAN READ THE GUARDS' LIPS FROM HERE... OH, DEAR!
THEY'RE SAYING THE PLANET IS DOOMED! THAT A FIRST ORDER ARMADA HAS ARRIVED!
OH, WHY DIDN'T I STAY BEHIND WITH ARTOO?
WE'VE GOT TO GET YOU TO THE MILLENNIUM FALCON, GENERAL ORGANA!
NO. YOU, SEE-THREEPIO AND CHEWBACCA PREP THE FALCON FOR EVACUATION.
I'M NOT LEAVING WITHOUT THOSE MON CALAMARI SHIPS!
FIRST AN ASSASSINATION ATTEMPT ON GENERAL ORGANA WHILE SHE IS ON A DIPLOMATIC VISIT...AND NOW THE FIRST ORDER?
I WARNED YOU ALL THAT RECEIVING A RESISTANCE DELEGATION WOULD BE TROUBLE. SHE HAS LED THESE STAR DESTROYERS STRAIGHT HERE!
ACTUALLY, IT SEEMS THAT THEY ARE HERE BECAUSE OF YOU.
THIS TIME YOU WILL SHOW GENERAL ORGANA THE PROPER RESPECT!
THIS IS AN OUTRAGE! SHE WAS ORDERED TO LEAVE MON CALA--
THE HOUR GROWS SHORT FOR POLITICAL JOUSTING, GENERAL RI, SO I WILL SKIP AHEAD--

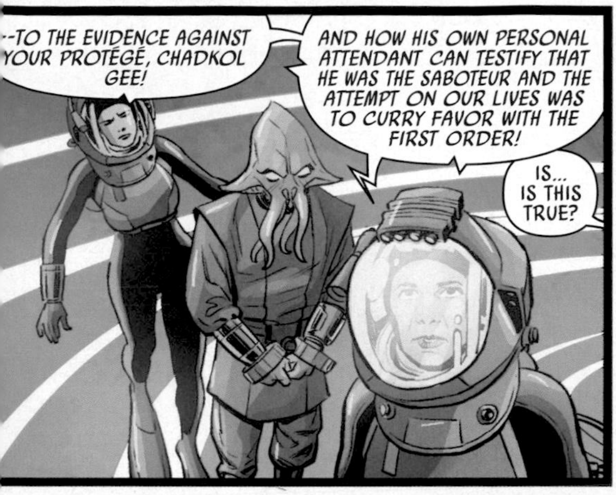
--TO THE EVIDENCE AGAINST YOUR PROTÉGÉ, CHADKOL GEE!
AND HOW HIS OWN PERSONAL ATTENDANT CAN TESTIFY THAT HE WAS THE SABOTEUR AND THE ATTEMPT ON OUR LIVES WAS TO CURRY FAVOR WITH THE FIRST ORDER!
IS... IS THIS TRUE?

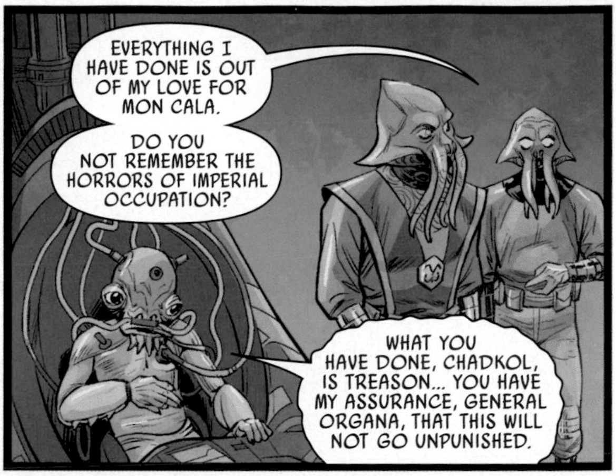
EVERYTHING I HAVE DONE IS OUT OF MY LOVE FOR MON CALA.
DO YOU NOT REMEMBER THE HORRORS OF IMPERIAL OCCUPATION?
WHAT YOU HAVE DONE, CHADKOL, IS TREASON... YOU HAVE MY ASSURANCE, GENERAL ORGANA, THAT THIS WILL NOT GO UNPUNISHED.

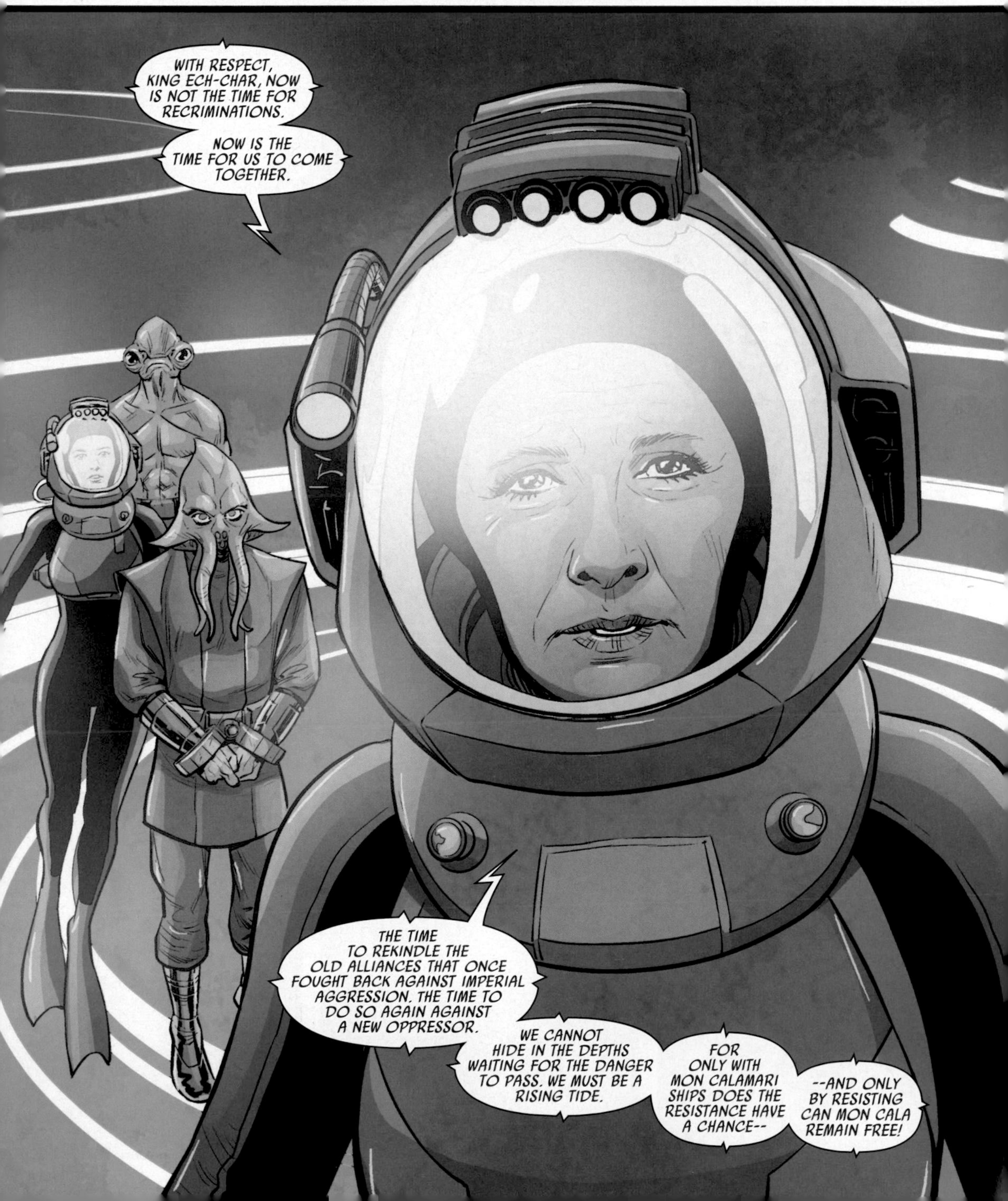
WITH RESPECT, KING ECH-CHAR, NOW IS NOT THE TIME FOR RECRIMINATIONS.
NOW IS THE TIME FOR US TO COME TOGETHER.
THE TIME TO REKINDLE THE OLD ALLIANCES THAT ONCE FOUGHT BACK AGAINST IMPERIAL AGGRESSION. THE TIME TO DO SO AGAIN AGAINST A NEW OPPRESSOR.
WE CANNOT HIDE IN THE DEPTHS WAITING FOR THE DANGER TO PASS. WE MUST BE A RISING TIDE.
FOR ONLY WITH MON CALAMARI SHIPS DOES THE RESISTANCE HAVE A CHANCE--
--AND ONLY BY RESISTING CAN MON CALA REMAIN FREE!

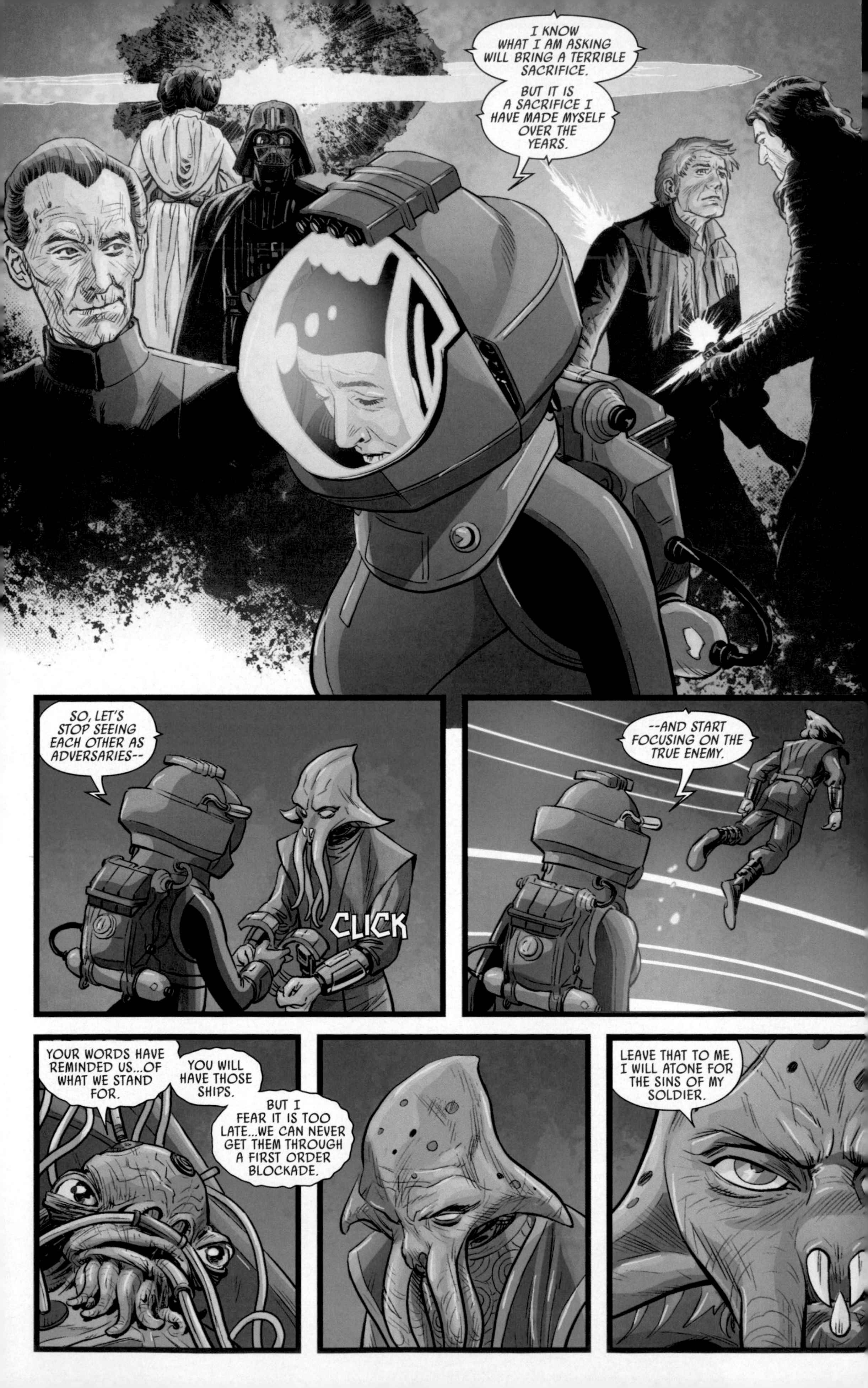
I KNOW WHAT I AM ASKING WILL BRING A TERRIBLE SACRIFICE.
BUT IT IS A SACRIFICE I HAVE MADE MYSELF OVER THE YEARS.
SO, LET'S STOP SEEING EACH OTHER AS ADVERSARIES--
CLICK
--AND START FOCUSING ON THE TRUE ENEMY.
YOUR WORDS HAVE REMINDED US...OF WHAT WE STAND FOR.
YOU WILL HAVE THOSE SHIPS.
BUT I FEAR IT IS TOO LATE...WE CAN NEVER GET THEM THROUGH A FIRST ORDER BLOCKADE.
LEAVE THAT TO ME. I WILL ATONE FOR THE SINS OF MY SOLDIER.

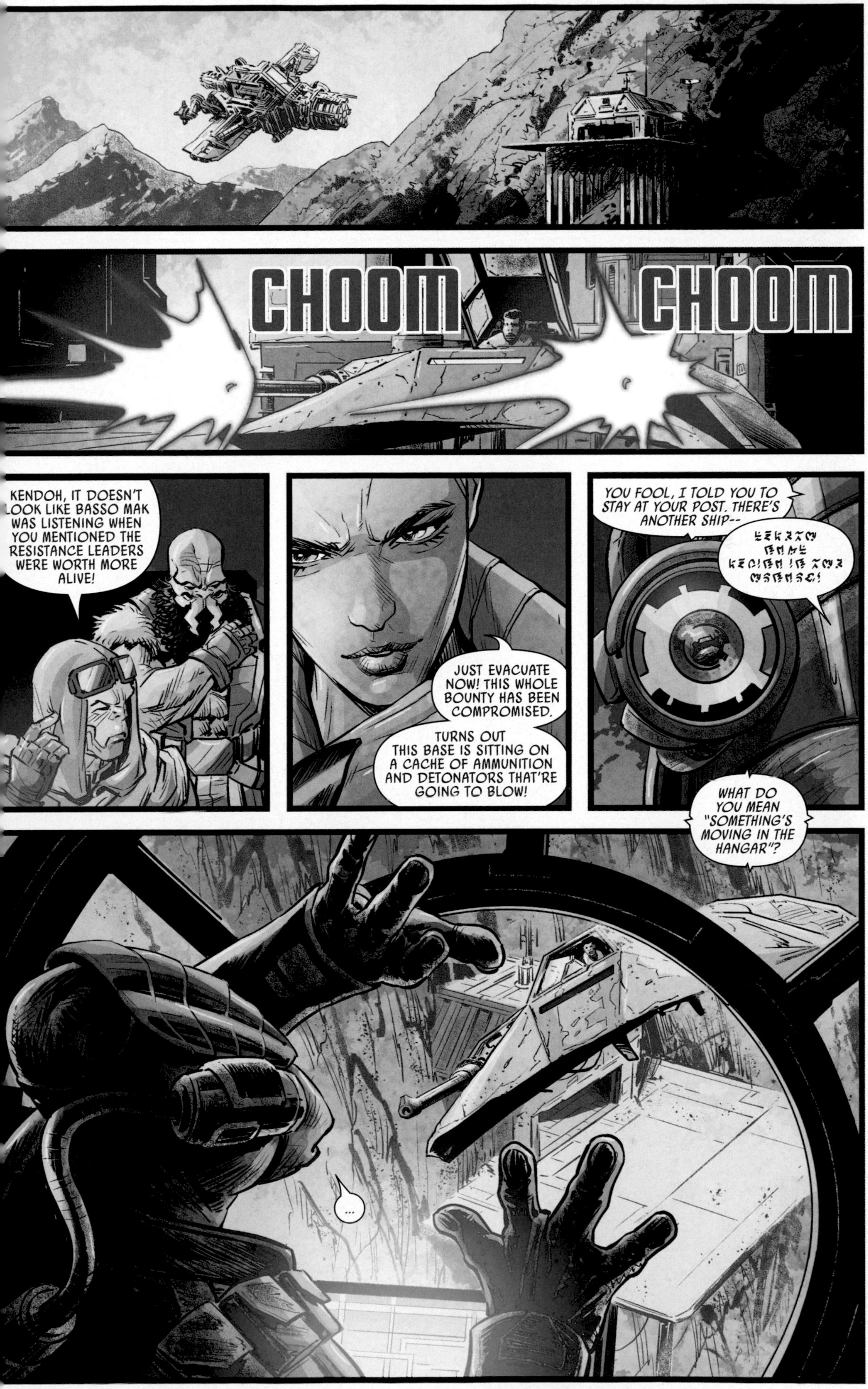
CHOOM
CHOOM
KENDOH, IT DOESN'T LOOK LIKE BASSO MAK WAS LISTENING WHEN YOU MENTIONED THE RESISTANCE LEADERS WERE WORTH MORE ALIVE!
JUST EVACUATE NOW! THIS WHOLE BOUNTY HAS BEEN COMPROMISED.
TURNS OUT THIS BASE IS SITTING ON A CACHE OF AMMUNITION AND DETONATORS THAT'RE GOING TO BLOW!
YOU FOOL, I TOLD YOU TO STAY AT YOUR POST. THERE'S ANOTHER SHIP--
WHAT DO YOU MEAN "SOMETHING'S MOVING IN THE HANGAR"?
...

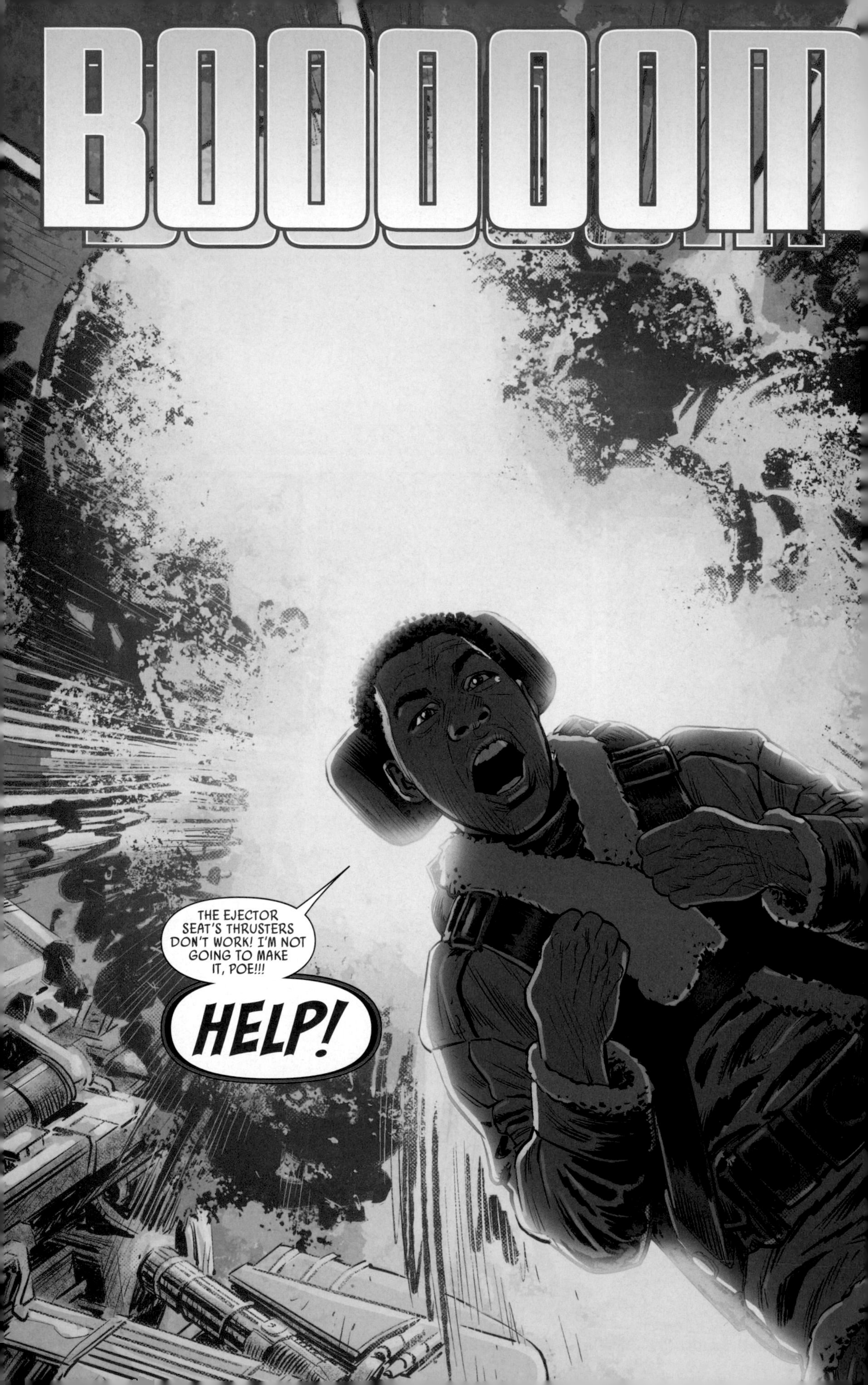
BOOOOOM
THE EJECTOR SEAT'S THRUSTERS DON'T WORK! I'M NOT GOING TO MAKE IT, POE!!!
HELP!

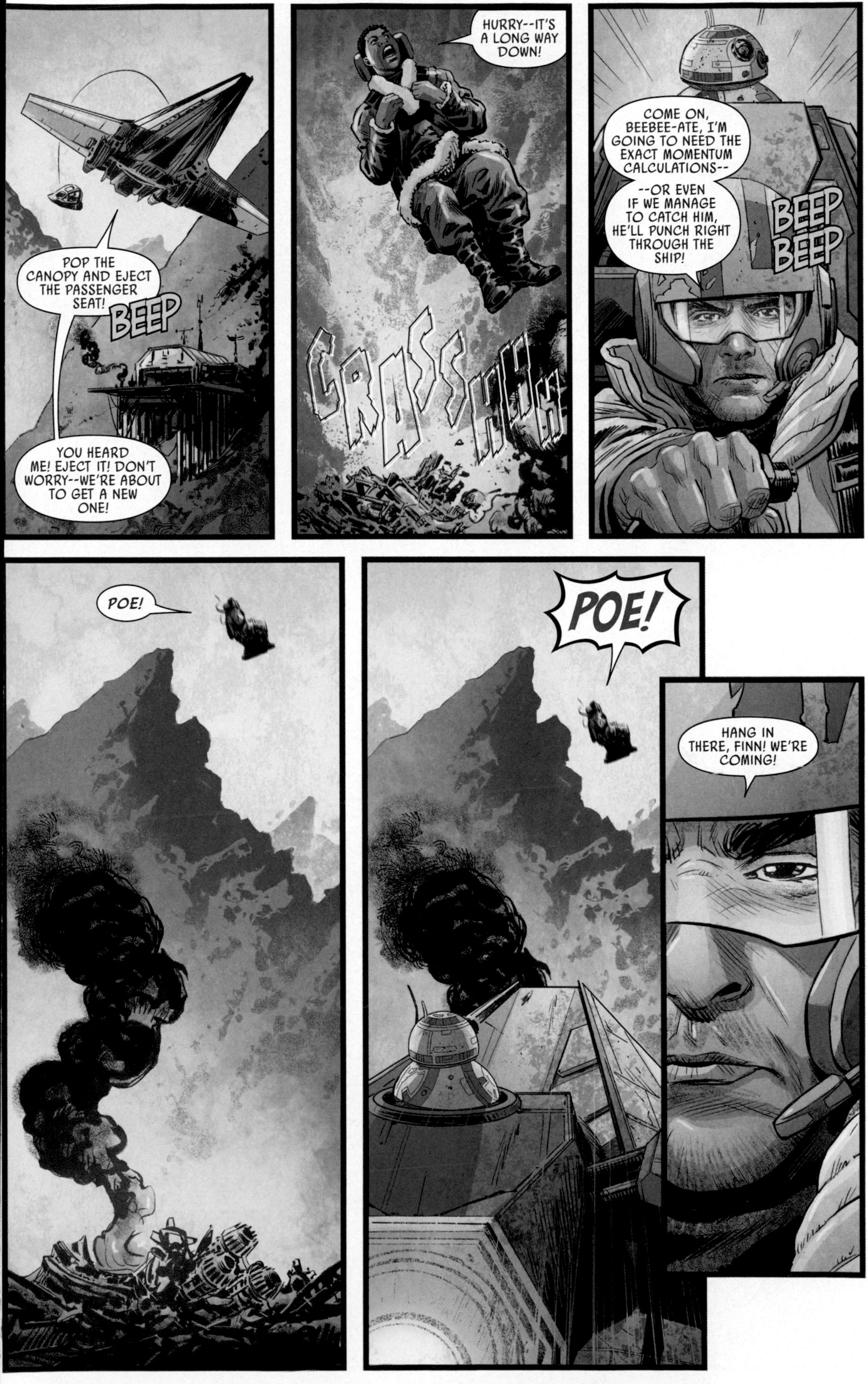
POP THE CANOPY AND EJECT THE PASSENGER SEAT!
BEEP
YOU HEARD ME! EJECT IT! DON'T WORRY--WE'RE ABOUT TO GET A NEW ONE!
HURRY--IT'S A LONG WAY DOWN!
CRASSHHH
COME ON, BEEBEE-ATE, I'M GOING TO NEED THE EXACT MOMENTUM CALCULATIONS--
BEEP BEEP
--OR EVEN IF WE MANAGE TO CATCH HIM, HE'LL PUNCH RIGHT THROUGH THE SHIP!
POE!
POE!
HANG IN THERE, FINN! WE'RE COMING!

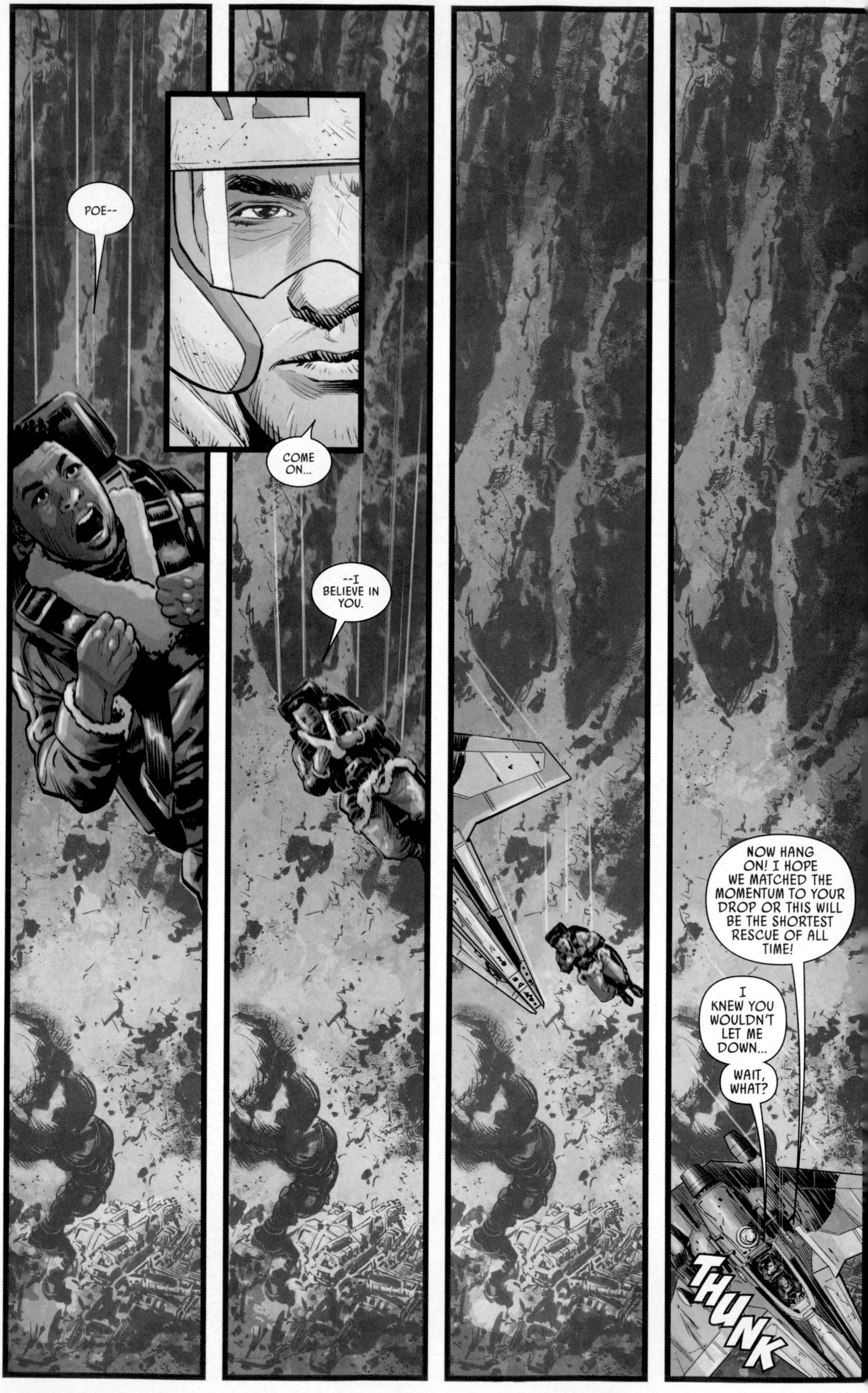
POE--
COME ON...
--I BELIEVE IN YOU.
NOW HANG ON! I HOPE WE MATCHED THE MOMENTUM TO YOUR DROP OR THIS WILL BE THE SHORTEST RESCUE OF ALL TIME!
I KNEW YOU WOULDN'T LET ME DOWN...
WAIT, WHAT?
THUNK

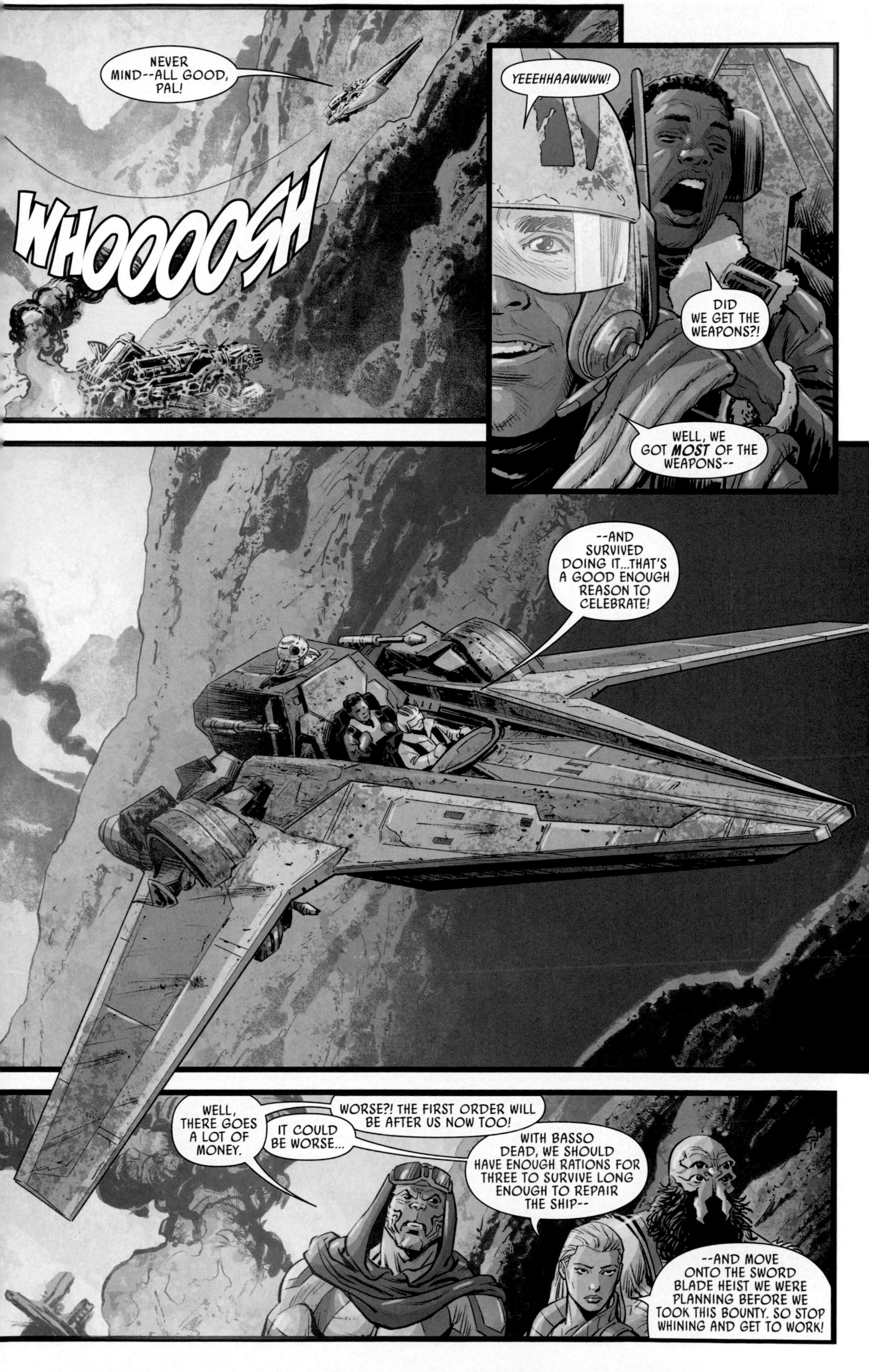

NEVER MIND--ALL GOOD, PAL!
WHOOOOOSH
YEEEHHAAWWWW!
DID WE GET THE WEAPONS?!
WELL, WE GOT *MOST* OF THE WEAPONS--
--AND SURVIVED DOING IT...THAT'S A GOOD ENOUGH REASON TO CELEBRATE!
WELL, THERE GOES A LOT OF MONEY.
IT COULD BE WORSE...
WORSE?! THE FIRST ORDER WILL BE AFTER US NOW TOO!
WITH BASSO DEAD, WE SHOULD HAVE ENOUGH RATIONS FOR THREE TO SURVIVE LONG ENOUGH TO REPAIR THE SHIP--
--AND MOVE ONTO THE SWORD BLADE HEIST WE WERE PLANNING BEFORE WE TOOK THIS BOUNTY. SO STOP WHINING AND GET TO WORK!

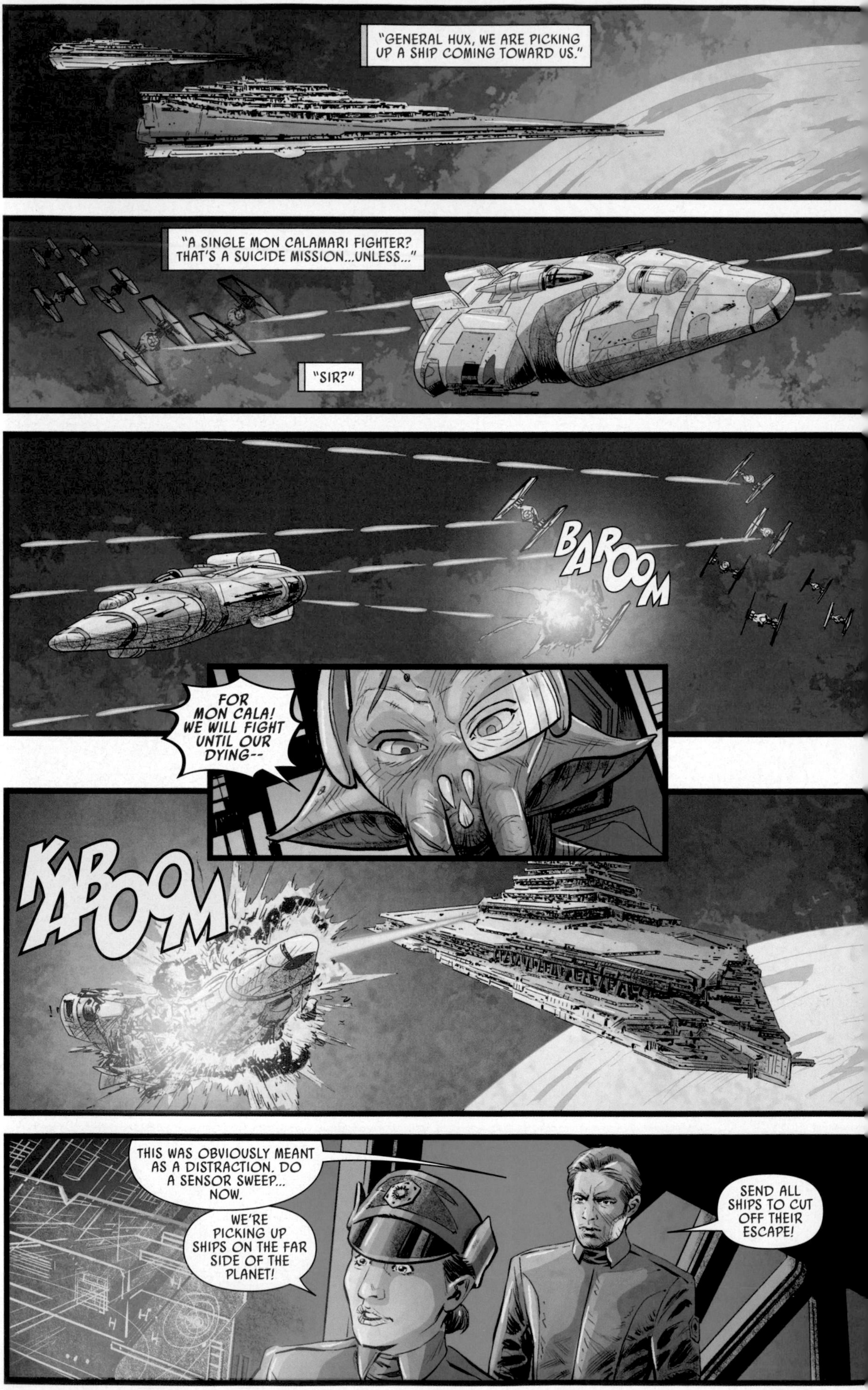
"GENERAL HUX, WE ARE PICKING UP A SHIP COMING TOWARD US."
"A SINGLE MON CALAMARI FIGHTER? THAT'S A SUICIDE MISSION...UNLESS..."
"SIR?"
BAROOM
FOR MON CALA! WE WILL FIGHT UNTIL OUR DYING--
KABOOM
THIS WAS OBVIOUSLY MEANT AS A DISTRACTION. DO A SENSOR SWEEP... NOW.
WE'RE PICKING UP SHIPS ON THE FAR SIDE OF THE PLANET!
SEND ALL SHIPS TO CUT OFF THEIR ESCAPE!

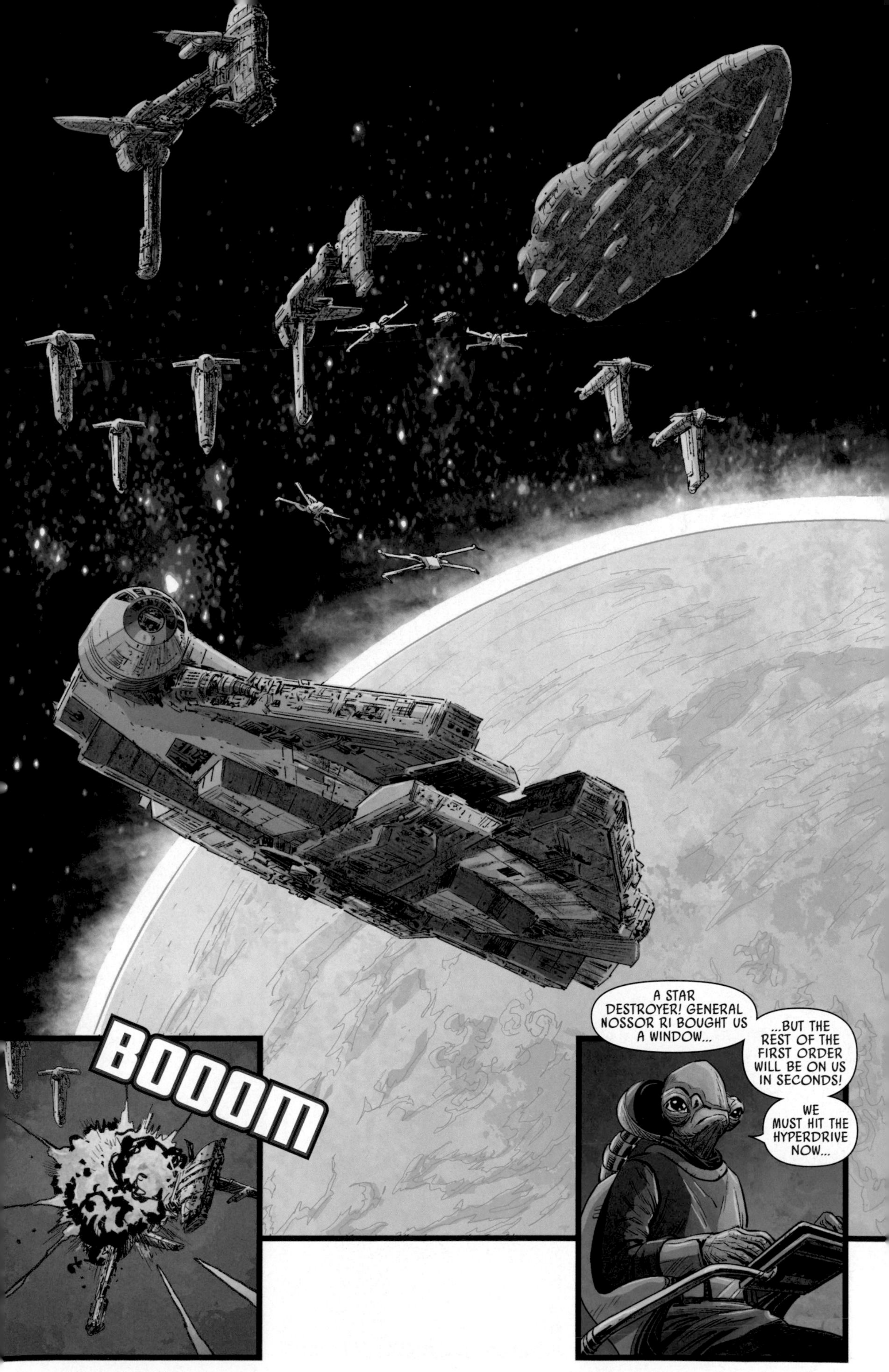
BOOOM
A STAR DESTROYER! GENERAL NOSSOR RI BOUGHT US A WINDOW...
...BUT THE REST OF THE FIRST ORDER WILL BE ON US IN SECONDS!
WE MUST HIT THE HYPERDRIVE NOW...

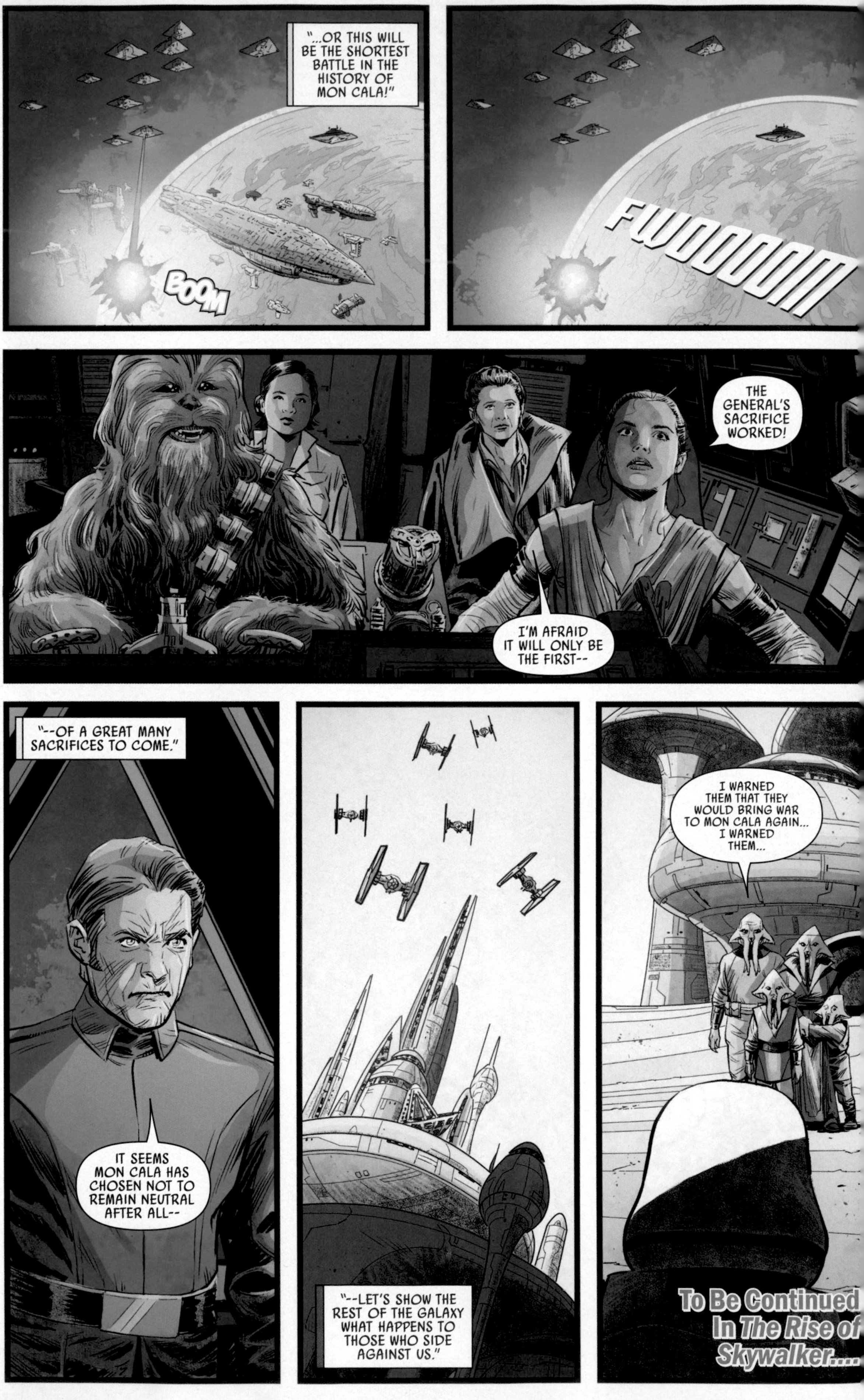
"...OR THIS WILL BE THE SHORTEST BATTLE IN THE HISTORY OF MON CALA!"
BOOM
FWOOOOM
THE GENERAL'S SACRIFICE WORKED!
I'M AFRAID IT WILL ONLY BE THE FIRST--
"--OF A GREAT MANY SACRIFICES TO COME."
IT SEEMS MON CALA HAS CHOSEN NOT TO REMAIN NEUTRAL AFTER ALL--
"--LET'S SHOW THE REST OF THE GALAXY WHAT HAPPENS TO THOSE WHO SIDE AGAINST US."
I WARNED THEM THAT THEY WOULD BRING WAR TO MON CALA AGAIN... I WARNED THEM...
To Be Continued In *The Rise of Skywalker*....

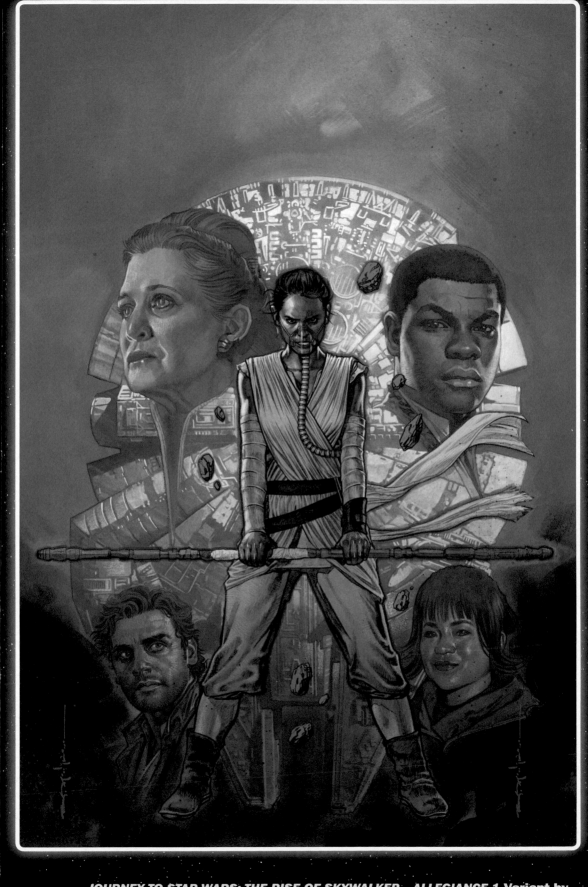

JOURNEY TO STAR WARS: THE RISE OF SKYWALKER – ALLEGIANCE 1 Variant by
BRIAN STELFREEZE

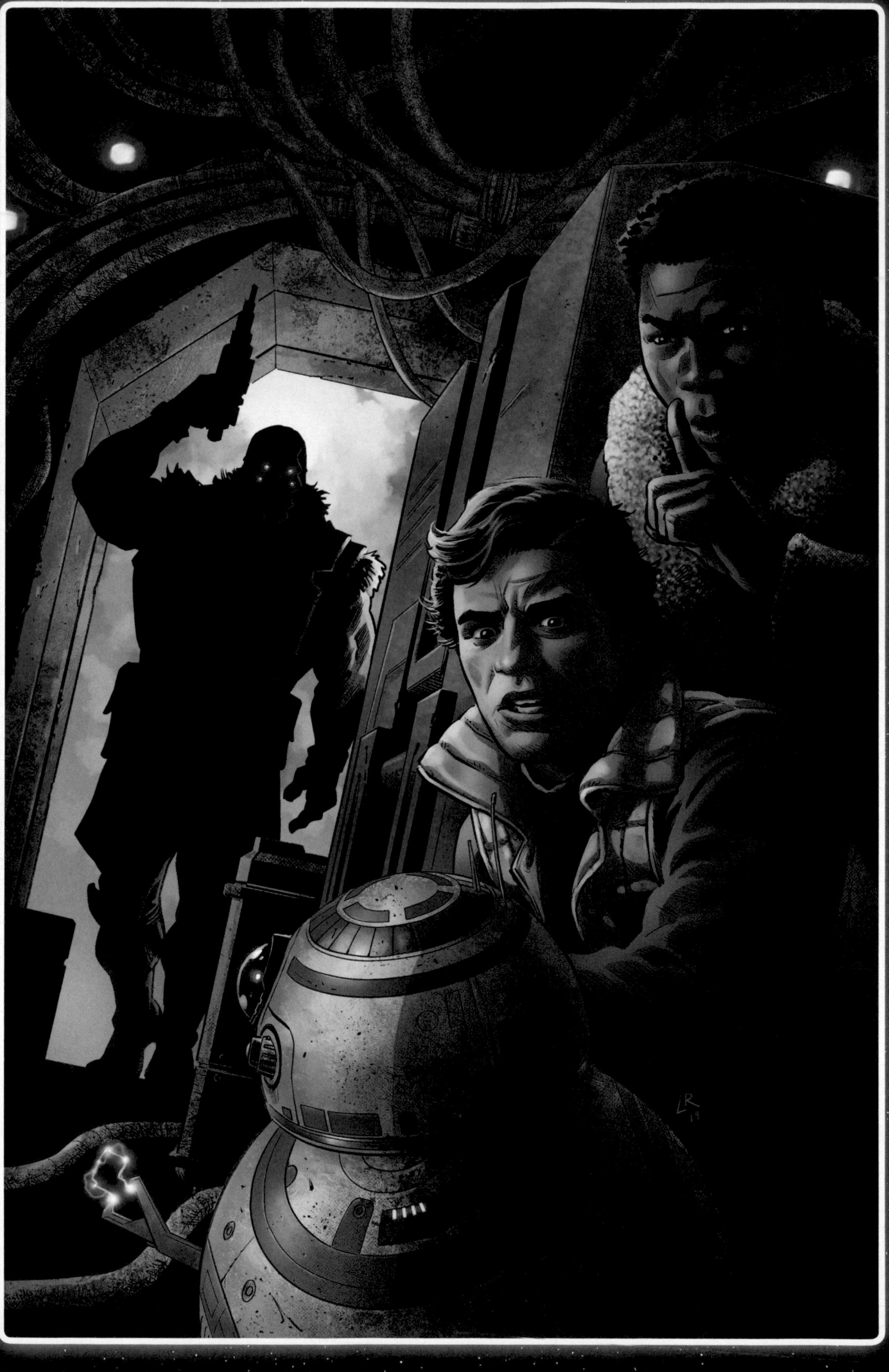

***JOURNEY TO STAR WARS: THE RISE OF SKYWALKER – ALLEGIANCE 2* Variant by**
LUKE ROSS

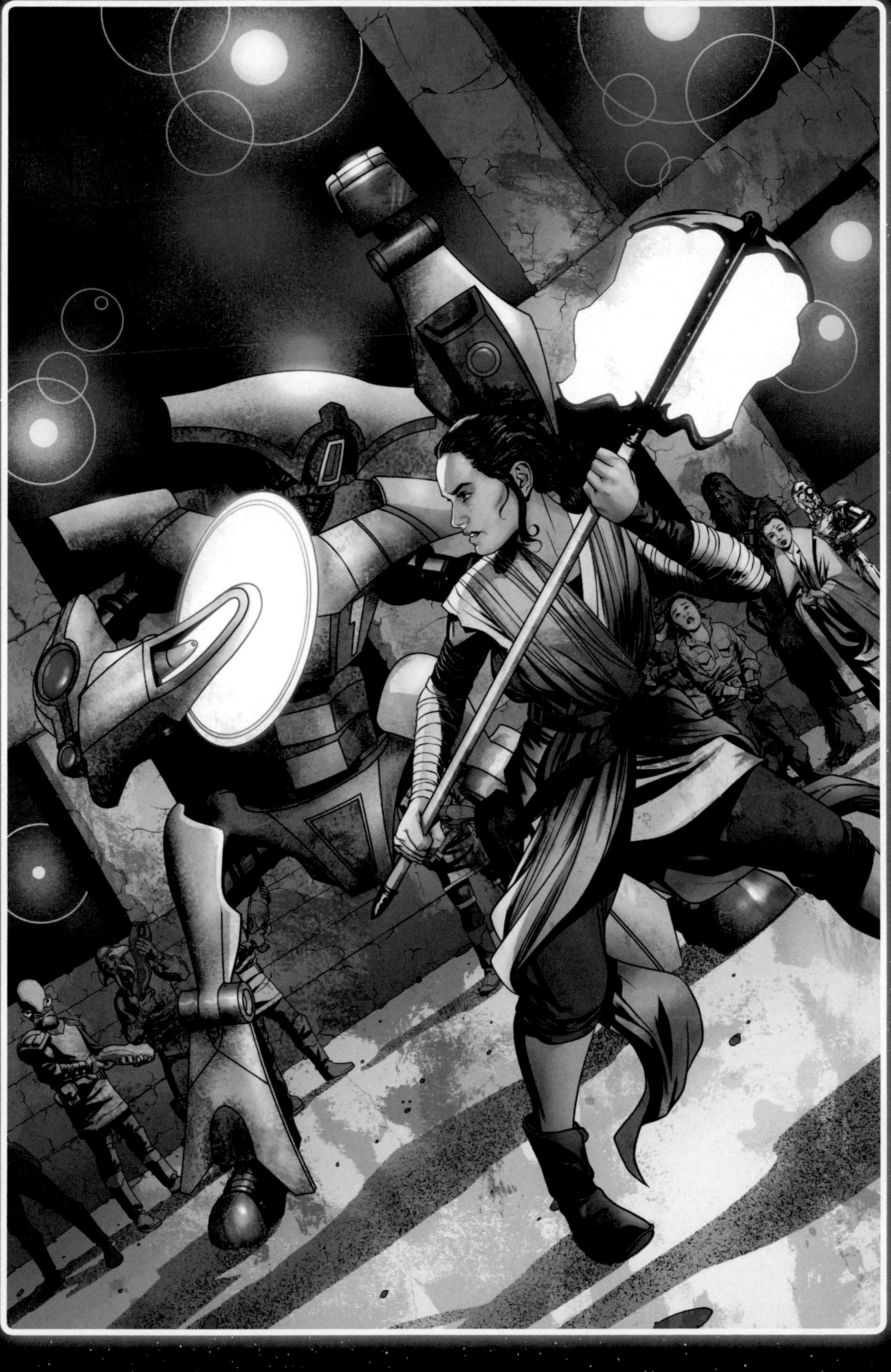

JOURNEY TO STAR WARS: THE RISE OF SKYWALKER – ALLEGIANCE 3 **Variant by**

MIKE MCKONE & JASON KEITH

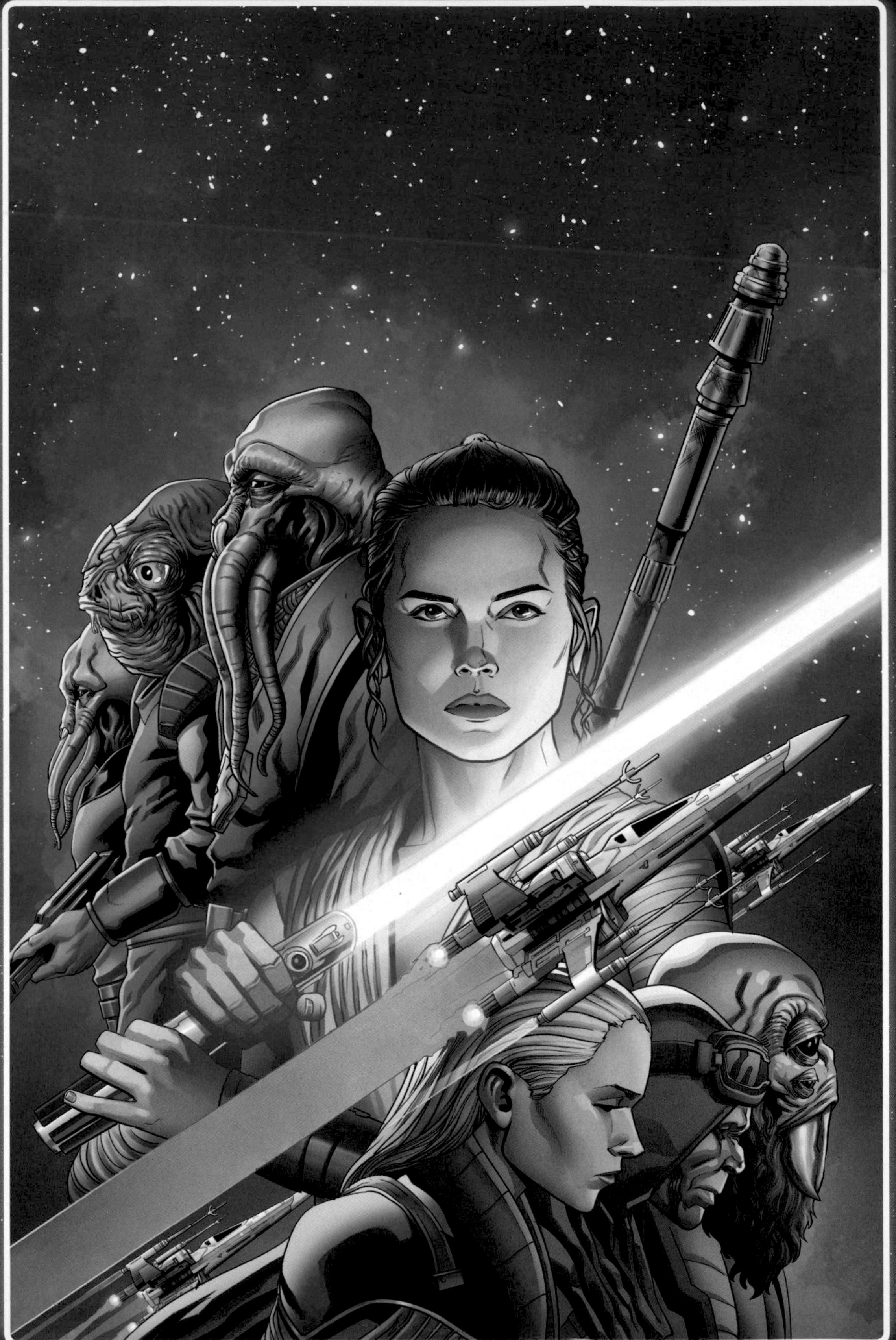

***JOURNEY TO STAR WARS: THE RISE OF SKYWALKER – ALLEGIANCE* 4 Variant by**
WILL SLINEY & GURU-eFX

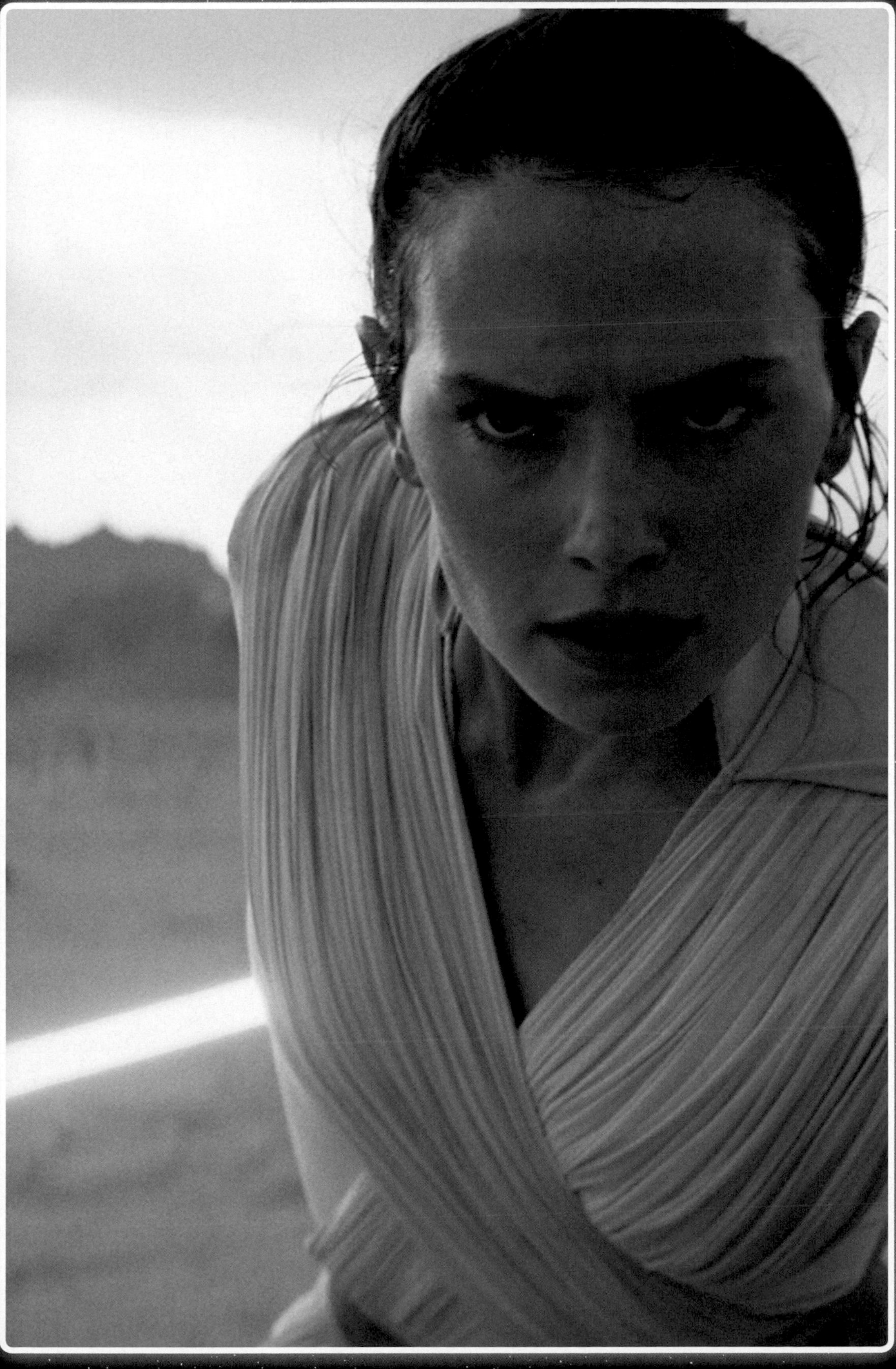

JOURNEY TO STAR WARS: THE RISE OF SKYWALKER – ALLEGIANCE 1 Movie Variant

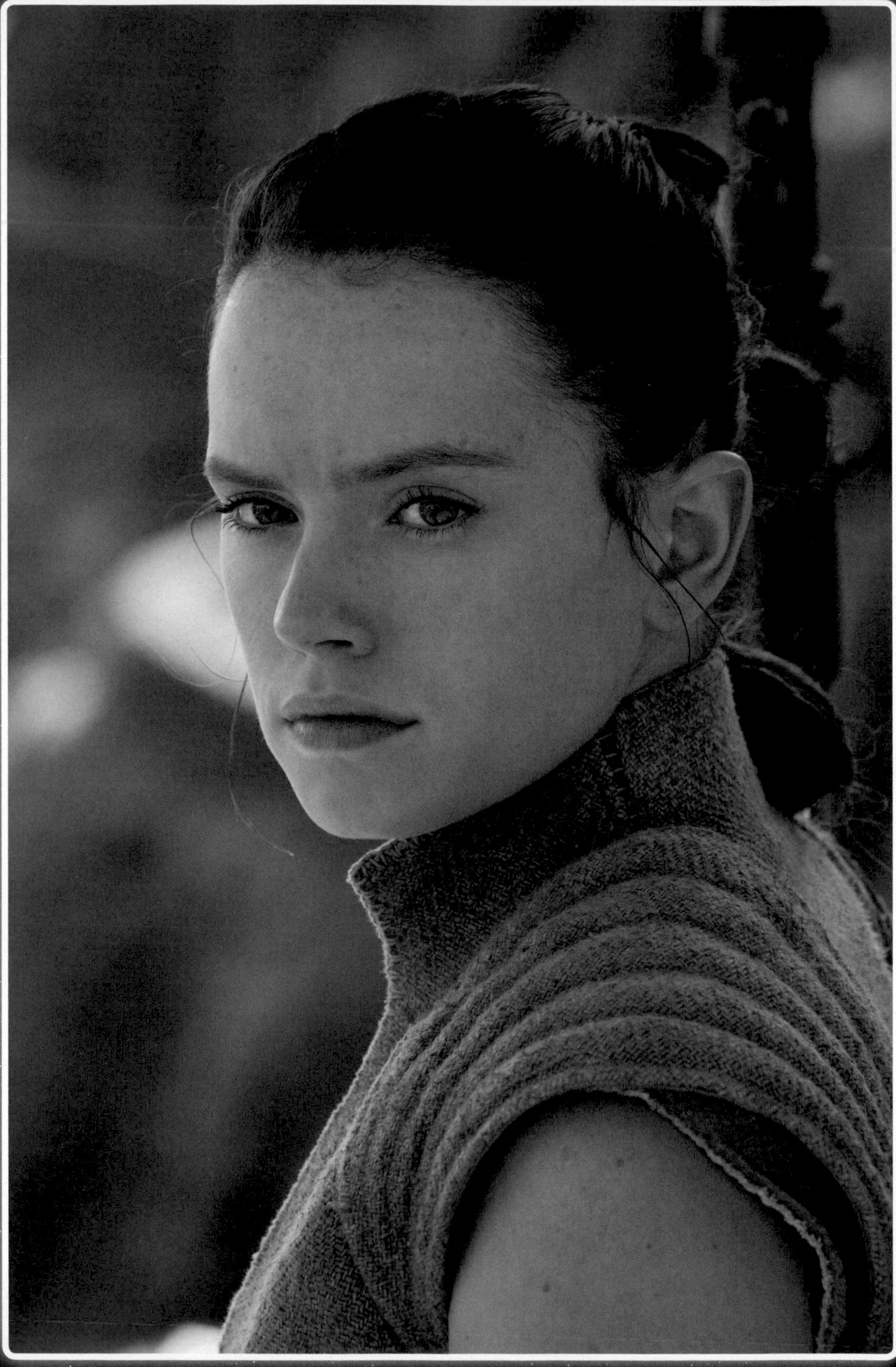

JOURNEY TO STAR WARS: THE RISE OF SKYWALKER – ALLEGIANCE 2 Movie Variant

THE JOURNEY OF
STAR WARS
ALLEGIANCE

njoy a sneak peek behind the creative process of **ALLEGIANCE**. Writer Ethan Sacks is here to shed some light on his mazing work with a look at an earlier draft of the script and on the collective creativity of artist Luke Ross and colorist e Loughridge. They, along with Clayton Cowles over at VC, really gave this story their all. Take it away, Ethan!

**PAGE TWO & THREE
(TWO-PAGE SPLASH WITH
THREE RIGHT INSETS)**

Splash. Taking up the vast majority of the two pages, a flotilla of First Order Star Destroyers and one of the Episode VIII Dreadnaughts are setting up a blockade of the planet. The amount of firepower should look intimidating. This is our chance to show just how powerful a threat the First Order is.

Right Inset 1: A medium shot shows a communications transmission projected before Hux of a heavily robed Tah'nuhnan leader, the whiskers showing her age. Her two dozen arms are clasped in the universal sign for prayer. Even in the transparency of the broadcast, we can see she's begging.

> TAH'NUHNAN LEADER:
> Please, do not do this, General Hux. The Tah'nuhna are neutral! Not even the Empire ordered the invasion of our planet.

Right Inset 2: Cut to the bridge of the lead Star Destroyer. We see GENERAL HUX talking to a hologram projection of the Tah'nuhnan leader. The hologram is not opaque, so we can see part of Hux through it.

> GENERAL HUX:
> A Resistance transmission was traced here...that does not seem very neutral as far as the First Order is concerned.

> TAH'NUHNAN LEADER:
> We...we welcome all travelers in need ...

> TAH'NUHNAN LEADER:
> It...it has always been our way.

> GENERAL HUX:
> That always was your way.

Right Inset 3: Tight shot of General Hux, head slightly tilted forward in a menacing manner. There is a tight sneer across his face.

> GENERAL HUX:
> And who said anything about invasion?

We wanted to open the series with a horrific example of what the First Order could do to innocent civilizations in their tireless pursuit of the remnants of the Resistance. They are determined to wipe out anybody who might harbor or assist their enemies for any reason. So we introduced the peaceful species of the Tah'nuhnan, with their beautiful glass architecture carved over generations and long history of science and philosophical contributions—only to wipe them out of existence several pages later. I just loved the visual of what Star Destroyers would do to these glass structures, and Luke Ross drew the carnage perfectly.

PAGE NINE (FOUR PANELS)

Panel 1. Cut outside the camp, in the midst of a large garbage mound. We recognize REY, despite her poncho and regulator, holding her trademark staff with both sides in an aggressive posture. We see why: She's on the verge of being attacked by a large bearlike creature with horny protrusions from its head. It's large — about eight feet tall — and fearsome looking, but its skin is full of blisters — a side effect of what the toxic pollution has done to the local wildlife. It has four eyes. Let's call it an Anoatian pit beast for dialogue purposes. There is a blaster hanging from a holster at Rey's hip. They are facing off in profile on opposite sides of the panel.

CAPTION:
"...and something tells me Rey is getting bored just scavenging for spare generator parts all day."

PIT BEAST:
GRRRRRRRRR!!!

Panel 2. The horned pit beast lunges forward, snarling teeth first, with Rey leaping upward over the creature's head just in time as it closes its jaws on the air at the spot she had just been standing...

SFX:
SNAP!

Panel 3. Rey uses the top of the creature's head to spring upward onto higher ground. And by ground, we mean a cluster of garbage. Below, in the background, the pit beast looks enraged.

REY:
Come on, is that the best you can do? I thought Anoatian pit beasts were supposed to be dangerous!

Panel 4. The garbage she lands on wasn't too secure and gives way, causing Rey to lose balance and look like she's about to fall downward.

REY:
Whoaaahhh.

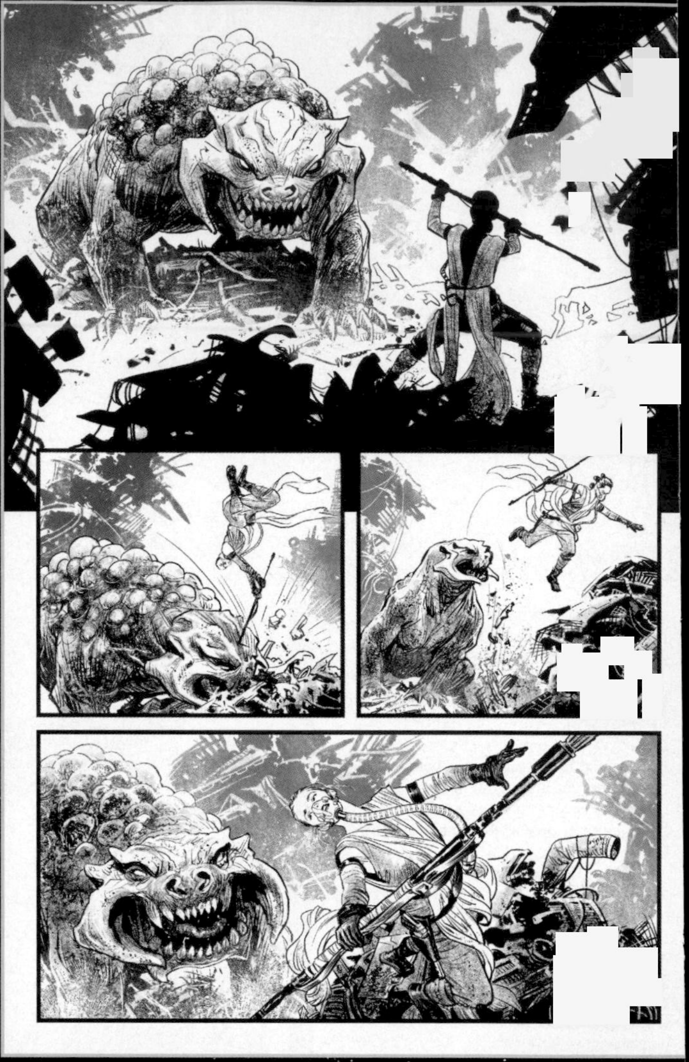

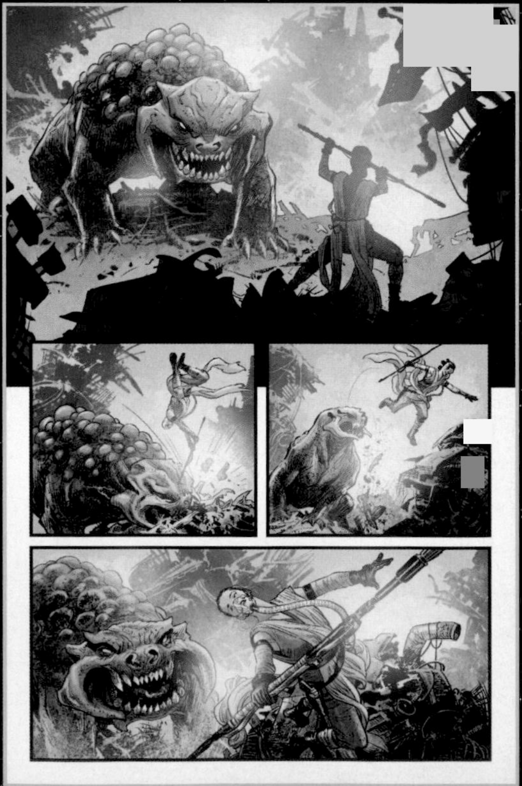

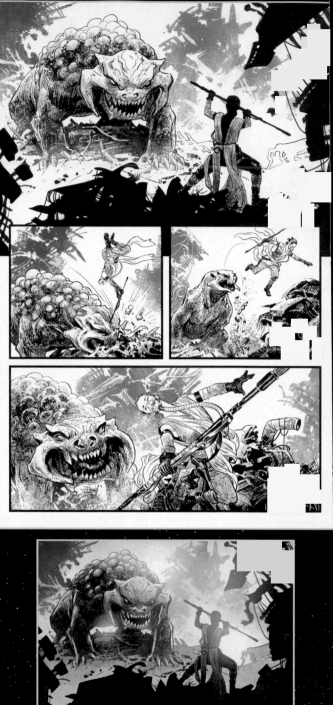

As the First Order terrorizes systems across the galaxy, the Resistance survivors left after the events of *The Last Jedi* are hiding. And what better place to hide than the garbage planet of Anoat? A poisoned trash heap of a world between the Bespin and Hoth systems. (Yes, the *Millennium Falcon* passed by it but didn't stop in *The Empire Strikes Back*.) We couldn't resist the symbolism of hitting rock bottom by living in garbage. For the Rey fight, we wanted to design a creature that looked something like a horned bear, but Luke Ross outdid himself with the Anoatian pit beast, a monstrosity that looks like it could hold its own against a rancor.

PAGE FOURTEEN (FOUR PANELS)

Panel 1. Cut to a Mos Eisley-like smugglers haven on a space station. FINN is in the midst of getting punched out by a large Dashade thug in what looks from the background to be a seedy bar. Finn was rolling with the punch or he would be in a lot more trouble. Behind them, an assorted motley crew of scum and villainy are cheering. BB-8 is visible in the background.

SFX:
Whamm!

CAPTION:
"...it sounds like Finn is having all the fun."

CAPTION:
The Wayward Comet. Refueling Station.

Panel 2. Finn, his mouth bloodied, falls backward into the arms of a pair of Yarkora contraband runners who look surly.

FINN:
Unnn... Thanks for the assist. We smugglers have to stick togeth —

Panel 3. The Yarkoras push Finn back toward the reader and back into the fray. That heartless act has caught him by surprise.

FINN:
—eeerrrrrr!

Panel 4. Finn ducks as the bigger Dashade misses on his swing.

FINN:
I don't suppose we could just call this a draw?

Though the main plot of the series follows Leia, Rey and Rose, there's a side story that sends Finn, Poe and BB-8 off on their own escapade. This was a combination that everyone wanted to see because they've been established as good friends but haven't been together on an adventure since their escape in the TIE fighter in *The Force Awakens.* I loved their back-and-forth banter when they did share screen time and wanted to capture that in **ALLEGIANCE**.

PAGE SEVENTEEN (THREE PANELS)

Panel 1. The Twi'lek dancer is now revealed to be none other than REMEX IO, the Clawdite shape-shifter from *STAR WARS: GALAXY'S EDGE*. He is speaking into the wrist communicator.

REMEX:
Is the bounty big enough on that Resistance leader to make it worth it, Kendoh? I kind of have a soft spot in my heart for underdogs.

Panel 2. Inside the cockpit of Kendoh's ship — last seen in *STAR WARS: GALAXY'S EDGE* — KENDOH, WOORO and a fourth member of the gang, an Utai warrior with a cybernetic eye named BASSO MAK. They are looking at a small hologram of Remex on the console.

KENDOH:
A big enough bounty to buy you a new conscience...or a new heart.

KENDOH:
Follow him to his ship, Remex, and then tag it with a tracker. We'll take him when he lands.

BASSO MAK:
(Alien gibberish)

CAPTION:
"Are you sure you know what you're doing? The First Order is —"

KENDOH:
Just punch up a direct channel, Basso...and pray that I do.

Panel 3. Cut to inside the bridge of the Star Destroyer seen earlier in the issue. General Hux is standing over a communications console watching a nervous junior officer who is reporting news that his superior finds distasteful.

CAPTION:
The *Finalizer*. First Order Star Destroyer.

GENERAL HUX:
Do not waste my time with every rumor of a Resistance sighting from every drunken scoundrel in the sector.

OFFICER (off-panel down):
But, sir, the intel checks out.
I think there is a good chance—

GENERAL HUX:
Think? An officer of your rank isn't tasked with doing the thinking, lieutenant.

Readers of the **GALAXY'S EDGE** comic will immediately recognize the shape-shifting Clawdite Remex Io, who was introduced in that series. That's a tip-off that the Kendoh Gang, which was created by artist Will Sliney and me, are the ones contracted to hunt down Resistance members like Finn. In fact, eagle-eyed fans who read **GALAXY'S EDGE**, which takes place after **ALLEGIANCE**, will catch that this bounty was referenced in that series.

PAGE TWENTY (SPLASH)

Splash. That contingent we briefly saw last panel crossing the bridge dominates the image. It is a group of four Quarren and two Mon Calamari. At the head is a grizzled Quarren, GENERAL NOSSOR RI (a nod to that *Clone Wars* saga, "Battle for Mon Calamari," though we won't delve into that deeply) and his fiercely isolationist advisor, also a Quarren, CHADKOL GEE. The latter and the underlings are pointing guns at Leia and company, who can be glimpsed from behind a little bit where possible in the foreground on the side of the panel.

CHADKOL:
You shouldn't have come after all you have done, General Leia, after all the death you brought to our waters.

CHADKOL:
So tell us why we shouldn't kill you where you stand?

CAPTION:
To Be Continued.

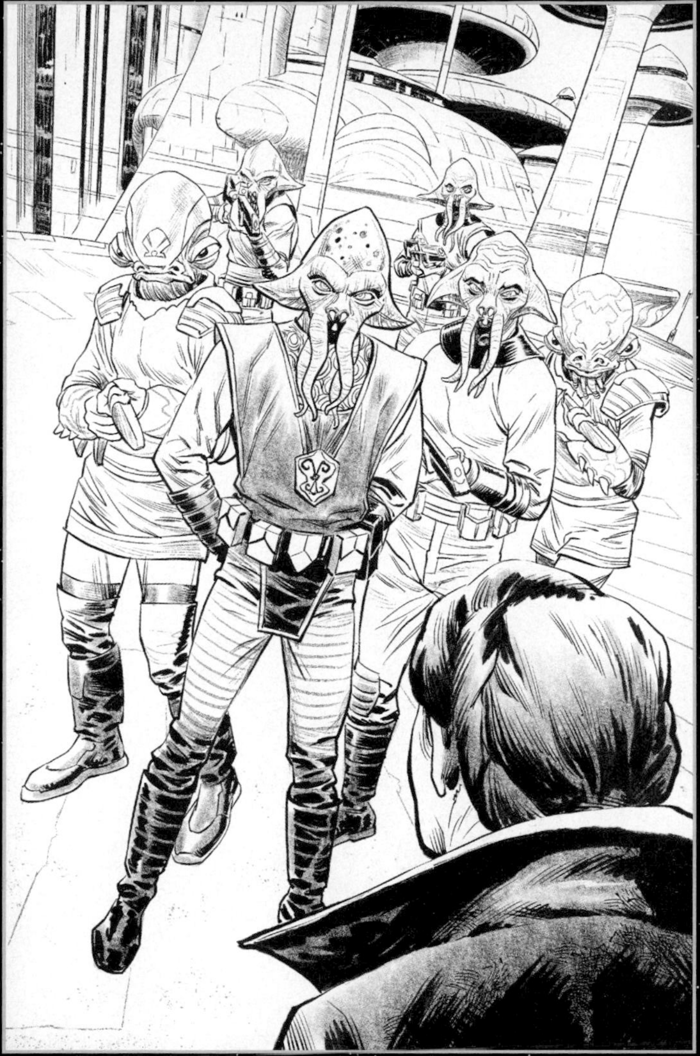

Leia and company don't get the welcome that they were expecting when they land on Mon Cala. Having been occupied by Imperial forces three decades ago, many Quarren and Mon Calamari don't want to get drawn into another war. The leader of the isolationists, the Quarren seen in the center of the splash page, is Nossor Ri, a veteran of that classic season four episode of the *Star Wars: The Clone Wars* animated series, "Water War."

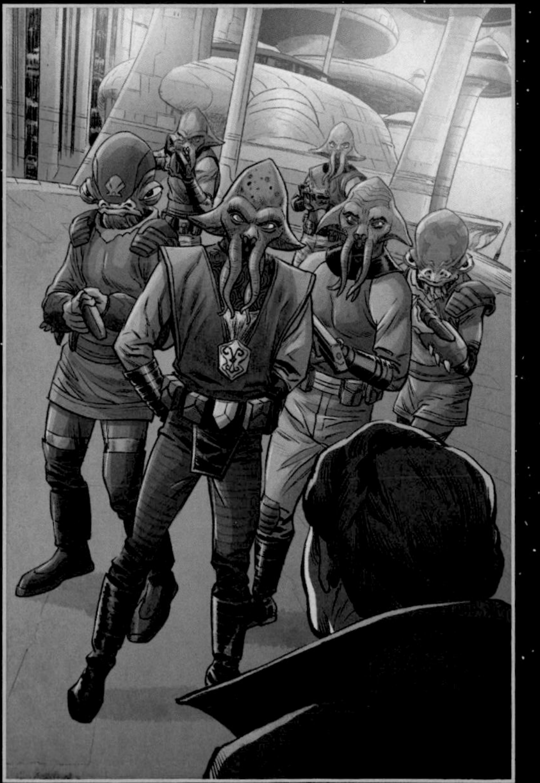

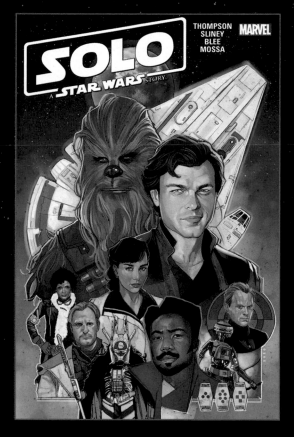

STAR WARS™

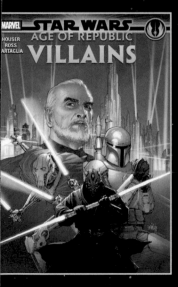
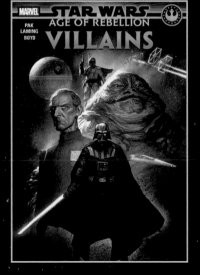
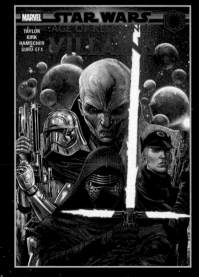

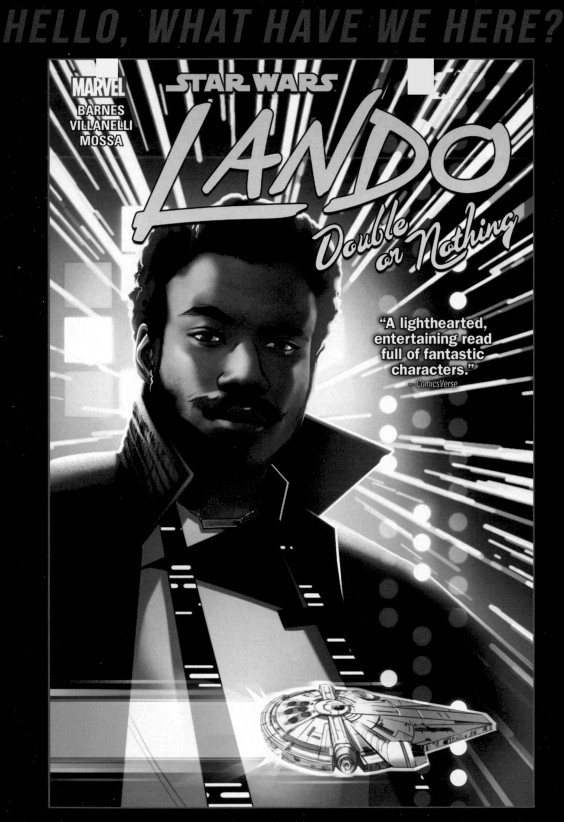